URBAN RECYCLING AND THE SEARCH FOR
SUSTAINABLE COMMUNITY DEVELOPMENT

URBAN RECYCLING AND THE SEARCH FOR SUSTAINABLE COMMUNITY DEVELOPMENT

Adam S. Weinberg, David N. Pellow, and Allan Schnaiberg

PRINCETON UNIVERSITY PRESS   PRINCETON AND OXFORD

Library of Congress Cataloging-in-Publication Data

Weinberg, Adam S.
    Urban recycling and the search for sustainable community
development / Adam S. Weinberg, David N. Pellow, and Allan
Schnaiberg.
        p.   cm.
    Includes bibliographical references and index.
    ISBN 0-691-05014-7 (cloth : alk. paper)
    1. Community development. 2. Sustainable development.
3. Recycling (Waste, etc.) I. Pellow, David N., 1969– II.
Schnaiberg, Allan. III. Title.

HN49.C6 W437 2000
307.1'4—dc21   00-021055

This book has been composed in Sabon

www.pup.princeton.edu

Printed in the United States of America

10   9   8   7   6   5   4   3   2   1

Contents

Acknowledgments _____

THE ROOTS of this work go back to a variety of people and ideas. Hugh Stretton's (1976) innovative writing about alternative paths for social development gave us a sociological framework for thinking about pathways for communities and sustainable development. In carrying out our fieldwork in the several organizations referenced in this book, a number of leaders and staff in these settings gave us thoughtful and attentive responses. Many of these individuals not only gave us "data"; they also imparted new ways of thinking about recycling and community development that later informed our work.

Similarly, we have presented a number of preliminary papers to professional social science audiences in recent years. We were asked provocative and often ill-informed questions that alerted us to common misperceptions and missed perceptions about recycling and urban redevelopment. But we were also asked constructive and thoughtful questions that forced us to dig further and think harder about the issues. Sometimes our audiences were partly drawn from various levels of recycling organizations, and their questions convinced us to go back and interview them, since their perceptions were quite different from ours. And this in turn led us to revise some of our observations and interpretations.

Perhaps most important in these endeavors was the companionship provided by the President's Council on Sustainable Development (PCSD). From 1998 to 1999, two of the authors served as task force members for the PCSD as it prepared its final report for the White House. The work of the PCSD shaped our thinking about sustainable development, and we in turn helped shape the PCSD's vision of sustainable communities. This group also gave us hope, as we met an impressive array of individuals and organizations working toward sustainable community development. Our thinking in these pages is often some form of conversation with them.

Finally, several reviewers of successive versions of this manuscript challenged some of our thoughts and the organization of our arguments, and led to what we consider a much- improved manuscript. Tom Rudel of Rutgers University, along with anonymous reviewers was a source of much reflection and constructive criticism. Though we sometimes gnashed our teeth in frustration, in retrospect there is no doubt that the reviewers deserve a good deal of credit in this regard. Though we have been through a long process of deliberation with Peter Dougherty of Princeton Press on this manuscript, the faith he exhibited early during the often-frustrating process of revision and resubmission kept us persevering, seeking to generate a more transparent argument and accessible manuscript. We thank all these contributors to this work.

We also wish to thank our families. They suffered through our periods of "keeping our heads in the dumpsters" and bemoaning the ill will of our critics, and continued to give us encouragement. On a more personal level, each of our families has gone through a variety of transformations during this time—events that will coexist in our memories years from now when we look back on the period during which this manuscript was researched and written. We have endured the journey together.

URBAN RECYCLING AND THE SEARCH FOR SUSTAINABLE COMMUNITY DEVELOPMENT

One

Urban Recycling:
An Empirical Test of Sustainable Community
Development Proposals

IN THE FALL of 1997, the President's Council on Sustainable Development (PCSD) issued a report that called for the United States government to commit itself to building sustainable communities. The report emphasized that any vision of sustainable development must begin with efforts to "encourage people to work together to create healthy communities where natural and historic resources are preserved, jobs are available, sprawl is contained, neighborhoods are secure, education is lifelong, transportation and health care are accessible, and all citizens have opportunities to improve the quality of their lives" (PCSD 1997:3). The report went on to call for new approaches to community development. In short, the council posed a very straightforward vision: communities could simultaneously achieve economic vitality, environment protection, and social equity. This is often referred to as balancing the three Es of community development.

In this book, we examine the potential for sustainable forms of community development to emerge within the United States. To do this, we reconstruct the recent history of urban recycling programs in the United States. In particular, we examine the relationship between politics and markets as they first created and later destroyed recycling programs in the Chicago metropolitan area. We note two shifts in the history of recycling. First, there was a shift away from the focus on waste as a panacea, something that could "save the environment" and/or provide job opportunities for the desperately poor. Instead, waste became treated as a commodity that could generate revenues. Second, there was also a shift away from recycling as an activity in which marginalized social groups and community-based organizations engaged toward its control by large firms, many of which now operate in global markets.

This analysis of recycling allows us to theorize more generally about sustainable development. The same economic and social policies that distorted recycling have also influenced other processes involving urban communities, workers, consumers, and local governments. They will ultimately influence any efforts to create sustainable community development. Our account of recycling differs substantially from popular views of recycling as an activity generated by the goodwill of people who are trying to do something beneficial for society. We concentrate on the interplay between economic agendas and political power. As in all forms of urban development, recycling should be understood as a site of conflict among a variety of social actors who are using political arenas to control a resource in order to meet their different economic agendas.

We agree with the President's Council that many communities would benefit from a stronger economy, an environment that can preserve life, and strong social systems that enhance the quality of life. Urban development programs should be directed toward achieving each of the three Es: *economy, equity,* and *environment.* Moving in this direction, however, will not be an easy task. Any serious analysis of sustainable community development must address a series of vexing intellectual questions. Our analysis of recycling outlines these questions and provides a social context for beginning such theorizing.

In the next chapter, we outline our theoretical framework. In this chapter, we familiarize the reader with the concept of sustainable community development and the rise of urban recycling programs.

Sustainable Community Development

The concept of sustainable development was popularized by the World Commission on Environment and Development, a United Nations entity usually referred to as the Bruntland Commission. In 1987, the commission issued a report that defined sustainable development as those forms of development that allow people "to meet the needs of the present without compromising the ability of future generations to meet their own needs."

Over the last decade, the concept of sustainable development has been used, misused, and fiercely debated (see, e.g., Willers 1994). As early as a decade ago, Pezzy (1989) had already identified twenty-seven distinct definitions of the term. In general, the debates over sustainable development have evolved into two separate discussions. Within the environmental sciences, a dispute has emerged over the extent to which economic growth can occur while maintaining the viability of ecological systems and their biological diversity.[1] Economist Herman Daly has been the most vocal public intellectual in the post-Bruntland debate. His

---

[1] Interestingly, within the bio-ecology scholarly community, the original concept before the Bruntland report was not sustainable *development*, but rather sustainable *bio-diversity* (Clark 1995; IUCN 1980; cf. Lele 1991), indicating a shift in who had control over the framing of this issue.

general position is summarized in the title of a recent article "Sustainable Growth? No Thank You" (1996b). Daly defines sustainable development as "development without growth . . . beyond environmental regenerative and absorptive capacity" (1996a:69). Drawing a distinction between sustainable growth and sustainable development, Daly has led the charge among environmental science scholars arguing that sustainable *development* is a code word for sustainable *growth,* and that sustainable growth simply cannot exist within ecological limits. He and others argue that any economic growth as we now measure it simply continues to deplete ecosystems. Thus, any form of economic growth will destroy the earth's capacity to sustain life (Daly 1996a, 1996b; Daly and Cobb 1994).

A second use of the term *sustainable development* has focused on community development. Here the emphasis has been on developing projects that achieve the three E's of economy, equity, and environment. Activists and scholars working in this area have placed equity and environmental concerns on the community development agenda. They have struggled to do this in a political economy marked by increasing social inequalities (Audirac 1997; Green 1997; Hoff 1998; PCSD 1997). These scholars have been highly critical of post–World War II forms of community development in the United States. During this period, the primary goal of community development has been to generate aggregate economic growth in communities. Even equity and environmental problems are thought to depend on such augmented economic growth. Growth is believed to generate the revenues and technological advancements needed to solve all social (and indeed environmental) problems (for a defense of this position, see Peterson 1981).

Sustainable development partisans have been critical of this argument. They have instead argued that "the economy" cannot be separated from "equity" and "environmental" concerns (e.g., Longworth 1998). Most of the environmental and equity problems arise from particular forms of economic growth. Hence the *process* of generating growth is causing the very *problems* it is supposed to solve. Sustainable community development advocates articulate a vision for generating forms of economic development that lead instead to more humane social equity and ecological outcomes (Shuman 1998). The President's Council on Sustainable Development report states, "The key to building sustainable communities — those that get better and stronger over time — will be to recognize that economic opportunity, ecological integrity, and social equity are interlocking links in the chain of well-being" (PCSD 1997:7).

Whereas the first debate over sustainable development centers primarily on preserving ecosystems, the focus of the second debate is on reviving communities. Adherents to the latter school of thought do not assume that current practices are the only tools that society has to work with in dealing with long-term ecosystem limits. Proponents of sustainable community development are looking for forms of community development that simultaneously generate economic vitality, environmental stewardship, and social equity outcomes. The core intellectual question is: What are the conditions or practices that will actually enhance the local economy of struggling communities while also rebuilding strong social systems and preserving the environment? Our examination of recycling is our grounded attempt to develop some new theoretical underpinnings to help answer this question.

Scholars working in the environmental sciences have been highly critical of this line of reasoning, arguing that many of the practices advocated as sustainable community development are not truly sustainable for ecosystems. Proponents of sustainable community development are aware of this problem. They counter by arguing that we need to create new ways of thinking, which will lead to projects that achieve measurable progress along all of the sustainability dimensions. Hence their focus is not primarily on ecological throughputs. Rather, they seek to integrate *multiple* needs of communities into every project. Theirs is a political project centered on creating new forms of community development. Jonathan Lash, the president of the World Resources Institute and cochair of the President's Council on Sustainable Development, responded to such a critique in a public meeting in Pittsburgh in the following manner:

> We realize that we are not solving every problem. There are still going to be environmental problems. The point of sustainable development is to get us past the political obstacles. . . . Over the course of the last couple of years, people from government, the private sector and the NGO [nongovernmental organization] community are learning to sit at the same table and work together. In doing so, we are seeing initiatives that push the 3E's forward. (PCSD Town Meeting, October 1998)

Our attempt to distinguish between the two debates over sustainable development may seem like splitting hairs. But it is very important for the framing of this book. There are virtually *no* widespread practices that meet the first criterion of *ecological* sustainability. Politically and culturally, we are so far from being able to achieve these results that it would make little sense to write an empirical book at this time. Debates over sustainable *community* development, however, relate to more operational cases, and are thus somewhat more amenable to empirical examination. We are, however, making some progress toward sustainable community development.

We also believe that sustainable community development would mark a dramatic departure in the future development of capitalism, so much so that a truly sustainable society might be entirely noncapitalist. To quote the PCSD report, "Sustainable development is one of those rare ideas that could dramatically change the way we look at 'what is' and 'what could be'" (1997:2).

Recycling as a Case Study in Sustainable Community Development

Recycling constitutes a model of sustainable community development in two ways. First, recycling is one of the few common elements in discussions among scholars, policy makers, and activists concerned with sustainable community development. Over the last decade, we have followed and participated in hundreds of discussions of sustainable development at every level of government. These ranged from rural town meetings in upstate New York to presidential task forces in Washington, to urban city council meetings in the Chicago area. We have also been active in several community-based organizations and nonprofit enterprises that advocate and practice recycling. In all of these contexts, we have been struck by the breadth of the discussions about sustainable community development that incorporate some form of recycling. Recycling is almost always raised as an important part of a community's transition toward sustainable community development.[2]

Recycling also constitutes a model of sustainable community development because it is one of the very few ideas proposed by advocates that embraces all of the three Es. Most proposals or working models of sustainable development fall short of the three Es and focus mainly on ecological sustainability. The Institute for Local Self-Reliance, a nonprofit organization that advocates sustainable community development, promotes recycling. The banner line for its recycling campaign is, "Recycling is an economic development tool as well as an environmental one." The social benefits of recycling are implied in the term *economic development*, which from a sustainability perspective connotes socially responsible economic activity.

For analysts seeking to either study or promote sustainable develop-

[2] For example, we found recycling to be an important part of current discussions about federal indicators of sustainable development, local political strategies for sustainable community development, international strategies for creating sustainable markets, private sector commitments to sustainable practices, and social movement agendas for legislative changes around sustainable development.

ment, the lack of data has often been a problem.[3] There are few available data sources on sustainable community development because most projects are still on the drawing board. Researchers have responded in two very different ways. Social theorists have outlined sweeping visions for sustainable worlds (Daly 1996b; Hawken 1993; Hutchinson 1997; Redclift 1987). These texts have often been highly inspiring but usually quite abstract. They leave the reader to wonder how we might get from our current practices to these idealized ones. Other researchers have been more empirical. They have produced collections of short case studies that seek to introduce "best practices," which approximate sustainable development conditions (Audirac 1997; Hoff 1998). These collections are interesting but they are often built on a diversity of short-term case studies. From these limited contexts, it is hard to gauge long-term effects. It is also difficult to draw comparisons between these case studies.

In this book, we have tried to do something more systematic, employing a comparative longitudinal analysis of a few rich case studies. Recycling is one of the few practices that gives us that abundance of data. Currently more than eight thousand communities in the United States are engaged in recycling over 100 million tons of materials each year. Moreover, we have a long history of recycling in the United States, stretching back for almost a century.

Our overall argument in this book is straightforward. In chapters 3–6, we will present a series of fruitful case studies. Our basic findings there are as follows:

> **1.** Recycling has become a commodity-based, profit-driven competitive industry in which large private firms using public dollars are squeezing the life out of smaller nonprofit and family-owned recyclers.
> **2.** Some programs achieve modest economic gains but distribute them primarily to the private sector.
> **3.** Ecological gains are modest. While large volumes of materials

---

[3] A small number of social scientists have been working around these problems for some time, including Redclift (1987), Reddy (1979), and Dickson (1975). There is a somewhat richer empirical and theoretical tradition for an earlier version of sustainable development — *appropriate technology*, initially put forward by E. F. Schumacher (1973). Much of this literature is based in Third World contexts. We have previously drawn upon this body of social scientific work concerning applications of both appropriate technology and sustainable development in industrialized nations (e.g., Schnaiberg 1997b; Schnaiberg, Weinberg, and Pellow 1998; Weinberg, Pellow, and Schnaiberg 1996). Appropriate technology research is far more grounded in programs from the 1970s, while sustainable development research is more concerned with potential applications and a handful of quite recent programs. One recent social scientific conference (Baker et al. 1997) offers some European empirical and theoretical contributions to this debate as well.

are diverted from landfills and incinerators, it is a small percentage of the total urban waste stream. This diversion rate is well below what most advocates anticipated and built into their expectations. Furthermore, recycling does not address an array of other ecological problems that revolve around pollution and toxic chemical exposure.

4. Equity issues are also quickly dismissed in most recycling programs. Particularly troublesome, the quality of the jobs produced is poor.

5. Where we did find that recycling programs have the potential to achieve truly sustainable community development, they are turning out to be politically unfeasible. Most of the programs that do achieve sufficient progress along each of the three E dimensions are being driven out of the recycling market by large municipal programs contracted out to private sector firms, which achieve little progress along any of these dimensions.

In the final chapters, we synthesize these observations to theorize more generally about sustainable community development. We will argue that the current political economic structure will resist and crush existing or proposed efforts to create sustainable community development practices. At best, the political economy is likely to support only a very weak form of sustainable community development. In the rest of this chapter, we sketch out the recent history of recycling in urban communities. Our brief introduction is meant to provide the reader with a historical backdrop against which our case studies can be better understood. Many of our arguments will become clearer as we introduce the case studies.[4]

The Rise of Recycling: "Why Waste a Resource?"

Precursors to Recycling: The Political and Historical Construction of Waste

Historically, waste was not viewed as a social problem. Prior to the 1890s, it was often seen as a potential source for the future, as the junk could be sold, given away, or mined for spare parts (Melosi 1981: introduction and 37–39; Rathje and Murphy 1992: chap. 2).

Community perceptions of waste shifted between 1880 and 1910, as cities became a locus for new industries. The industrialization of urban

---

[4] In earlier versions of this book, we included an extensive history of solid waste disposal practices in the United States. However, following the advice of students and colleagues, we cut the material to a brief section. For interested readers, we suggest Melosi 1981.

areas increased the demand for urban land, which was needed for factories and for housing the new workers who migrated to the cities seeking jobs. Thus, population densities increased, with people living closer to one another than ever before. In essence, this created a "friction of space." The "backyard" virtually disappeared. People found their neighbors' wastes less acceptable. People's wastes could not be segregated from the living spaces of others, nor were they as easily segregated from people's own living spaces (Melosi 1981: introduction and chap. 1).

In addition to the low-skilled factory workers, new concentrations of skilled craftsmen and white-collar workers became attached to the new factories. People started to travel from their "nice" neighborhoods to new jobs in the industrialized parts of the city. A new middle class of entrepreneurs and clerical workers in these cities—American "burghers," in effect—had to traverse streets filled with garbage to reach their businesses. They demanded those local governments "do something" about these dirty public spaces. These concerns were often rationalized on the basis of *miasmic* theories (a new pseudoscience, which suggested that a kind of air pollution was generated around solid wastes) and by *filth* theories (which suggested that direct contact with wastes was the cause of disease). Both concerns targeted wastes in poor neighborhoods (Melosi 1981: chaps. 2–3). These theories had social credibility because they appeared to be consistent with emerging medical research that linked a range of diseases, including cholera and typhoid, to the contamination of urban water and food supplies by human waste.

Another factor influencing changes in waste disposal was culture. Attitudes toward "dirty work" changed as white-collar workers in retail trades and service sectors began to enter the labor force and provide an alternative occupation to manual labor. Even if incomes for many of these workers were not very high, they identified with the urban elite rather than with the urban working class. In fact, many members of the white-collar class viewed the lower classes as unhygienic and mired in filth.

A generalized concern with dirt and community hygiene especially characterized the Progressive Era of urban change (Hays 1969). Urban reformers' view of "messiness" included their uneasiness with ethnic diversity and with poverty in tenement areas. Visible wastes in poor people's neighborhoods merely confirmed many affluent citizens' views of these groups as second-class urban citizens and their living spaces as "blighted" with trash. This gave rise to a movement by middle-class women's groups to "beautify the city."[5] They framed the issue as "municipal housekeeping."

---

[5] This was a kind of "cosmetological" approach (Schnaiberg 1973) that has continued to influence subsequent antilitter campaigns and contemporary recycling programs.

Each of these factors gave rise to a strong middle-class distaste for all forms of visible waste. It also placed significant pressures on urban government to address the solid waste problem. These sentiments coalesced in a "good government movement" that called on urban governments to clean up the city in order to improve the "quality of life" for poor people. Just as human waste could poison the body, solid waste was now viewed as poisoning the community. The good government movement was going to "clean up" poor neighborhoods as a social relief strategy (a connection still made today). The noted sanitarian Samuel Greeley would go on to "speak with high praise of the activities of women in city-cleaning projects distributing leaflets to every household decrying the practice of throwing wastepaper into the streets . . . and provid[ing] trash cans for their towns" (Melosi 1981:119–21).

Initially, waste-hauling enterprises offered private services. Individual citizens and producers paid for this removal. Haulers generally took waste away to either a publicly or a privately owned dump site. Sites were near but not in the community. The movement from this system to mandatory municipal garbage pickup was slow. But visible refuse and its unpleasant odors continued to stimulate middle-class citizens groups' social and political demands. They continued to push for increased public cleanliness in the form of mandatory waste disposal practices. Urban governments resisted as much as was politically feasible because they did not want to take on the increased financial responsibility.

The real catalyst for change was the emergence of private sector firms who began to recognize that considerable profits could be extracted from waste disposal if they collected fees from the city and from private clients to finance these services. Firms became involved in a variety of roles: the collection of garbage, the management of public dumpsites, and the development of equipment and supplies (and even labor). These contracts became highly profitable. So profitable were many of these that they attracted the attention of organized crime in some cities. Rather than offering superior or more cost-effective collection services, these groups kept competitors in check with direct intimidation. Thus, garbage was an intensely contested terrain of urban resources.

The emergence of a larger private market for waste disposal was generally viewed as positive by middle-class constituencies, urban government, and the private firms. However, it was not always good for the local environment or for low-income neighborhoods. Private firms attempted to maximize their payments from the city officials while minimizing the labor power and other inputs needed to collect and haul garbage by horses and wagons. As in many rural and urban areas today, they recognized that they could reduce costs by locating dumps closer to cities. They began to dump wastes in pockets of land around neighborhoods inhabited by the poor and racial minorities.[6] This practice was cheaper than hauling the wastes to somewhat more distant dumpsites (Melosi 1981:27–30). Firms also began to incinerate wastes more frequently.

Thus, the history of waste was shaped by the intersection of politics, economics, and culture. First, waste collection and disposal represented some dimensions of class conflict. In particular, class differences led to different forms of waste management — from the minimalist orientation of the poor, who may have dumped garbage just outside their homes, to that of the more powerful rising middle class, who were able to mobilize municipal governments to get wastes "off their streets."

Second, waste now offered considerable market exchange opportunities for private entrepreneurs. Mobilization of waste-hauling organizations led to the increase in political pressures on city officials, designed to enable these firms to capture this potential wealth and to retain access to waste disposal contracts. This fact, as much as any other, has become a central historical constraint on the modern recycling programs of U.S. cities; while garbage was out of sight of citizens, it was rarely out of mind for entrepreneurs in the waste collection field. Such entrepreneurs would maintain their interest in these market exchange values even when waste disposal ideas were superseded by new concepts of recycling.

The Promises of Early Recycling Programs in the United States

Modern recycling first emerged in the late 1960s. The original programs grew from environmental movements at the time, which created small local operations. They recycled waste as a vehicle for addressing equity and environmental concerns (we will explore this history in more depth in chapter 4). Recycling provided income for some of the most marginal urban populations. Homeless, immigrant, and low-income populations were encouraged to take items from trash cans in a process that became known as "dumpster diving." The materials were then taken to drop-off recycling centers run by the social movement groups. At these facilities, people could exchange the materials for a small sum of money. The social movement group would then package the materials and resell them to regional firms that would use the materials in manufacturing operations. This practice allowed marginal social populations to squeeze out an existence when few other options existed. From the late 1960s through the early 1980s, most postconsumer waste recycling took place

---

[6] This is one of the earlier forms of "environmental injustice" and "environmental racism" (Bullard 1990; Gottlieb 1993).

within these community-based recycling centers. This began to change in the 1980s, as a series of political, social, and economic crises started to unfold in urban areas.

By the early 1980s, urban governments were confronting a range of issues arising from the restructuring of the American economy. From a sustainable community development perspective, these events were problematic and culminated in the following:

1. The dismantling of inner-city urban communities due to deindustrialization. Many manufacturing firms were fleeing the inner cities, with devastating results for low-income and working-class populations. Job insecurity led to family instability. Inner-city stores closed as residents' incomes plummeted. Middle-class whites fled the city to the suburbs, taking their resources with them. In short, urban mayors were confronted with communities that were poor and spiraling downward. (Squires 1994; Wilson 1996)

2. A rising awareness of the accumulating pollution of urban air and water systems that created new challenges for environmental protection of communities. It was clear by the 1980s that urban governments were dealing with potentially massive challenges to providing clean water and air for urban residents. It was also becoming clear that surrounding suburbs were not immune to these problems.

3. New social and political concerns that arose to address the disappearing "green space" within and around urban and suburban communities. Middle-class populations placed tremendous pressure on urban governments to protect some open space for recreational purposes.

4. Political pressure from growing environmental groups who used the "energy crisis" of the 1970s to raise new questions about the sustainability of American consumption patterns in the face of limited global supplies of nonrenewable resources.

5. Scientific concern about atmospheric emissions of greenhouse gases, which created new concerns about global warming. This concern in part reinforced environmentalists' desire to preserve more trees, since they absorbed carbon dioxide, the most diffuse greenhouse gas. Environmentalists thus resisted both domestic and overseas invasions of forest preserves to extract timber, wood pulp, and energy and mineral resources.

By the early 1980s, these crises had produced two vocal constituencies. The first included representatives of community-based organizations, especially in minority neighborhoods within central cities. They called for new economic opportunities to raise the standard of living of unskilled and low-skilled workers. William J. Wilson quoted a twenty-nine-year-old unemployed African American man from Chicago who lamented the recent economic changes: "You could walk out of the house and get a job. Maybe not what you want but you could get a job. Now, you can't find anything. A lot of people in this neighborhood, they want to work but they can't get work" (Wilson 1996:36). The calls by community groups for new opportunities coalesced around strong local organizations that had proliferated in most inner-city areas, demanding that urban governments to create jobs (Squires 1994; Stoecker 1994).

At the same time, a rising cadre of mostly middle-class constituents was calling for a "cleaner, greener" city, a political activity concentrated in suburbs and selected urban neighborhoods. This middle-class constituency consisted of professionals and managers working in the downtown cores. They were employed in financial services and corporate headquarters, or in new business service ventures catering to these corporate clients. One of the early successes of this group was to create pressure to gentrify rundown neighborhoods close to their work settings. Once the blighted housing was replaced with more attractive middle-class housing, more affluent professionals began to relocate back into in the downtown core into gentrified neighborhoods (Anderson 1990; Stoecker 1994).

Once ensconced in the city, these new or returning residents added their voices to the urban political agenda. They sought a beautiful and livable city with nice parks, clean streets, little crime, and pleasant neighborhoods. They did not seek new urban manufacturing ventures. Indeed, they often fought against their proponents, since they feared such endeavors would pollute their neighborhoods and reduce the value of their residential properties. However, they did favor new service and retailing enterprises, particularly those dispensing recreational and gastronomic opportunities for the new gentry. But these establishments offered relatively few jobs for unskilled workers, and those available did not help workers gain new skills, upward mobility, or even a living wage.[7]

These two constituencies were at odds over many issues. One issue that united them, however, was concern about toxic chemicals. Revelations of toxic waste contamination around the nation and the world were emerging in a number of well-publicized cases, including Love Canal in New York and Times Beach in Missouri. Internationally, citizens read about the dispersion of radioactive wastes from Chernobyl's

---

[7] This drama continues to shape urban areas. While the contemporary battles are too extensive for elaboration here, we encourage the reader to read Zukon 1995 and Anderson 1990.

nuclear power plant, as well as about the toxic disaster at the Union Carbide plant in Bhopal, India. There was also a host of more localized incidents (Brown and Mikkelsen 1990) in the same period, often discovered when agencies began to implement the Resource Conservation and Recovery Act (RCRA) of 1976.[8]

Another incident, or "eco-event," was the infamous Mobro 4,000, or the "Garbage Barge" journey. In 1987, this barge filled with municipal waste from New York City sailed down the East Coast. It continued to the Bahamas, Belize, and Mexico looking for a place to dump. The barge was denied entry at each port. After six thousand miles of sailing, the ship returned to New York City, where its wastes were buried on Long Island.

An academic initiated another event that received media attention. William Rathje, a noted anthropologist from the University of Arizona, started to mine landfills for old garbage. Rathje found garbage buried ten years previously — newspapers, hot dogs, and chicken drumsticks — still intact, even though they had been buried long enough to have biodegraded. These findings put to rest any debate over whether landfills were environmentally sound ways to dispose of refuse. They did not return their contents to the soil. Instead, they took up potentially useful land areas and reserved them solely for waste dumping.

All the while, urban governments struggled with increasingly polarized constituencies in their desires for dealing with solid waste disposal. Most citizens (affluent and working class) sought economic development, but they were at odds over which types of development to promote. Less affluent citizens worked lower-status jobs and lived in less-desirable neighborhoods; more affluent citizens were able to find sanctuary in "clean" neighborhoods. These areas were unpolluted by smokestack industries and were populated by upscale restaurants, boutiques, and high-paying service-sector jobs. Both groups fought incinerators and new landfills.

Within this context, recycling programs became attractive because they appeased both constituencies. Recycling also addressed the financial burdens on urban mayors, who were struggling to discover ways to do more for both political constituencies with fewer fiscal resources. Thus, recycling emerged as a kind of "urban alchemy." Much as alchemists had promised to turn base metals into gold or silver, proponents of recycling promised to convert garbage into a valuable resource. Ur-

[8] All of this made the siting of new landfills or incinerators nearly impossible (Szasz 1994). During the 1980s, local mobilization successfully prevented the siting of hundreds of landfills and incinerators across the United States. This prompted many observers to declare a "landfill crisis." The media began to report that major urban areas would start to run out of landfill space some time in the next decade.

ban mayors were attracted to recycling's promise to reduce the municipal costs of garbage disposal (this will be a major theme of chapter 3).
Instead of paying a "tipping fee" to place all municipal solid waste into
a landfill, cities could collect some of the materials, sort them, and sell
them to firms who used them for manufacturing new goods.

The core of this process was the creation of Material Recovery Facilities (MRFs, pronounced "murf"). MRFs are large facilities where workers stand on an assembly line and sort, clean, and eventually bale large
amounts of recyclables (see chapter 3). Recyclables usually arrive at a
MRF in some sort of truck, with different materials mixed together.
Workers use a combination of physical technology and manual labor to
sort this stream into distinct categories (e.g., paper, metal, glass). Contaminated materials have to also be identified and removed from the
recycling stream. This labor-intensive process allowed mayors to pitch
recycling as a job growth program. Not only would low-skilled workers
be hired to pick up recyclables, but they would be employed in large
numbers to staff the MRFs.

In the late 1980s and 1990s, bolder municipal proposals called for
still more employment potential through the creation of recycling industrial parks and zones (chapter 5). Proponents of these plans envisioned
large complexes where garbage would be sorted and remanufactured
on-site. For example, paper could be removed from the waste stream,
repulped at an adjacent paper company, and resold to the local newspaper, producing jobs in the MRF and in the manufacturing facility. It
would employ enough people to generate spin-off economic activity in
local stores and restaurants that could revive urban neighborhoods.
This was the ultimate strategy for mayors, who envisioned being able
to avoid conflicts over landfill and incinerator siting while creating
jobs and making the city a "cleaner, nicer" place to attract relocating
professionals.

While citizen workers and governments became converts of the new
recycling gospel, many firms also saw political and economic opportunity. Contemporary production practices produce considerable volumes of waste, most of which comes from production changes that have
saved firms money. For example, bottling companies have derived substantial savings in labor costs by switching to "disposable" containers.
Likewise, packaging is a cheap form of advertising. These changes,
however, have increased the flow of solid waste to consumers, and
thereafter into the waste stream. In earlier years, producers reduced the
visible social problems of publicly discarded packaging waste by developing a public interest organization called Keep America Beautiful
(KAB). KAB encouraged consumers to "pitch in" by using litter cans

and to "give a hoot, don't pollute."[9] In the past decade, these same firms have diversified this campaign to support curbside recycling. These firms anticipated that recycling would be helpful to them because it would create a market for their wastes. Rather then being a part of the *problem*, the packaging would become part of the *solution* — an essential input into a recycling program, which in turn created jobs and protected the environment.

Moreover, many of these same packaging organizations have been consumers of the recycled materials. For example, bottling companies use recycled materials to make aluminum cans and other packaging. They urge municipalities to develop large recycling programs. Although this may seem to be a "community service," the organizational motive is to increase the aggregate volume of recyclables, thereby lowering the price these firms pay cities for the materials.

This history will become clearer as we document the details in chapters 3–6. For the moment, we note that recycling emerged with considerable potential for its diffusion, including:

1. curbing environmental impacts of current consumption by reducing the need for virgin materials,

2. reducing the need for taking land around urban communities for landfill use,

3. decreasing pollution from expanded landfills by reducing the solid waste placed into landfills,

4. reducing municipal costs of waste disposal by reducing tipping fees (and, in many cases, reducing property taxes),

5. generating new jobs in MRFs and remanufacturing facilities, and

6. building important political coalitions around an issue viewed as benefiting all social classes.

This vision of recycling amounted to a fantasy that communities would be getting something for nothing — that recycling offered a kind of free good to urban communities. This was especially appealing in the United States of the 1980s, a period of fiscal and environmental conser-

[9] Interestingly, the trade associations involved in the Keep America Beautiful, Incorporated, organization started to funnel funding to local community organizations, which came to operate within municipal governments to support recycling programs. This "Trojan horse" model has permitted still greater penetration of political agendas with the corporate interests of the packaging industries. For example, municipal garbage trucks in Evanston, Illinois (see chapter 5), carry a recycling message from Keep Evanston Beautiful, Incorporated (KEB). KEB is primarily funded by Keep America Beautiful, Incorporated. But its funding is run through the state of Illinois or city of Evanston, under grants from KAB.

vatism in government. Urban governments faced declining federal support for a number of social programs, along with a federal retreat from enforcement and enactment of environmental protection laws. Social movement organizations litigated against administrators of environmental agencies who used their authority as environmental regulators to actually *undermine* the very legislation they were suppose to enforce (Landy, Roberts, and Thomas 1990; Szasz 1994).

Recycling, in contrast to the conflicts around toxic waste regulations, was a new kind of "environmental policy." It met the demands of some environmental groups that cities cut down on consumption and conserve resources. But it simultaneously satisfied the arguments of many capital owners and managers that all government officials had to act responsibly, by ensuring that environmental regulations did not distort the workings of "the market." Recycling promised to achieve the goals of vocal urban and suburban environmental constituencies while using the means of powerful business representatives, who did not have to alter their economic practices in any substantial way.

Thus, recycling was and remains very popular with the private sector, the state, and consumers. Indeed, one of the socially and culturally appealing dimensions of recycling was precisely its potential to "bring us all together" in a unified program. Moreover, unlike many environmental regulations, this program had a kind of divisible form of benefits: households could feel good about separating their recyclables. They could gain social approval by placing distinctive bins in front of their houses for their neighbors to see and feel community pride when clean municipal trucks came by to pick up and sort these raw recyclable materials. Finally, they also felt they were contributing to local fiscal stability by reducing the costs of trucking garbage to landfills and by donating their recyclables to the city's coffers. Likewise, city officials and the private sector felt good about engaging in an environmentally responsible practice in which both revenue and profit generation were anticipated.

The Disillusionment with Early Recycling Programs

Why did the earlier promises of recycling fade? Two quite distinct and simple arguments can be made. The first is that what initially appeared to be a free resource for communities was in fact much costlier to collect and reuse. New York City mayor Rudolph W. Giuliani has been perhaps the most visible advocate of this argument. Giuliani has maintained that New York's recycling program is too expensive. It requires staff to administer the program, constant public relations to educate the public about how to recycle, and extra crews and trucks to collect materials. Throughout the mid-1990s, he has threatened to downsize, outsource, and otherwise disrupt the growing system.

At one point, he proposed cutting $26 million dollars from the budget. Mayor Giuliani spent substantial political capital arguing that recycling was too expensive and that it had been sold on the promise of overly optimistic environmental and economic benefits. Other mayors and public officials began to articulate a similar view of recycling as "naive" or "promising good ideas that never materialized." In June of 1996, John Tierney proclaimed in the *New York Times Magazine*, "Rinsing out tuna cans and tying up newspapers may make you feel virtuous, but recycling could be America's most wasteful activity" (Tierney 1996).

A second view of recycling's failures has been advanced by community groups. They view the history of recycling as just another case of political goals being undermined by powerful economic interests. For them, the simplest argument is that recycling has become dominated by private industry's decision making. Many are philosophical — almost resigned — about this transformation (see our extended discussion on this in chapters 4 and 6). Caitlin, a member of the Chicago Recycling Coalition's Board of Directors, stated the following:

> Recycling has become big business now, but I think that's something that had to happen, because of the law [mandating recycling]. And because garbage haulers are not going to let little non-profit groups — the true believers — go out there and do all the recycling. Number one, they [nonprofits] can't, because there are not enough of them. And two, they don't have the capacity, they don't want to be business people who make money. They went into recycling for different reasons, so it's just a natural progression of how the economy grows. It becomes institutionalized, and it's not necessarily bad.

Caitlin, like many community activists, argues that the problems with recycling are political, not technological. For example, recycling opponents (such as Mayor Giuliani) argue that the prices for recycled paper are too low to make recycling profitable. Community activists counterargue that these prices are the result of the artificially depressed demand for recycled paper, a demand that is really a political decision. It changes dramatically based upon political decisions about: (1) the extent to which national forests should be logged; (2) the price to charge for emissions caused by logging and pulping; (3) state purchases of virgin versus recycled paper; and (4) regulations requiring certain percentages of recycled content in paper. From this perspective, the problem with recycling is that the wealthy have been able to use their power to skew recycling programs. Resulting programs have favored elite interests over the expressed interests of the communities that had initially called for recycling programs.

Yet a third argument, along related lines, can be made. Although recyclable materials from citizens initially were defined as something close to a free good, the historical reality is that they were an important raw material, or "feedstock," of the waste disposal industry. Thus, the attempt to divert solid waste from landfilling and incineration threatened to disrupt the operations of a large and profitable waste-hauling industry. This was not a trivial consideration. Waste-hauling firms generate profits from garbage pickup, incineration, and the creation of privately run landfills. They are dependent upon a large and steady waste stream. This was especially true for Waste Management and Browning-Ferris Industries (BFI), who are central actors in our telling of the Chicago-area story.[10]

One way of synthesizing all three of these arguments is to understand that while proponents initially saw recycling as largely unrelated to the economic structure, firms viewed recycling as both a threat and an opportunity. Recycling posed a threat to manufacturing concerns, who would have to retool in order to adapt to a mixture of recyclable and virgin materials. It also posed a threat to primary resource extractors, whose products might be in less demand if remanufacturers were partially substituting postconsumer waste for virgin materials in production. For example, logging companies were fearful that recycling would decrease demand for nonrecycled paper and, hence, for logs. Finally, recycling also posed a threat to waste haulers, who had slowly and quietly built a large, profitable enterprise around the hauling and disposal of solid postconsumption wastes from communities.

Thus, to some extent all of these entities had a stake in making recycling programs fail. Paradoxically, they also had a stake in seeing that only certain forms of recycling programs succeeded. In particular, producers were concerned that the failure of recycling might attract public attention to the processes that generated growing volumes of consumer wastes. In the 1980s, a slogan emerged, referring to the "three Rs: reduce, reuse, and recycle." If recycling failed, firms might face mandates to reduce the amount of packaging or to reuse it. Both of these options were potentially expensive.

---

[10] There is some confusion over the name to be assigned Waste Management. When we began our study, the firm was named as WMX, after some previous name changes — e.g., from Waste Management International. The firm, late in this study, returned to its earlier name of Waste Management. Toward the end of the study, the firm was acquired by USA Waste Services. Generally, we refer to the firm as either WMX or Waste Management, although most recently the firm returned to its earlier name of Waste Management International.

Thus, the stage was set for what we later describe as a kind of *constricted* recycling program. In this program, private interests were quietly attended to, while public agendas were more overtly set. Recyclables would become collected by waste-hauling corporations wherever feasible, to sustain the latter businesses. The processes of sorting and packaging recyclable materials were generally to be carried out by municipalities or community development groups. Much of the cost of preparing goods for remanufacturing would thus be covered by public budgets, and not corporate profits.

Moreover, to ensure maximum corporate benefits from recycling at the municipal level, trade associations for various packaging industries widely promoted recycling in all communities. These associations thereby generated a large volume of potential raw material for recycling. In so acting, they removed much of the pressure on local landfills, and thereby diminished potential political reactions against producers of these disposed waste products. Eventually, this would lead to a de facto competition among communities, allowing prices for recyclable goods to remain as low as possible. From the standpoint of recycling firms, the aggregate of communities would ideally produce somewhat more recyclables than the market actors wanted to absorb, thus maintaining low prices and supply reserves of the "urban ore."

During the past fifteen years, these conditions have held somewhat, albeit with variations. Market opportunities often have led to disruptions of this ideal. With the rise of surplus recyclables, for example, more remanufacturers became convinced that recyclables were cheaper to use as raw materials than were virgin materials. Growing numbers of paper mills, for example, created growing demand for recyclables. Likewise, when business conditions improved, demand for paper products (among other goods) rose so sharply that the "paper glut" of newsprint and other recyclable papers was eliminated, and prices rose fivefold.

When all these conditions were in place, we saw the establishment of a new "recycling industry," complete with its own trade journals, professional associations, and lobbyists. A growing market emerged for companies that developed recycling technologies. These firms produced a range of equipment from specialized truck bodies, with compartments for sorting at the curbside collection point, to conveyor belts, magnetic and nonmagnetic material separators, air "classifiers," and computer-based color recognition systems that separate metals and different types of glass, automated equipment for baling and moving sorted materials, and even equipment for laborers hand-sorting recyclable materials.

Rather than becoming primarily a "religion," recycling became an industry, with all the traits of typically large-scale organizations (see chapter 3). As one consequence of these developments, however, some municipal planners realized that the terms of trade were stacked against them. These city officials began to alter the ways in which communities were recycling and sorting waste. In other words, both market conditions and political conditions altered the trajectory of recycling. In the course of this process, both new opportunities for and constraints upon recycling emerged. What failed to emerge was any clear discussion about the choices over recycling outcomes. Locked out of the political discussion were the social movement actors with an interest in a less-market-driven recycling process, one that would instead meet social and ecological needs. This will be a hidden theme in chapters 3–6. We will return to it in chapters 7 and 8.

Contemporary Recycling Practices

The Increased Volume of Recycled Materials

Despite its contested terrain, recycling — both as a household practice and as an industry — has continued to grow. We note three major trends relevant to the discussion in this book. They are represented graphically by the three tables below. These trends include:

1. the continued rapid growth in recycling around the country;
2. constant market volatility and fluctuation in the price of commodities; and
3. the growth of large organizational actors in the recycling industry.

Table 1.1 makes it clear that recycling continues to grow in American society. Every year, more communities are engaged in recycling and a greater percentage of the American population is served by curbside recycling programs. Between 1990 and 1996 the number of curbside recycling programs more than tripled, and during that time the number of people being served by these programs jumped to more than half of the U.S. population. These figures provide support for the notion that recycling has become a "cultural mandate." As the editor of *Recycling Times* magazine once declared, "More people recycle than vote!"

The increase in recycling programs has been matched by a corresponding growth in the number of MRFs. The capacity of these MRFs had increased to 64,200 tons per day by 1996.

Table 1.2 substantiates the growth in recycling as a major form of waste disposal.

In the past four decades, we have recycled more and incinerated and landfilled less and less waste. In sheer volume, we now recycle more than eight times the amount of waste we recycled in 1960 — one-fifth of

TABLE 1.1
Indicators of Growth in the Recycling Industry and Recycling Programs in the
United States, 1990–1996

	1990	1995	1996
Number of MRFs	NA	310	363
Total MRF capacity (clean MRF + mixed waste MRF) (in tons per day)	NA	52,000	64,200
Clean MRF capacity (in tons per day)	NA	32,000	29,400
Mixed waste MRF capacity (in tons per day)	NA	20,000	34,800
Number of curbside recycling programs	2,700	7,375	8,817

Sources: United States Environmental Protection Agency 1996 and 1997; Carless 1992.

the municipal solid waste stream—and incinerate around one-half of
the waste we burned four decades ago. But we continue to landfill more
than half of our waste, although that figure has also declined.

Thus, every year recycling is increasing both in terms of volume and
as a percentage of the waste stream.

Market Volatility for Recyclables

Table 1.3 indicates that recycling continues to be a volatile sector with
fairly large and frequent price variations. End user prices for any one

TABLE 1.2
Materials Recycled, Incinerated, and Landfilled from the Municipal Solid
Waste Stream in the United States, (in thousands of tons) and Percentage Total
Generation, 1960–1996

	1960	1970	1980	1990	1996
Recycled	5,610 (6.4%)	8,020 (6.6%)	14,520 (9.6%)	29,650 (15%)	46,610 (21.9%)
Incinerated	27,000 (30.6%)	25,100 (20.7%)	13,700 (9%)	31,900 (16.2%)	36,090 (17.2%)
Landfilled	55,510 (63%)	87,940 (72.6%)	123,420 (81.4%)	131,550 (66.7%)	116,240 (55.4%)

Source: Franklin Associates, Ltd. 1996.

TABLE 1.3
End User Prices for Recycling Commodities, 1990–1998 (in Dollars per Ton in January of Each Year)

	1990	1992	1994	1996	1998
Aluminum containers	975	750	600	1200	1125
Green glass cullet	48	49	15	20	10
HDPE plastic	180	125	150	150	300
Corrugated cardboard	25	24	22	25	100
PET plastic bottles	180	110	145	400	100
Steel	64	57	68	60	59

Source: United States Environmental Protection Agency (USEPA) 1997.

commodity can change dramatically from month to month and are often linked to global markets. For example: the supplies of bauxite reserves in Russia and the timber is Asian forests are often linked with the
fate of recyclers all over the Untied States. The one commodity on table
1.3 that seems to have maintained a relatively steady value over time is
the steel container. Aluminum prices are always the highest of all commodities but remain subject to volatility. Between 1990 and 1998,
prices for green glass dropped fivefold while corrugated cardboard
prices increased fourfold. This type of volatility has been blamed for the
death of many small recycling firms and has resulted in efforts by government agencies to lend a hand in creating more markets for materials.

There are several factors that determine how well markets will do.
The first is economic conditions. Many commodities are sensitive to
economic conditions, and in bad economic times the demand for products — particularly newspapers and cardboard — will fall. Furthermore,
since local, state, regional, national, and global economies are all
linked, there may be significant changes at any one of these levels (such
as a recession or new legislation) that can have a major impact on markets for a particular material.

The second factor is consumer demand. Sometimes consumers may
resist purchasing products made with recycled materials because of real
or perceived questions about product quality. For example, producers of
deinked pulp have had this type of problem, which has resulted in several mill closings.

The third factor is exports. Export markets for many materials are
erratic and difficult to predict. They are determined by a variety of political and economic factors in importing countries, compounded by the
general state of the global economy.

The fourth factor influencing markets is the discontinuity between supply and demand. For products like paper, the supply and demand are often out of synch. That is, oftentimes a single foreign nation may begin purchasing large quantities of recovered paper, resulting in a sudden supply shortage and price increases. The demand for this export could also abruptly drop, resulting in swift price plunges and oversupply. The rapid growth of recycling and processing infrastructure in the United States in the 1990s might eventually create an oversupply, contributing to a fall in prices if the demand does not keeps pace.

The fifth factor is legislation. Sometimes the passage (or threat of passage) of legislation favoring recycled content products at the state or federal level can help create demand for these products. Legislation has become one of the most popular ways for policy makers and recycling industry officials to develop markets. There are a number of other factors influencing recycling markets, including producer capacity and transportation costs, but it will suffice to say that while recycling appears to be here to stay, it will be some time before the terrain becomes more predictable.

The Consolidation of the Recycling and Solid Waste Management Industry

Due to the great price fluctuations and large sums of money at stake, waste hauling and recycling have come to be dominated by large waste haulers operating most urban/suburban programs through curbside collection. For example: every year, *Waste Age* magazine produces a "Waste Age 100" list that ranks firms on the basis of reported annual revenues. These companies are either publicly owned or private firms involved in the collection of municipal solid waste or the processing of recyclables in the United States. The 1996 Waste Age 100 list represents total revenues of $23.77 billion. While mergers and acquisitions are the order of the day, the solid waste industry is extremely fragmented. The four largest companies account for only 30 percent of total industry revenue, and seven midcapacity public companies represent 40 percent of revenues. However, the industry trend is toward consolidation. Higher capital requirements, arising from increasing and more stringent environmental regulations, are affecting the smaller private companies' and municipalities' ability to operate in compliance with these regulations. Between 1994 and 1996, twenty-eight Waste Age 100 companies were acquired or merged with other Waste Age 100 companies (Jones 1996).

Our analysis of the Waste Age 100 also revealed that most of the large solid waste firms are also the largest recyclers, in keeping with the history of local solid waste management noted earlier. There *are* companies with an exclusive or principal focus on recycling. However, most of them are quite small and are not considered powerful "players" in the industry. Even so, there has been a marked increase in these companies within the Waste Age 100 list. From 1994 to 1996 the number of recycling companies making the list increased from eighteen to thirty-five and is expected to continue to grow.

Another trend in both solid waste and recycling is the changing ownership of these industries. Sixty percent of the waste collection business is still operated by either local governments or family-run enterprises. But that is rapidly changing as bigger, more "efficient" private companies take over publicly run operations and family-run firms (see chapters 2, 3, and 5). In 1995, 74 percent of MRFs were privately owned and 84 percent were privately operated. While more and more taxpayers' dollars pour into recycling programs, recycling profits have disproportionately gone to private industry rather than into public agencies.

The globalization of the solid waste and recycling industries is another trend we anticipate will continue. WMX Technologies was based in Oakbrook, Illinois, before its acquisition by USA Waste Services, and had operations on five continents. Waste Management International, plc, was a British division of WMX Technologies and recently began construction of a large waste transfer station in Hong Kong. The project is being completed through a partnership with two Asian-owned waste firms. Browning-Ferris Industries, a Houston-based firm, has also been successful at achieving a global reach, much of which has been decades in the making. For example, BFI has been operating waste hauling and recycling in Puerto Rico since the late 1970s.

Many solid waste and recycling firms in the United States and around the world are making inroads into Asian nations because these countries are opening their growing consumer markets. Edwin Falkman, chief executive of Waste Management International in 1993, was quoted as saying, "The growth markets for us are Asia, Asia, Asia, and Asia" (Chakravarty 1993). WMX and its subsidiaries have also been directly involved in the drafting of new environmental regulations in nations like Indonesia and Mexico. A final indicator that solid waste recycling is becoming a global opportunity for private firms is that the locations of several recent recycling and waste management trade association conferences span the globe—Munich and Cologne, Germany; Monterrey, Mexico; and Las Vegas, Nevada.

While globalization is expected to continue, we must emphasize that the various branches of the recycling industry are still intimately linked with local and regional economies. The pulp and paper industry, for example, is an important part of the southern U.S. economy and the national economy, ranking eleventh among all manufacturing industries in contribution to the gross domestic product (Miller Freeman, Inc. 1996). Market volatility in this sector can produce significant positive or negative ripples, particularly in the South.

The Chicago Region as a Locale for Examining Recycling and Sustainable Community Development

The following chapters represent a decade of observations and data collection. Over this long period, our methodological approaches spanned the spectrum of field research strategies, including fieldwork at each of the recycling facilities, formal and informal interviews, ethnographic data collection in the surrounding communities, and participant observation with the Chicago Recycling Coalition, Uptown Recycling, the Resource Center, the Illinois Chapter of the Sierra Club, and several community organizations involved in recycling politics, including Westsiders for a Safe and Toxic-Free Environment, Citizens for a Better Environment, the Mexican Community Committee, and People for Community Recovery. Our fieldwork was supplemented with a decade of active scholarship in the recycling field, which included attending and participating in professional meetings along with reading and coding the trade literature on recycling.

In chapter 2, we briefly outline the theoretical points that frame our analysis. While we have clear theoretical goals, we also want this book to be accessible to a variety of readers. Hence, we have not suffused the substantive chapters with theoretical interpretations. Despite this, our framing of these chapters is heavily informed by social theory. We outline these starting points in chapter 2.

In chapters 3–6, we examine four different types of recycling programs that came into existence (or at least were planned) in the Chicago area during the 1989–99 period. As noted earlier, the body of research on sustainable community development has focused on either highly abstract visionary theories or short case studies. What we see as sorely needed in this literature are approaches that present useful theoretical models grounded in rich, comparative case-study data. In this project, we set out to collect such data on recycling.

We chose Chicago as our research site because each of the researchers was based in that city during the core data collection years. Thus, we had the opportunity to gather the sort of longitudinal local information about the cases that makes qualitative case study work rewarding and useful. Chicago also had at that time a diversity of recycling programs that were representative of larger national trends.[11] These programs ranged from an old neighborhood drop-off center to a state-of-the-art mixed-waste processing MRF.[12] This diversity afforded us a unique opportunity to do comparative work across a range of cases within a single industry.

In chapter 3, we discuss the history of the largest municipal waste recycling operation in the United States. Waste Management operates four facilities in Chicago's blue bag program, where millions of tons of recyclables and raw garbage are processed. These "mixed-waste" recycling systems depend upon large volumes of a municipal waste stream being processed to extract recyclables. A combination of high technology and labor-intensive production exists in these facilities. These programs have become more popular with municipalities in the United States during the 1990s. Their apparent cost-effectiveness (Longworth 1998) has led city officials to replace most of the other forms of programs that we outline in the later chapters. Table 1.1 reveals that, in a single year (1995–96) the number of these "dirty MRFs" increased by nearly 75 percent.

In chapter 4, we examine the Resource Center (RC) and Uptown Recycling, Incorporated (URI), as examples of community-based recycling programs. Their programs were much more modest than Chicago's blue bag. But they did integrate the equity, economic, and environmental goals of sustainable community development theory into their operations. They often functioned as social movement organizations, operating in a field with little organized competition. But they were undermined by the political and economic influences of the most powerful solid waste firm in the world—Waste Management.

In chapter 5, we document a variety of attempts to develop recycling industrial zones and recycling industrial parks. These projects attempted to use recycling to take items out of the waste stream and remanufacture on-site. This model was at the cutting edge of efforts to achieve sustainable community development through technological solutions, a form of industrial ecology that is often advocated by ecological modernization theorists.

In chapter 6, we present the city of Evanston's recycling facility to illustrate the use of recycling "linkage" programs. These programs built

---

[11] At the initial stage of this research, we conducted an exhaustive search of the trade literature on recycling to get a sense for the range of recycling programs across the nation. We found Chicago, and our cases, to be representative of larger national trends.

[12] We attribute this diversity to the industrial, midwestern politics of Chicago. It is progressive enough to have embraced recycling, yet is not so progressive or politically unified that it embraced any single model. The diversity of political life and neighborhoods in the Chicago area produced a multitude of recycling programs.

upon larger urban development models to balance private industry's needs with community needs for innovative investments in human capital. Evanston teamed up with the Private Industry Council (PIC) to run a MRF as a job retraining facility for young people receiving General Assistance (i.e., welfare). After only about six years of operation, though, the municipal program was outsourced and privatized because it "couldn't pay for itself."[13] This paradox of a municipal program initially created with the intention of achieving environmental, social, and economic goals being dismantled because it simply was not "profitable" is a dismal and painful case study.

In chapter 7, we return to the theoretical starting points outlined in chapter 2. Using the substantive chapters, we develop a theoretical understanding of recycling. In doing so, we outline a political economy of sustainable community development.

In chapter 8, we outline the ways in which the history of recycling in Chicago reflects larger national trends in the industry and what this means for sustainable community development in the United States. When we began this research endeavor around 1990, there was a diversity of recycling programs in the Chicago and around the nation. Over the last decade, most of these programs have succumbed to the large-scale, publicly funded, privately owned recycling model. Chicago is a good case study for this general pattern. When we began our study, each of these programs figured to be major models in the Chicago recycling arena. When we ended our study in January 1998, only the Chicago blue bag program, run by Waste Management, remained.

---

[13] Ironically, this is very different from the theory and practice in a number of social and environmental policy arenas, where the social and/or environmental benefits are estimated for programs through "shadow pricing" the outcomes (Schnaiberg 1980: chaps. 5–6). This allows such programs to appear as efficient vehicles for achieving social or environmental ends. For recycling, though, the demands of its economic "supporters" have been that recycling must "pay for itself." This is a shadow *cost* of treating recycling as a win-win program: it became viewed as an essentially apolitical and nondistributive policy.

Two

The Challenge to Achieve Sustainable Community Development: A Theoretical Framework

The Treadmill of Production as a Modern Political-Economic Model

We view the rising interest in sustainable community development as very promising. The fact that the White House created a Council on Sustainable Development signifies genuine political and social interest in some forms of sustainability. However, as social scientists, we also want to stress that sustainable community development efforts are but the latest in a long history of urban and environmental reform movements. These include the Progressive conservation movement at the turn of the last century, the appropriate technology movement in the 1970s, and the grass-roots environmental movement of the 1980s. For almost three decades, we have followed the diversity of such movements, and the outcomes of their efforts to reshape a variety of social, economic, and environmental practices in communities (Gould, Schnaiberg, and Weinberg 1996; Schnaiberg 1973, 1980, 1994a; Schnaiberg and Gould 1994). In the course of this research, we have studied the social and political context in which these movements have to operate—the *treadmill of production*.

The treadmill of production is a model that we use to represent political economic dynamics shaping natural resource usage in local, regional, national, and transnational spaces. The logic of the treadmill is as follows. As corporations and individuals invest and reinvest capital to seek maximum profit and economic growth, there are concomitant strains on the ecosystem and the social system. Economic growth is fueled by the continuous withdrawal of natural resources for industrial feedstocks. Industrial production and citizen consumption practices create effluents, waste, and other pollutants, producing further ecological disorganization. Capital intensification and automation become the most profitable path in most industries, resulting in increased worker displacement and underemployment. Both the ecological and social strains place pressure on the state, communities, workers, and corporations to address these ills—often, ironically, through more pro-growth policies. Each interest operates under the assumption that advances in public welfare are achieved primarily through economic growth.

Schnaiberg's initial (1980) articulation of the treadmill of production arose from two observations. First, there appeared to be a major change in the actual impact of production processes upon ecosystems in the last half of the twentieth century. Second, social and political responses to these impacts seemed to be quite variable and volatile. While some people rebelled against modern production, others embraced new technologies as the best hope for solving environmental problems.[1]

Schnaiberg later observed that another shift in the U.S. production system was the changing status of workers. After World War II, the United States was being transformed from a working-class society to a middle-class society, albeit one still marked by considerable poverty. Workers gained new income and occupational opportunities through the expansion of production and trade, and while the modern factory needed fewer workers, the new production workers were more educated and more skilled than their predecessors had been. They also tended to earn middle-class salaries.[2]

The new production systems differed with regards to the environment in two fundamental respects:

1. Modern factories tended to need higher material inputs. The modern factory was capital-intensive, and hence more energy was needed to run machinery. Likewise, the increase in production levels meant that more raw materials were needed. This feature of this new production system helped explain why ever-greater levels of *withdrawals* from ecosystems were required. Expansion in production required more natural inputs. These ecological withdrawals led to one set of environmental problems — natural resource depletion.

2. Modern factories used many chemicals in the production process. The modern factory used new "efficient" energy/chemical-intensive technologies to transform raw materials into finished products. Thus, workers were increasingly engaged in managing energy and chemical flows, and directing their flows through complex machinery, which created marketable products. This feature led to a second set of environmental problems — pollution — that Schnaiberg termed *additions* to the ecosystem.

---

[1] His earliest work (1973) had delved into the components of the "evironmental movement." He identified four different forms of environmental organizations: cosmetologists, meliorists, reformers, and radicals. Each of the groups perceived the causes of environmental problems in quite different ways. The groups also differed in their views of the severity of environmental problems. Thus, they offered quite different remedies for *environmental protection*.

[2] For excellent analyses see Reich 1991 and B. Rubin 1996.

Two forms of "treadmills" emerged in this new system. As firms made more products using more efficient technologies, they also garnered rising profits, which could be invested in still more productive technologies. This suggested a kind of *ecological treadmill*. Profits were thus invested in new technologies that would support still greater production expansion. This expansion required greater inputs (raw materials and energy) and hence greater withdrawals of natural resources. It also led to greater additions (toxic chemical pollution and other forms of liquid and solid waste). The implications of this model were that ecosystems were increasingly becoming used as sources of raw materials and as "sinks" for toxic wastes, thereby increasingly degrading ecosystems while enhancing profit levels.

The second form of the treadmill was social. After each cycle of production, a growing share of profits was allocated to upgrading the firm's technological "efficiencies." Analogous to the fate of ecosystems, workers were helping to sow the seeds of their own displacement. By generating profits in one cycle, they would help set in motion a new level of investment in labor-saving technology. In turn, this would ultimately lead to many workers' removal from the production process (Rifkin 1995). Some workers gained opportunities in this process, as skilled technological workers. Others gained employment as their firms expanded, creating new job prospects more remote from direct production. Still other workers in smaller firms gained income as the production system expanded, requiring inputs from a diversity of firms. The overall effect, however, was a dramatic reduction in the need for skilled human labor.

Moreover, as this treadmill of production expanded, it created new sources of revenue for governments. Some of this revenue was used to provide some displaced workers social and economic compensations. Governments now provided more services to workers and families, as they lost their jobs, through new "safety nets" of income supplementation. In addition, government agencies themselves expanded, absorbing some displaced workers and providing alternative employment opportunities. Thus, there were both losses and gains as the treadmill expanded, replacing earlier forms of production, natural resource utilization, and employment.

Yet the treadmill of production's current practices are inherently *un*-sustainable, on both ecological and social dimensions—an outcome of this current economic and political arrangement (Gould, Schnaiberg, and Weinberg 1996; Schnaiberg 1980; Schnaiberg and Gould 1994).

Our concept of the treadmill visualizes a political economy increasingly driven by five goals. The first of these objectives is the expansion of industrial production and economic development. Economic expansion is generally viewed as the core of any viable social, economic, or environmental policy. Economic expansion is thought to increase the profits that corporate managers and their investors require for capital outlays. Workers are believed to benefit from these outlays because they lead to increased production, which creates new local employment opportunities both in direct industrial production and more indirectly in the construction and service sectors. The service sector is thought to grow most rapidly due to the economic multiplier of more workers with higher wages living and spending within a community. Capital outlays also lead to higher levels of productivity, which is a precondition for rising wages. Government agencies need to ensure that national production is generating enough profitability to induce investments by capital owners, provide enough additional market values to maintain a level of wages adequate to sustain consumer demand, and generate enough tax revenue to cover the state's social expenditures. Governments expect that tax revenues from the accelerating treadmill will rise more rapidly than citizen demands. Thus, government officials and agencies increasingly share a stake in the economic expansion of the private sector.

The second aim is to increase consumption. Many of the developed world's production systems were destroyed by World War II. Transportation and communication technologies were also still quite cumbersome in 1945. This limited the scope of production in many industrial countries. Initially, many of the national markets could not absorb even the limited postwar supply (Thurow 1996). If economic growth were to come about through increased production of the amount of goods, consumers needed to have the disposable income to purchase the goods. Therefore the state, along with private capital, worked to make low-interest loans available to consumers for the purchase of homes and other items. This would ensure a continued cycle of production and consumption. Coupled with this fiscal policy were the marketing efforts industry launched, aimed at legitimating the purchase of "new and improved" products even when older goods were equally suitable (Rifkin 1995).

Solving social and ecological problems by accelerating the treadmill is the third goal. Social and ecological problems are increasingly thought to be best solved "through the market." Thus, there is an untenable, almost magical, sense that any type of economic expansion will address these ills. Poverty will be reduced by a growing economy because there is an expanded job base and increased wages at the bottom. A growing economy also supports government social expenditures (for education, housing, and other needs of the poor). Furthermore, economic growth and concomitant technological advances provide the funds and tools required to address environmental degradation.

The fourth goal is to build economic expansion around large-scale capital agents. Economic expansion is seen as fostered primarily through the growth of large firms, the Fortune 500, or "core firms." Large firms are thought to be the driving engine of the economy. Their growth creates the most demand for jobs, and it also creates secondary demand for supplies, which fuels the growth of smaller entrepreneurial firms. The wages paid to the large labor pools provide consumption capacity among consumers who keep Main Street American merchants in business. The earlier popular slogan "What's Good for General Motors Is Good for America" captures this thinking.

The final objective is to construct a political alliance of private capital, labor, and governments. The post–World War II political economy was held together largely by an implicit contract or compact. Private capital's need for a steady and reliable labor force and workers' need for jobs and their general satisfaction with unprecedented amounts of material gains led to a "no strike" pledge with management. The state played its part by expanding public education in order to produce a higher quality labor force, while also expanding consumer credit to make sure that domestic demand for goods kept pace with the increase in production.

Thus, the driving force behind this treadmill has been the growth in market value interests. *Market values* refers to profits sought by economic organizations and to levels of share prices or dividends for public investors in these organizations. Market values stand in stark contrast to *use-values*, which refers to people's biological and social needs outside of markets, such as subsistence (clean air and water, safe soil), cultural (e.g., open space), and recreational.

The treadmill paradigm traces the heightened influence of agents with market values over other community actors whose values include clean air, land, and water, and recreational opportunities. Thus, market interchanges come to dominate almost every decision made about urban areas (Logan and Molotch 1987; Squires 1994; Zukon 1995). Even those aspects of community life that were not previously related to market activity, such clean air and water, are reduced to market commodities. For example, emissions from power plants can now be traded on specialized markets, allowing high-polluting firms to buy the surplus pollution-reduction permits from lower polluting firms.

From both these physical and social processes, Schnaiberg (1980) argued that the diffusion and expansion of the treadmill of production helped to explain *both* the increase in environmental problems *and* the ambivalence of many people about how much to concern themselves with these new problems. Workers, as well as investors and managers, saw the treadmill's heavier use of ecosystems as a kind of "goose that laid the golden egg," producing wages and wealth and new government services. Most people were reluctant to address the concomitant environmental problems. Their welfare increasingly depended upon market *expansion*. The environmental problems, and some of the attendant social problems of rapidly changing production systems, were played down relative to the sense that the "market" was producing social, economic, and political solutions.

Ours is not the only political-economic model relevant to sustainable community development. Among others is Logan and Molotch's (1987) "urban growth machine" model. They have argued that urban areas are driven by a select group of real estate developers who create wealth by developing land, thus continually shaping urban agendas and debates around growth. MacIonis and Parrillo summarize: "Urban growth coalitions — typically made up of bankers, businesspeople, corporate property owners, developers, politicians, and investors — seek to spark population growth, increase the market value of land, and stimulate the city's economy through investment and development" (1998:204). Logan and Molotch argue that urban governments support growth machines because they view development as generating more tax revenue. However, development also brings more people who drive up the costs for city services (e.g., new schools, sewers, and police) faster than revenues are increasing, thereby straining city budgets (Logan and Molotch 1987).

Many of the elements in this model are congruent with the treadmill of production. The differences lie in their range of objectives and focuses. The urban growth machine is focused primarily on land-use policies within cities and on conflicts over the use of space, rather than on the range of natural resources that is incorporated within the treadmill (land, water, air, and their degradation and interaction with society). Moreover, the urban growth machine examines only localized land-use outcomes, while the treadmill includes the ecological impacts of such outcomes at the local, regional, national, and transnational levels. The two theories are most similar in their conception of the role of political and economic power in the use of natural resources, and most dissimilar in the range of social impacts of such natural resource patterns within communities. Finally, while both can be helpful in anticipating roadblocks to sustainable community development, the treadmill has broader potential to anticipate distant influences as they impact indirectly on community decisions and structures.

Conflict, Power, and Dialectics: A Political Economy Perspective

Political economy perspectives tend to be built around three assumptions about social processes: (1) local actions can be understood only within larger regional and global processes; (2) the driving force of action is conflict among social groups over scarce resources; and (3) political and economic processes are not analytically separate. Most often, social actors are using the political arena to shape economic markets in ways that are advantageous to them. As these social actors accrue further market advantages, they in turn use these economic gains as sources of power in the political arena. This process permits economically successful actors to generate still more favorable market situations for themselves.

With the backdrop of this political economic model of the treadmill, we suggest that community development tends to be shaped by three important factors:

1. divergent social interests, which lead to conflict,

2. the dialectical relationship between the environment and society, and

3. the ambivalence of the state as it seeks to reconcile competing and dialectical interests among its constituencies, which include both treadmill economic organizations and citizen-workers.

Political-economy perspectives are often used by macrostructural social researchers, who argue that these three central features of community development are often overlooked by students of local development, by policy makers, and by other social analysts who work on microstructural dimensions of community development.

Community Development Is Shaped by Divergent Interests: Conflict and Power

Community development is neither an evolutionary nor a benign "win-win" process. It is a conflictual process, where groups with different motives and means battle to shape the urban landscape (Logan and Molotch 1987). Thus, any effort at implementing a sustainable community development initiative will have to emerge from within a broader set of arrangements that shape urban politics.

Urban actors can be distinguished by their inherent interests in the urban landscape. On the one hand there are actors concerned with using the urban landscape (especially natural resources) to support their subsistence needs. For example, with regards to sustainable community development, we find environmentalists who call for lakes to be kept clean so that residents can drink the water and eat the fish. Homeless advocates call for abandoned lots to be turned into community gardens for low-income families.

On the other hand, there are urban actors in search of market exchanges that yield profits; they continually search the urban landscape to locate elements that can be transformed into anything that will generate revenue or profit. Firms are interested in lakes as potential places to store industrial by-products. Developers are interested in vacant lots as places to build new homes and commercial buildings.

Urban conflicts are often driven by these diametrically opposed interests. Most actions favor one set of values to the detriment of the other. One example is local waterways. For residents, these waterways provide safe drinking water and places to swim and fish. For firms they provide essential places to store the waste generated in the production process. Once industrial chemicals are dumped, the water is no longer safe for drinking or swimming — hence, the inherent conflict between these two types of urban stakeholders.

Proponents of sustainable community development often argue that individuals are both members of firms and community residents. These observers also argue that if we can root people to place and convince them of the value of sustainable community development, they will take these personal values into their workplaces (Shuman 1998). Although it is true that people play multiple roles, it is remarkable how often we come to separate these roles. In an earlier project, we came to know a man who worked for a pharmaceutical company during the day, helping them to evade environmental regulations (legally, of course). At night, however, he worked as the head of a local environmental organization, trying to strengthen those same regulations. It would have made more sense for him to use his intellect to bring the two roles together. This, however, might have led to his being fired from the firm or impeached by the environmental organizations. We thus note two common sociological observations: (1) social action arises from people's institutionally shaped roles and not solely from their personal values, and (2) urban conflicts are often shaped by these roles.

Community Development Is Shaped by the Dialectical Relationships between Environment and Society

To understand the origins of modern environmental problems, we also need to appreciate how the environmental interests of actors outlined above relate to the physical-biotic organization of ecological systems. The history of expanding industrial production has provided the data to outline a dialectical conflict between social and ecological organization in advanced industrial societies (Grove 1992; Schnaiberg 1980:423–24). Dialectical conflicts emerge whenever social systems have two or more goals that cannot simultaneously be met. Essentially, the dialectical tension in relationships between modern societies and their natural environments emerges from two axioms: (1) most elements of ecological systems cannot meet both market value needs and use-value needs; and (2) the treadmill of production places a primacy on market value uses of ecosystems, despite the fact that other uses of ecosystems are biological and social necessities for all classes of people. Chart 2.1 outlines a series of propositions that delineate the dialectical connections between social and environmental structures.

There are three possible governmental responses to this dialectical system — each of which is a type of *synthesis* in that it represents a response to multiple stakeholders. The first is an *economic* synthesis, which has predominated in the history of the United States and most other industrial societies. In this arrangement, the state largely fosters capital accumulation and supports primarily the exchange values of ecological systems. Only severe ecosystem disorganization is attended to, and only when it immediately threatens productive systems or is the object of significant public outcry. State "environmental" policies are localized and short-term.

A second state response is what we term a *managed scarcity synthesis*, where the state attempts some minimal regulation of access to ecosystems by various categories of users. State agencies seek to maintain some balance between environmental market values and use-values for competing actors and social classes (Hawkins 1984). To some extent, this characterizes the modern era of "environmental protection" in the United States and elsewhere.

A third state response is the *ecological synthesis* (Evernden 1985; Schumacher 1973). Here the state attaches a primacy to ecological sys-

CHART 2.1
The Societal-Environmental Dialectic

i. Production (the process of turning ecosystem elements into social resources) in industrial societies involves withdrawals from and additions to natural ecosystems, thereby producing profit (i.e., market value).

ii. Such withdrawals and additions disorganize the physical-biotic structure of these ecosystems while generating these market values.

iii. Ecosystem disorganization decreases the use values of ecosystems, restricting, among others, social access to recreational habitats, health-sustaining biological supports (air, water, land), and also decreases future levels of social production (market values).

tem protection, emphasizing use-values (including the value of preservation of existing species and habitats) over market values. This is consonant with the proposals of "deep ecologists" (e.g., Devall 1980) and neo-Marxists, who advocate a reorganization of the social relations of production (e.g., Buttel and Larson 1980; O'Connor 1988). Their goal of a sustainable society is, however, rarely supported by modern U.S. state policies (cf. Hays 1969).

The determinants of the above state responses to these dialectical conflicts include the following: social, economic, and political actors' interests in various elements of ecosystems; the power that each group of actors has to forward its interests in various economic markets and political arenas; and emergent institutional structures that reflect these interests and powers. In short, we need to understand how the motives (consciousness) and power (control capacities) of various social class segments shape the dynamics of political-economic conflicts and lead to particular state responses (i.e., syntheses) as these groups seek to control ecosystems for their own interests.

Beyond this environmental-society dialectic, moreover, the state must also create conditions that *allocate* ecological resources to organizations and social groups. In our detailed analyses of recycling programs in chapters 3–6, we note how government actions altered both the levels of recycling and the degree to which social groups received benefits from these forms of recycling. Central to this notion of the role of government is the concept of *scarcity* — both of natural scarcity within ecosystems and of socially created scarcity of access as a feature of environmental protection laws. Below, we outline how the modern treadmill of production produces an enduring bias that pushes state policies closer to an economic synthesis and away from any approach to an ecological synthesis.

Community Development Is Shaped by the State's Ambivalence about Use-Values

The state is both a facilitator of capital accumulation and a legitimator of the socioeconomic structure for the citizenry (O'Connor 1973, 1988). In its role as facilitator of a prosperous economy, the state needs unlimited access to natural resources for market values. Thus, the state comes to depend upon the treadmill, and the treadmill needs to ensure that national production is generating enough surplus to support outlays to capital owners; that it is providing enough additional market values and social surplus to supply an adequate level of wages to maintain consumer demand; and that it is generating enough tax revenue to cover the state's social expenditures (Gould, Schnaiberg, and Weinberg 1996; Schnaiberg 1980; Schnaiberg and Gould 1994).

Contrarily, the state must also regulate the treadmill. In order to achieve and maintain social legitimacy, the modern democratic state has to play a role in ensuring some degree of distributive justice (Schnaiberg 1994b). Thus, for example, it must maintain sufficient resource levels to meet the use-values of many of its voting constituents. It must ensure clean air and water, safe parks, and other quality-of-life concerns. Typically, though, this is not a win-win situation. In order for community residents to obtain access to natural resources for their own needs, firms must be denied certain kinds of access, in order to preserve air and water quality and sufficient open space for recreational needs. Yet the interests of firms are actively represented in the political arena by lobbyists and trade associations and are underscored by the contributions to campaigns made by large-scale firms.

Likewise, interest groups representing a range of citizen, labor, and environmentalist constituencies have also adopted the practice of lobbying political leaders. In fact, one of the authors worked for one such organization and lobbied Illinois legislators to repeal a law that would encourage cities to attract waste incinerators. Environmental groups have also modified these earlier approaches by highlighting voting records of candidates and disseminating this information widely to potential voters (through the Internet and new World Wide Web sites as well).

The economic power of large firms is by no means a perfect guarantee that state officials will universally favor pro-treadmill economic policies. Yet the predictive power of economic influence remains very high. Moreover, even if the much debated "campaign finance reforms" were to take hold, our analyses above suggest the multiple pathways by which the impacts of treadmill expansion have percolated down to both political leaders and their constituents already.

Allocating Scarcity: A Central Parameter

Following the above discussion, it is crucial that we understand the *mechanisms* by which both ecosystems and political systems permit or restrict access to natural resources. An ecological perspective on scarcity emphasizes that production involves withdrawals from and additions to ecosystems, which produce pollution and depletion of these ecosystems. These withdrawals and additions create ecological imbalances, altering the composition of living species or of nonliving substances and upsetting dynamic equilibriums of ecosystems (Schnaiberg 1980: chap. 1). Some natural resources are renewable (sunlight, wind) while others are nonrenewable (petroleum), thus creating different degrees of scarcity by type of resource.

But from a political-economic perspective, there is an even broader concept of scarcity. Most classes, class segments, and institutions experience and define scarcity as the increased difficulty attaining use-values or market values from ecosystems.

For example, firms hold complex relationships to the ecosystem. In the 1980s for instance, there was a major conflict in Waukegan, Illinois, over chemicals (PCBs) dumped into a harbor in Lake Michigan. The controversy came to a head when residents of the community expressed concerns about the potential negative human health effects of the dumping. These residents organized a protest campaign targeting the polluter. The PCBs were dumped by Outboard Marine, a firm that had fought environmental cleanup for the obvious economic reasons (the company had already spent millions in cleanup costs). Yet another high-tech firm, ATD, grew as it developed a new technology designed to extract pollutants like the PCBs from Waukegan. Likewise, many waste firms have made fortunes from their ability to extract harbor sediment and either bury or incinerate it. Thus, while the major response of capitalist actors has been to resist environmental regulation designed to enhance the use-values of other classes, another segment of this dominant class has extracted new market value from the state's environmental protection activities. Another way to think about this would be to argue that the modern environmental movement (in this case embodied in the citizens' organization in Waukegan) represents a broader range of challenges to the dominant capitalist producers, generating a series of complex conflicts and responses (Buttel and Larson 1980; Dowie 1992; Schnaiberg 1980: chap. 8).[3]

These conflicts become more complex as private citizens hold a range of views. On a purely economic level, environmental protection technology has to be funded either directly through taxation or by firms who pass along the costs to the consumer. Each of these processes reduces the discretionary income of and transfer payments by the state to working- and middle-class segments of society (Bryant and Mohai 1992; Bullard 1990). Environmental movement organizations often see themselves as acting to redistribute use-values to a broader social constituency (Buttel and Larson 1980; cf. Mitchell 1980). But many working-

[3] In an earlier period, during the conservation-efficiency movement (Hays 1969) the conflicts were between competing large-scale capitalist and smaller-scale precapitalist producers. The goal of the former was to maximize long-term sustained-yield production, rather than simply maintaining a limited level of production. Much of the conflict was within the capitalist class, between competing market-value interests. The rise of organizations devoted to environmental preservation introduced a more complex set of conflict. But this preservation movement itself was also largely elitist, with conflicts located within the dominant class, and largely localized.

and middle-class segments of society resent and resist the resulting costs and scarcities of environmental protection (Buttel 1985, 1986; Buttel and Larson 1980; Schnaiberg 1983b; Stretton 1976).

To explain contemporary political-economic conflicts, then, we need a deeper understanding of scarcity. A particularly helpful way of thinking about scarcity is to view it through the eyes of social interest groups. We can map out this relationship as follows.

One defining element of the environmental dialectic is the fact that ecosystem elements usually have limited capacity to meet the competing demands of political-economic interests (Schnaiberg 1994b). This is a central dilemma for state policy makers, who are increasingly called upon to intervene politically in what have historically been capitalist market transactions (Lindblom 1977; O'Connor 1988). This history of an economic synthesis, moreover, exerts a strong institutional bias in favor of market values, as opposed to citizens' use-values of ecosystems. However, there are political conditions that can partly offset this bias.[4] Accumulated disruption of ecological use-values, disseminated scientific research detailing this disorganization, and the rise of a modern environmental movement industry (McCarthy and Zald 1977) have all served to provide some of these political conditions. This explains why the United States and other advanced societies have moved some distance toward the managed scarcity synthesis of the environmental dialectic, rather than in the direction of economic synthesis.

Our example above underscores this point. The harbor in Lake Michigan can be used to provide market values for capital owners who use the water as a physical or chemical component of their production, as a cooling resource, or as a site for dumping waste products. Conversely, it has use-values for residents around the lake, ranging from potable water, a site for fishing and other recreational activities, and a sink for dumping human and domestic wastes (Catton and Dunlap 1989).

Hence scarcity is an interactive outcome, reflecting biological properties of ecosystem elements and social users' criteria for use. A final element is relative cost. For users with either very small volumes of need or with ready availability of monetary resources, the scarcity experienced will be smaller for a given degree of ecosystem disorganization. Because of the inequalities of fiscal resources in the highly stratified treadmill of production, this further biases policy making toward capitalist class segments.

---

[4] Our understanding here is somewhat similar to Skocpol's (1980) analysis of state policy making in that the state is often pulled in several different directions, but also seeks to retain its own autonomy.

Political Consciousness in the Managed Scarcity Synthesis

Political conflict initially arose from tensions within the economic synthesis. Withdrawals from and additions to ecosystems from larger-scale production had diminished other users' market values and use-values from these U.S. ecosystems (Hays 1969; Schnaiberg 1980). Environmental reform legislation emerged within a new managed scarcity synthesis in the Johnson and Nixon administrations. In turn, these policies were implemented by the Nixon, Ford, and Carter administrations, and led to both anticipated and unanticipated scarcity consequences (see Landy, Roberts, and Thomas 1990).

While representing a change in state policy and some relations of production, this managed scarcity synthesis left intact most of the class structure and institutional arrangements that created and reproduced the treadmill of production (Buttel 1985; O'Connor 1988). To some extent, however, state policies altered both the degree and the costs of access by capitalists to ecosystem elements. This "solution" to the scarcity of environmental use-values produced by the economic synthesis itself imposed new scarcities, as the ecosystems could not satisfy simultaneously all the users competing for the values and functions of a given ecosystem element.

Managed scarcity syntheses can thus reduce but not eliminate dialectical tensions. Political-economic conflicts recur as struggles between interest groups competing for access to the same ecosystem elements. What often happens in these conflicts is that one or more stakeholder groups may initially introduce or control a system of resource management, but over time other groups may eventually supplant them. Both use-values and market values are at stake in these conflicts and are guarded with "eternal vigilance" (Schnaiberg and Gould 1994) because at any time they could be challenged. These are many of the underlying dynamics that have shaped the history of recycling in the United States.

The Treadmill of Production and Recycling: Overt and Covert Conflicts

On its surface, recycling seems to have emerged as a consensual policy in the United States. With its promises to reduce landfilled waste, create jobs, and produce revenue for cities and profit for businesses, recycling represented a win-win proposition, which garnered support from a variety of public- and private-sector organizations. Testimony to this appeal is the fact that over eight thousand U.S. communities have developed some form of recycling programs. Ironically, during this diffusion of recycling a number of tensions have risen to the surface of public consciousness. Foremost among these is the fact that "recycling doesn't pay for itself." A number of early recycling program leaders have discovered that the costs of collecting, sorting, and baling recyclable materials exceeds the prices that local organizations receive from brokers or remanufacturers. In the many recent articles published in the popular press, observers have bemoaned such disappointing fiscal outcomes. However, there has been little political or social analysis of recycling's fall from grace.

However, from the perspective of the treadmill of production, such conflicts are both easier to predict and far weightier than merely some "miscalculations" by city officials or environmentalists. The superficial morality play about "landfills filling up" and the "need to reduce wastes" misrepresents the history of "problems" for which recycling appeared to be the solution. Such problems represent the organized interests of treadmill producers, whose production decisions led directly to landfill and other environmental disruptions. Central to this drama are the bottling and packaging industries, whose shift to disposable containers and packaged goods has produced the single largest increase in solid wastes. The major rationale for creating disposable containers and packaging is simple and direct: to reduce labor costs. Both the collection and cleaning of refillable containers is somewhat labor-intensive. And the rise of consumer packaging has permitted retail merchants — especially larger discount stores — to reduce their labor costs by hiring fewer and less-skilled clerks whose main tasks have now been reduced to passing packaged goods through a scanner to compute costs to consumers.

Moreover, these packaging organizations have mounted a disinformation campaign about their production process for nearly forty-fivce years, through their "public interest" organization, Keep America Beautiful. Finally, they concentrated their efforts to oppose public referendums about "bottle bills" during the 1970s. Bottle bills would have added a surcharge to all containers, providing incentives for consumers to return these containers to merchants and incentives for producers to refill these containers rather than make new ones for future disposal. Estimates range as high as $50 million spent by these packaging interests to defeat campaigns in most states to add a bottle charge for containers. From an ecological standpoint, these major producers had strong interests both in extracting virgin materials to make packaging (petroleum for plastics or wood pulp for paper) *and* in ensuring that communities provided sufficient disposal sites to permit such packaging to get off city streets and out of sight.

Interestingly, these treadmill organizations quickly organized to support local recycling in the 1970s and 1980s. Keep America Beautiful created local and national organizations to encourage recycling (and other forms of waste disposal exceeding recycling capacity). However, their encouragement was very focused on allocating responsibilities for recycling to consumers and municipalities, rather than to producers. These industries were well aware of the expenses involved in the collection and sorting of recyclables, and by promoting consumer-municipality obligations, they could evade the high costs of such processing.

Moreover, by widely promoting recycling, they ensured that their own remanufacturing plants would have a large volume of future feedstocks, permitting remanufacturing managers to pay lower prices to reprocess such recyclable feedstocks. So successful were these treadmill agents that many communities that recycled were faced with a glut of recyclables on the market. They had a choice of either selling their own recyclables for a minuscule price or spending still more money to landfill these recyclables.

In line with the arguments we made in chapter 1, there is a second category of interested organizations involved in the shadow plays around recycling programs: the solid-waste companies that have a strong stake in garbage processing. The primary revenue-generating activity of these firms has been the hauling of solid wastes for cities and private businesses. A secondary source of earnings has been the operation of private and public landfills, as well as incineration of various forms of solid waste (including burning wastes to generate electricity). To a considerable extent, this industry has gone through a long period of consolidation leading to the emergence of large national and multinational waste management conglomerates. To some extent, these firms have an interest in increasing solid wastes, since this generates more profits for them. In this regard, they have little or no conflict with the major underwriters of Keep America Beautiful, who produce much of these disposable containers and other packaging.

A third economic entity has also been concerned with recycling. Scrap dealers have traditionally been localized firms, with large land plots available for storing scrap materials. Their primary suppliers have been small businesses and scavengers, and they typically sell to small- or medium-sized regional businesses. In the case of auto junkyards, they may sell to individuals as well as to remanufacturers of auto parts. With the rise of a competitive recycling industry, many of these scrap dealers have faded from existence.

Recycling was initially placed on the public agenda by environmental movement organizations as early as the 1960s. However, this movement gained more attention in the late 1970s and early 1980s as the public attention to toxic wastes and other landfill problems emerged in the

United States. Recycling *within* industrial facilities was initially proposed as part of the Resource Conservation and Recovery Act (RCRA)
of 1976, aimed at toxic chemicals in use in manufacturing. When industrial interests blocked this proposal in favor of improved landfilling and
incineration, some environmental groups shifted their advocacy toward
three production pathways: the Three Rs — reduction, reuse, and recycling, preferably in that order. While they had some modest success with
some firms on the first two pathways, their major "victory" was in the
area of recycling postconsumer solid wastes, which were requiring ever-
growing landfill space to match rising levels of municipal wastes. Wastes
were to be reduced by consumers or they were to be reused in some
other socially useful way. Only as a last resort was recycling to be used.

Very quickly, however, recycling began to be proposed as the major
solution to the rising volume of solid wastes and the relatively fixed
amount of landfill space. Each of the major business groups reacted
according to its perceived interests. Packaging companies quickly realized that recycling could serve their interests, and they used both the
"public interest" Keep America Beautiful organization as well as advertising budgets to promote recycling as one alternative to communities'
problems with solid wastes. Their interest in recycling was twofold: (1)
anything that could remove municipal waste more effectively than landfilling would permit continued expansion of disposable containers and
packaging, with less opposition; and (2) if recycling campaigns worked,
the packaging industries would eventually find it profitable to retool for
remanufacturing, provided that recyclable feedstocks would be both
plentiful and cheap. Hence, the packaging industry helped diffuse the
message of recycling as a major solution to urban waste problems in
municipalities all over the country. Both of these strategies provided
cost containment for these industries and deflected potential pressures
on them to return to refillable containers and unpackaged consumer
goods.

Waste management firms were much more reticent about recycling,
since few of them had any experience with it. Initially they feared the
advent of recycling as the beginning of a process that would reduce
solid wastes and thus depress their profits. However, because of their
long-standing connections to municipal governments through their
waste-hauling and landfilling activities, they also set out to position
themselves quickly as a new profit center in the recycling field. As chapters 3–6 will make clear, they achieved some success in this entrepreneurial role by using their capital, expertise, and influence on solid
waste planners in a variety of communities.

In contrast, local scrap dealers, anticipating that they would have a
powerful role mediating between municipalities and remanufacturers,

welcomed recycling proposals. They were the only organizations that had business experience with collecting, sorting, and selling waste materials, and they felt they would become the local experts in the new recycling era. Fairly quickly, though, they became peripheralized in most larger cities, as the new volume and content of the recyclable waste streams appeared to overwhelm their limited capacities. Although they had the experience, they lacked the capital and influence of the large waste management firms, who rapidly repositioned themselves as recycling experts, despite their lack of direct experience. In addition, the rapid rise in volume of recyclable materials also drew new materials brokers into the recycling game, mediating between cities, waste management firms, and remanufacturers.

Much of the early history of environmental recycling proposals finds some echo in the chapters that follow. Yet far more dominant is the role of major waste-hauling firms, packaging industries, and municipal solid waste officials. Recycling has the veneer of an environmental policy aimed at creating sustainable communities. However, it quickly emerged as a market-oriented activity, reinforcing many of the treadmill of production's unsustainable goals and means. Thus the logic of recycling as currently practiced is quite remote from some of the dreams and expectations of environmentalists and local community organizations that were aiming at economy, equity, and environment. Of these three objectives of sustainability, economic goals have, through recycling programs, once again been prioritized at the expense of equity and environmental protection. Of the three environment-society dialectical syntheses, recycling has come to most represent a weak form of managed scarcity and, in some of the cases we examine, it approaches the economic synthesis. In none of the current programs that we review has there emerged anything like a stable ecological synthesis, although community-based programs approached this at their peaks.

Limitations of Our Analysis

Sustainable development may be a noble concept, but it remains unclear how our industrial societies will move toward this goal. We chose recycling as the central focus of this book in part because recycling appeared to be a first step on the path to building materially and socially sustainable communities. Perhaps the deciding factor in our focusing on recycling was that it was operating across many communities and within a variety of economic and social environments. When we started our field research, recycling already had a decade of history behind it, and thus was potentially a "leader" among sustainable programs and policies.

But these very features that attracted us to recycling may also give us pause to consider how strong a model recycling is, particularly for sustainable development activities. For example, recycling coexists with a variety of unsustainable economic and political activities in these communities. Its very adaptability may make it a poor candidate for the changes that sustainable development requires (i.e., to restructure the treadmill). And yet the opposite argument is also valid, namely, that movement toward sustainable development will come in increments, rather than as a socially cataclysmic transformation of the treadmill. As we have argued elsewhere, such movements have two problematics: (1) how do we *attain* this new form of social and environmental development? and (2) once attained, how do we *maintain* these new forms of productive organization? In this regard, the fact that we have attained several incarnations of recycling allowed us to examine how these were to be maintained or altered once in operation.

This latter question is a pressing one for us. Within months of submitting the first draft of this manuscript, there were major changes in some of the cases we present in chapters 3–6. They required us to rethink the conditions under which initial recycling programs had been attained, and what these entailed for their future maintenance. In this reconsideration, we were compelled to remind ourselves how our study's recycling programs were only a *part* of a production system. For example, in a recent interview with a former Chicago official, he emphasized that recycling was only a part of the city's broader concern with solid waste management. Thus, in chapter 3 the vagaries of the recycling program were bound up with larger issues of solid waste flows and their management. Likewise, in all of the chapters, the fates of recycling organizations in part hinged on the prices that remanufacturers paid for recyclable feedstocks. Few of the environmental movements supporting recycling have challenged the treadmill's market approach to recyclable materials, and yet the fate of a number of our programs was often dictated by low and volatile prices for recyclables.

Thus, recycling, in being a partial reform, has the strength of representing other sustainable development activities in cities. And it has a major weakness, in that neither the origin nor destination of recyclable materials is under the control of recycling agencies. Short of developing isolated sustainable communities, we must deal with the nature of communities as they really exist and seek ways of understanding them in order to help change them.

In the following chapters we present a range of case studies that reveal the promises and pitfalls of recycling programs in the United States. We will use the model of the treadmill to frame our discussion of the case studies. Two other issues will underlie our case studies. The first is the continued push toward the globalization of the economy and its negative impact on social systems and ecosystems (e.g., Longworth 1998). The second issue is the growing disparity in political power between stakeholders (citizens, labor, private capital, the state) in the community. Those actors who have the political will to change the presently unsustainable organization of capital, labor, and natural resources generally do not have the political power to do so. This is true of the progressive community groups and social entrepreneurs we discuss in chapters 4–6. We will return to these issues in chapter 7.

Three

Chicago's Municipally Based Recycling Program: Origins and Outcomes of a Corporate-Centered Approach

Who Is Riding the Tiger? The Alliance between the City of Chicago and Waste Management, Incorporated

In 1990, the city of Chicago announced a Request for Proposals (RFP) for developing a comprehensive, citywide residential recycling program. The RFP was surprising to people in the city's recycling community. First, the RFP specified that the program was citywide. By arbitrarily refusing to consider bids for separate sectors within Chicago, it ipso facto excluded an array of community-based centers. For example, the two community-based recycling centers we will discuss in chapter 4 (the Resource Center [RC] and Uptown Recycling, Inc. [URI]), had operated successful recycling programs in nearly a dozen different neighborhoods. But neither had the resources to write a comprehensive RFP detailing a citywide program, much less the capacity to implement such a program. Thus, the city's RFP excluded the range of progressive community-based recycling programs that had become important centers of economic and waste recycling activity in many of Chicago's low-income communities.

Second, the RFP appeared to be tailored to the capacities of Waste Management, a large international waste management firm anchored in Oakbrook, a suburb of Chicago. Ann Irving, the executive director of the Chicago Recycling Coalition, called the RFP process an example of "bald-faced power playing by a corporation with a monopoly." Irving and others hinted that the RFP was carefully written to target Waste Management as the ultimate contractor. Her charge stems from her observations that (1) Waste Management was headquartered in the Chicago metropolitan area and played an influential role in local politics; (2) William Daley, the brother of Chicago's mayor Richard Daley, served on the board of directors of Wheelabrator Technologies, a firm then partly owned by Waste Management (currently a wholly owned subsidiary); and (3) for several years, Wheelabrator's Northwest Incinerator in Chicago was embroiled in a legal battle that finally spelled its doom when it shut down in April of 1996. City officials knew long before this date that the incinerator's closing would necessitate a compensatory municipal waste management system. Echoing this sentiment, the corporate watchdog group INFACT noted in a widely quoted report, "William Daley, in fact, once sat on the company's [Wheelabrator's] board, where he was paid $40,000 annually. Mayor Daley's Chief of Staff represented WMX (Waste Management) in negotiations on Chicago's recycling program, and Daley's wife participated in charity work with the spouses of WMX executives" (INFACT web site 1997:3). Thus, at the very least, it seems clear that senior Waste Management officials had the ear of Chicago's mayor, Richard M. Daley. They often seemed to act as informal advisers on Chicago's waste disposal matters, as well.

Even so, Chicago's proclivity to contract with Waste Management appeared surprising, in part, given the company's less than desirable public image. Specifically, aside from the enormous economic clout Waste Management brought to the table, their operations around the nation have been dogged by a trail of lawsuits charging bribery of public officials, death threats to politicians, illegal dumping, and environmental racism — more lawsuits than those raised against any other large waste firms (*Rachel's Environment and Health Weekly* 1997).

A very different story emerged in our discussions with former officials of Chicago's Department of the Environment. Rather than Waste Management manipulating the city, it appears the blue bag design emerged from the city's long-term strategic discussions about solid waste management. Such discussions were initiated in the mid-1980s during the reign of Harold Washington, the city's first African American mayor, leading to a conceptual report in 1988. They were stimulated by a series of problems with the city's solid waste management facilities, including the odors and unsightliness of outdoor sorting centers, leaking landfills, and the rising costs of dealing with these matters. Initial reports about the future of solid waste management included a variety of local actors, including waste-hauling firms such as Waste Management and Browning-Ferris, but also incorporating labor unions and citizen groups as well as several city departments. It was decided that the city needed to upgrade its facilities to meet both Environmental Protection Agency standards and citizen complaints. This broad committee outlines some general principles for solid waste management.

However, by the time that detailed planning for solid waste began, this broader advisory group had lost its labor and citizen-group involvement. During the succeeding regime of Richard Daley, the detailed technical elements of solid waste management were hammered out, and in this period regular "players" such as waste-hauling firms had a more central role (Lowi 1979). This was the period in which recycling had appeared on the state of Illinois's agenda, and the city had to incorporate a 25 percent level of recycling as one goal of its new solid waste program. Although community groups in Chicago by then had developed some experience with localized recycling programs, city officials quickly decided that this limited involvement was largely irrelevant for scaling up to a citywide recycling program. In our interviews with one of these officials, he described the community-based programs as "boutique" operations, in contrast to the city's need for a "wholesale" approach to recycling.

Whatever the validity of such claims, they led the city to consider a rather different model for citywide recycling. Moreover, the recycling model was from the outset integrated within the broader goals of affordable and legally compliant forms of solid waste management by the city. In retrospect, one of the enduring conflicts between the city and citizen-action groups has been one about the centrality of recycling. For the city, recycling of its wastes from city residents was only a small part of the larger task of solid waste management of the residential and commercial activities in Chicago. For community-based citizen groups such as the Chicago Recycling Coalition, however, recycling was part of an environmental agenda. For the recycling organizations we will examine in chapter 4, recycling was an environmental, *social*, and *economic* activity, designed to offset wider social inequalities in Chicago.

Another central feature of designing a recycling program for Chicago was that the city was a relative latecomer to citywide recycling. This meant that city officials had the chance to observe the outcomes of recycling programs initiated earlier in large cities. In particular, New York City's experience appeared to loom large in the consciousness of Chicago officials. What they observed in such programs was a serious escalation of budgets, primarily because the revenues from sales of recyclables were much lower than anticipated. Moreover, Chicago officials also observed that the markets for recyclable materials were highly volatile, which meant that budgetary needs for recycling programs were unstable. Chicago's new mayor, Richard Daley, appears to have been especially concerned with these features, and urged his officials to find a way to buffer the city from such fiscal volatility.

What eventually emerged from these discussions was a "blue bag" model of recycling. Most curbside recycling programs are characterized by the collection of source-separated recyclables. These recyclables are put into bins for pickup by recycling trucks, not municipal garbage trucks. In contrast, Chicago's blue bag program required residents to place their recyclables in blue plastic bags alongside regular garbage bags containing household trash. Both types of bags would then be collected by municipal garbage trucks, not recycling vehicles. As with normal trash collection, the trucks would compress their loads with hydraulic crushers (to increase efficiency of pickup costs) and then dump them at Chicago's new Material Recycling and Recovery Facilities (MRRFs). Workers would then manually pull these bags off conveyor belts and separate their contents. Recyclable materials not in blue bags would also be pulled out of the garbage for sorting. There were to be four new enclosed MRRFs (or "sorting centers") to remove wastes from the public eye and nose, and a contractor would be sought to sort wastes, retrieve and package recyclable materials, and haul the remaining wastes to landfills in Illinois and Indiana.

The reasons for this program design appear to be largely economic and political. If Chicago was to control its recycling program costs, in contrast to the New York City experience, it needed a tightly integrated solid waste management system. Recycling would be embedded within the larger system. City officials appeared to accept the model of a treadmill of production, since they anticipated that they could not control markets for recyclables. And they also appeared to believe that large firms could better deal with this uncertainty, since such firms had experience operating in volatile markets. Thus, Chicago's RFP was specifically designed to attract bids from large firms to operate the city's entire solid waste sorting system (including Chicago's new recycling program).

Moreover, contrary to the charges of Waste Management domination by critics of Chicago's blue bag program, the company actually wanted to operate only one of the new sorting centers (according to a current manager there). WMX had a landfill in the Calumet Industrial District and sought to negotiate for a sorting center to be placed there, at a cost of $15 million. But Chicago had plans to build four such centers, at a total cost of about $60 million, and wanted a contractor to operate all of them (for economies of scale and to reduce city administrative costs). Thus, although WMX had never actually operated a MRRF, it anticipated large enough potential profits in hauling Chicago wastes to landfills that it eventually agreed to bid to operate all four MRRFs. Chicago appeared to have achieved its fiscal and program goals: it would more cleanly handle solid wastes, and do so for a relatively predictable cost of the four new MRRFs it was building.

In contrast to charges from the Chicago Recycling Coalition, the record also seems to indicate that Waste Management actually signed on to a losing proposition. Interviews with Chicago officials and the current manager of Waste Management's sorting centers indicate that WMX had never made a profit on the MRRFs, despite their early efforts to circumvent some of Chicago's goals. In dealing with this large firm, Chicago anticipated that WMX would not be committed to the same fiscal and material goals as the city would be. Therefore, the initial contract with WMX spelled out in great detail a variety of contractual provisions.

First, the city spelled out a sequence of "diversion" goals for the MRRFs. Starting with a goal of diverting 10 percent of the solid wastes, the MRRFs would later be required to divert 25 percent and higher levels of wastes passed through them. Failure to achieve these goals would make the contractor liable for financial penalties. The contractor would be paid about $36 per ton of waste hauled to landfills and $20 per ton of waste diverted from landfills. This price structure would appear to provide a disincentive for recycling, but Chicago negotiators anticipated that it would induce WMX to recycle even higher levels of wastes, since the difference in payments per ton of waste would be more than offset by revenues from selling recyclable materials.

Promises and Pitfalls of the Blue Bag Program

The city of Chicago added recycling to its new solid waste management system for reasons common in large cities. The environmental movement saw a huge upswing during the 1980s, as hundreds of communities successfully resisted the siting of landfills and incinerators (Szasz 1994). This massive resistance to traditional solid waste management practices precipitated what politicians and industry officials came to call "the landfill crisis." In Chicago, a similar campaign successfully passed a moratorium in 1984 on the expansion and siting of new landfills. This new law forced the city to rethink its future waste disposal plans. Siting an incinerator in the city was no longer socially or politically feasible because of community resistance.

The mayor's office also had to deal with a number of legal and political economic challenges. Included was a case being considered by the U.S. Court of Appeals for the Seventh Circuit, in which it was later ruled that Chicago's incinerator ash constituted hazardous waste. Chicago's Northwest Incinerator had been the city's principal waste management system since 1971. The tons of ash it produced every day were now subject to regulation under the Resource Conservation and Recovery Act. This created new expenses for the municipal disposal of solid waste. The city was deemed in violation of RCRA because the ash it buried in landfills did not legally constitute "proper disposal" of a toxic waste.

Siting a new landfill appeared to be equally problematic. Many of the city's white liberal elite were supporting "green" city policies. Annual Earth Day festivities were drawing several thousands of citizens into

Grant Park, making urban environmentalism highly visible. Recycling appeared, then, to be one of those rare win-win policies for the city. It would solve the landfill problem and please the environmental community. It might even provide jobs in some of the city's depressed areas.

To the city, the blue bag program seemed like a golden political opportunity. Recycling advocates, environmentalists, and some politicians (such as Alderpersons Burke and Hanson) had been calling for a comprehensive waste management plan for years. This seemed as good a time as any to respond to these arguments. Furthermore, the city of Chicago needed a system that would bring it into compliance with city and state laws. Illinois law required that Chicago have a recycling plan that would achieve a 15 percent recycling rate by 1994 and 25 percent by 1996. The Chicago Recycling Coalition and Citizens for a Better Environment, two of Chicago's most progressive environmental organizations, supported Chicago's recycling ordinance. The ordinance required that by 1993 all low-density dwellings have "regular recycling service." One or more of the following methods defined this as the collection of at least four types of materials:

1. at least biweekly curbside collection of recyclables by the city or a contractor;
2. a buyback center located within one mile of any building not served by curbside programs;
3. a network of drop-off boxes. (Office of Technology Transfer 1990)

The city was also eager to explore the prospect of new recycling centers for their job creation potential. Like many cities in the Northeast and Midwest, Chicago had faced a continuous exodus of blue-collar jobs since the early 1970s. Chicago's job drain rivals those in most U.S. cities. Entire neighborhoods and much of the city had experienced large-scale "deindustrialization" (Bluestone and Harrison 1982), leaving the urban core "hollowed out." Wim Wiewel (1990), a Chicago-based urban sociologist, estimated that from 1947 to 1963, jobs declined by 18 percent (122,000 jobs). And while there was a small gain between 1963 and 1967, from 1967 to 1982 the decline accelerated. The city's losses amounted to a 46 percent decline—a loss of about 250,000 jobs. By 1982, Chicago had lost 326,000 jobs, or 60 percent of its manufacturing jobs (Wilson 1996). New industries are highly sought after in urban centers like Chicago. For example, the blue bag program had an economic development component that the city valued. Chicago's four new MRRFs were slated to create anywhere from 50 to 100 jobs each, a total of 200–400 new city jobs. Current employment at the four MRRFs is approximately 850, as reported by a manager at Waste Management International.

Most of the needed infrastructure was already in place because Waste Management had been providing waste pickup service to commercial units for years. The company had a fleet of trucks and several transfer stations and landfills, including the Calumet Industrial District landfill. The blue bag program would fit right into this structure, with few major changes. Finally, after conducting a cost-benefit analysis, the city concluded that total annual costs for the public-private joint program were projected to be $31 million for a privately run curbside collection program. This compared favorably to the estimated $41 million for the cost of a publicly financed curbside program. And the public program did not include the costs of the 210 new trucks that would be needed.

Casting aside ecological and social criteria, then, "the primary reason given for adopting the commingled bag/MRRF recycling program [was] its affordability" (Office of Technology Transfer 1990). To quote a Waste Management manager: "In 1991 the city went out to look and see how should we recycle, and one of the things that they saw is that a lot of places have curbside programs and they looked at the cost of that. The cost — because you end up sending two trucks down an alley — it was cost prohibitive. So they looked at the blue bag program" (interview).

In our field research during 1996–97, we found that Chicago's program achieved relatively little headway towards the three Es of sustainable community development.[1] The blue bag program did divert a sub-

---

[1] Unlike the field conditions we faced in other recycling operations, we were essentially shut out of observing Waste Management's MRRFs. Although tours were open to us, we found that the working conditions of recycling-line employees were not visible to those touring the facilities. Moreover, despite the elaborate details about the physical capital and technology inside the MRRFs, few details about the actual labor conditions were made publicly available. Accordingly, details on the actual work conditions were derived from a series of interviews with workers and managers who spoke to us during nonwork hours. We also gathered considerable data from other local respondents and informants. These included members of the Chicago Recycling Coalition, a citywide nonprofit coalition supporting sustainable recycling practices in Chicago. Members sometimes referred us to other sources of information, including OSHA (Occupational Safety and Health Administration) records on safety violations at the four sites. Our previous research contacts included local ethnic community groups, who had enthusiastically supplied lists of potential workers for the MRRFs from their communities. They reported the discontent of these workers, and gave us names and contact numbers of both current and former employees of Remedial Environmental Management (REM), the subcontractor for lower-skilled workers in the Waste Management–run facilities.

Other informants directed us to former Waste Management foremen and lower-level managers, some of whom were discharged because they had complained about the unhealthy and unsafe work conditions for the REM employees on the sorting lines. They

stantial volume of materials away from landfills and incinerators. But despite the program's efforts, a very high proportion of local solid wastes was still placed in landfills in the early years of the program (variously estimated up to 94 percent), including in Waste Management's landfill. Thus the ecological efficiency of this capital-intensive program was rather limited. Moreover, our research indicated few equity or economic gains for the Chicago community and its population.

The following composite description of the MRRF operations reveals a graphic portrait of the social problems generated by the new program. The composite is based on our interviews with workers and foremen in their homes, who, like the majority of Waste Management's MRRF workers, were African American:

> It is 7 o'clock in the morning. You are a black woman. You are standing in a huge facility (several hundred yards long) It's freezing cold because there is no heat. You have just walked 1.5 miles because the facility is not accessible by public transportation and you are too poor to own a car. You are going to spend the next ten to twelve hours (often you do not know how long) standing on an assembly line sorting through raw garbage straight from trash cans. You may or may not have protective gloves, so you will have to be careful. Coming down the line could be hypodermic needles, dead animals, live rats, broken glass, and on the odd day a baby or other human body parts. You have seen coworkers splattered with battery acid and picking up leaking bags marked "biohazard." To quote one of your coworkers: "I can remember the first guy who got stuck by a needle. . . . The guy got stuck by a bloody needle. You don't know whose needle that was. Hopefully, he didn't get infected with HIV, or Hepatitis A or B." This worker goes on to tell us that this man was lucky compared to one of his coworkers who picked up a bag of asbestos that came down the line. For this you will be paid six dollars an hour, and guaranteed employment for eighty-nine days, at which time you will be fired one day before the ninety days needed for unionization and other benefits to start. . . . WELCOME TO CHICAGO'S BLUE BAG PROGRAM

Our field research on WMX's blue bag program was built around interviews with workers, supervisors, and managers at the MRRFs. Access to the site was unavailable during this period because WMX would

---

gave us detailed information, including some of the OSHA charges and investigations of the MRRFs. We validated and triangulated this information by using public documents, comparing statements by several informants and respondents, and obtaining rather detailed accounts of specific events.

However, after presenting our findings in 1999 to a group of scholars and city officials, we were invited to interview a number of city officials and Waste Management managers. We availed ourselves of this opportunity, updating the history of the program through the last stages of revision of the manuscript.

not permit us to closely observe or interview persons within the
MRRFs, other than in public tours offered at one facility (where it was
difficult to observe workers on the line). Workers were explicitly forbid-
den to speak with reporters and researchers, so much of these data were
gathered from individuals who spoke with us under secretive conditions. From these interviews, we developed a picture of the MRRFs that
was extraordinarily negative — the waste stream diversion rates were accordingly quite low, and workers operated in hazardous and difficult
conditions, as we detail in the following sections.

Early Problems with the Blue Bag: Miscalculating
Start-up Costs and Recovery Rates

Initially, Chicago's program design seemed to support its argument that
blue bag recycling in Chicago would be an efficient solution to a variety
of economic, ecological, and equity problems. Yet, in the initial years of
its operations, it became increasingly apparent that the city had mis-
calculated the subversion of the program. The current manager indicated that one of the reasons for the dismal performances at the MRRFs
in their early years was that they were put into full operation immediately after their construction was completed, without a start-up period of trial and correction, normal in most industrial plants. Former
Chicago officials who negotiated the initial contract added that another
problem was that the MRRFs came on-line during the period in which
George Soros and other major investors in Waste Management began
their attacks on higher management for producing too low a rate of
return for investors.

Whatever the background causes, three major problems surfaced
quite dramatically in the first years of the blue bag program's implementation. The first two problems were exorbitant start-up costs and low
participation rates. We will discuss the third problem — health and
safety issues — in the section below on occupational safety.

Start-up Costs

The first problem was the miscalculation of the cost of building and
operating the four MRRFs. These turned out to be much more expensive than originally estimated. Waste Management Incorporated designed, constructed, equipped, and operated the facilities. But the city of
Chicago compensated the company for its costs and services. Originally,
the city anticipated a capital burden payment of between $5 and $8

million for the company's construction of each of the facilities. The actual costs turned out to be closer to $16 million each (Office of Technology Transfer 1990). Chicago thus underestimated this figure by as much as $44 million.

The city agreed to compensate the contractor for hauling and disposing of nonrecycled refuse either to sanitary landfills or to the city-operated Northwest Incinerator (which had recently became out of compliance with RCRA standards and shut down). This turned out to be a far more expensive supplemental payment to Waste Management than Chicago had previously calculated. Recovery rates from the MRRFs were initially far lower than projected, resulting in larger volumes of materials sent to landfills. Waste Management nonetheless also retained all revenues derived from the sale of recycled materials, in addition to their fees for waste haulage to landfills.

Waste Management and the City of Chicago faced a battery of critics. The Chicago Recycling Coalition (CRC) led the way in attacking the blue bag as a fiscal and ecological nightmare. In an interview with Ann Irving, then executive director of CRC, we discovered some of the unflattering details of the city's marriage with Waste Management. Irving described how the political connections between the administration and the firm blocked any consideration of fiscal and environmental responsibility:

> There was a deal made behind closed doors—that this would be the new program. It's easy to see how this happened, in a sense. They also have a close relationship with the Daley family. Mayor Daley's brother sits on the board of Wheelabrator Technologies, which is a subsidiary of Waste Management—receives a fairly hefty forty thousand dollars a year stipend for doing basically nothing. And you know, Waste Management has been sponsoring a lot of city-greening activities and things of that nature. I think the most telling thing about the relationship between the city and Waste Management was that . . . the city chose this program [and] decided it was going to go ahead with this lengthy process of writing an RFP and during that process there was no open discussion about what this program was going to consist of. But the city was a little cagey as to what it was precisely going to ask for in the RFP. But what it was very up-front about was they were arguing that the contractor would be asked to provide the capital in order to construct the facilities. And that aced out a lot of smaller waste haulers in the area who might have been very interested in doing it. We've talked to people at Illinois Recycling Services—no great friend of the environment—but certainly a very growing company and a company that, I'm sure, would have been very interested in this contract. And we've been told privately by them that they *did* bid on the contract and were essentially just refused out of hand. And the city kept arguing that it

couldn't accept people like them because they just couldn't be sure that they would have the capital resources necessary to go with these very large facilities, the price of which of course would increase—even double—by the time it was built.

Further alienating taxpayers, environmentalists, and other firms, the city then made another unorthodox decision, Irving noted:

That was the idea, that the contractor would build the facilities and the city would pay the contractor on an annual or a regular basis for the processing of the materials and the disposal of the materials. And so the contract negotiations began and basically there were only two companies accepted into those contract negotiations—Waste Management and Ogden Projects (part of Ogden Martin corporation, a multinational firm). And midstream, halfway through the negotiations on the contract, the city announced that they felt they would save money in the long run if they paid for the capital construction of the facilities instead of asking the contractors to bear the costs. So that shows you how stacked the deck was in favor of Waste Management, where essentially the city set rules that would ace out any of the small waste haulers and halfway through the contracts—which seems almost incredible—decided "Oh, yeah, on second thought, we'll pay the lion's share of the financing." . . it's like $54 million the city is going to pay in capital costs. And then additionally Waste Management is going to make a lot of money on annual fees and, depending on how well the program works, in terms of the city's own costs, if the program does poorly, they'll pay more. So basically they're [the city] going to pay for half the facilities—even though it's a Waste Management–owned facility.

We discovered in interviews with Chicago officials that the original plan was that the city of Chicago would own three of the four MRRFs, and Waste Management would eventually own the fourth. The latter was situated on its own property in the Calumet Industrial District. Part of the discrepancy between critics' and the city's position of the MRRFs, however, remains that the city's goals for the MRRFs were for *total* solid waste management. Critics have focused only on the *recycling* component of the MRRFs. They noted that in addition to the high capital cost to Chicago's taxpayers, the early experience was that the blue bag program also failed to effectively recycle much of the city's waste.

Low Recovery Rates

The blue bag program was premised on two assumptions about keeping recovery rates high, and costs low: (1) Blue bags would allow for one

truck and a single work crew to collect both recyclables and nonrecyclables (i.e., garbage). This would lead to a higher percentage of recyclables being recovered from the waste stream as the nonrecycling bags
could be sorted for recyclables as well. In fact, the majority of recyclables recovered at the MRRFs originated in regular garbage bags and
were *not* from blue bags. It would save money by avoiding the purchase
of a separate fleet of trucks and the hiring of drivers. As CRC's Ann
Irving explained, "It just was appealing to streets and sanitation because there was no need to change the way they collect materials. It's
just garbage collection basically." (2) A high-tech facility would allow
for the hiring of cheap part-time labor without lowering recovery rates.

Both these assumptions turned out to be false, and generated unex-
pectedly low recovery rates. Although the city did not have to convert
to two sets of trucks (garbage versus curbside recycling), it did have to
purchase and maintain expensive garbage trucks. Furthermore, the sorting of regular trash at the MRRFs required expensive technological additions for the processing. This actually dwarfed the alternative costs of
a second set of trucks and drivers. The Chicago Recycling Coalition has
stated:

> The city claims that the blue bag program is cheaper because it avoids a
> separate pickup of recyclables. But the program will use expensive garbage
> packer trucks to pick up recyclables, where cheaper trucks and smaller crews
> could be used. Also, any savings on the collection costs will be lost because
> the blue bag program will have higher processing costs. This is because the
> labor and machinery involved in separating and processing the blue bags is
> more expensive than the processing of recyclables collected separately. (Chi-
> cago Recycling Coalition 1997)

The assumption the city and Waste Management made about recovery rates was even more inaccurate. The blue bag program was premised upon a high-technology production organization, staffed with
highly productive workers. But the program Waste Management implemented utilized a hiring process that relied on part-time, and largely
discouraged, labor. The initial assumption focused on the blue bags and
the trucks to be used to collect them. In order to reduce collection costs,
the city purchased trucks that compressed the bags. When the bags were
compressed, however, they broke. By the time the garbage arrived at the
MRRFs, there was a very messy mix in the trucks. The mess existed
both within the compressed blue bags themselves (commingling various
kinds of recyclable materials) and between the contents of the blue bags
and the contents of raw garbage bags.

Workers in the four MRRFs were then confronted with a truckload
of garbage mixed with the recyclables in (and outside) the blue bags.

Hence, most MRRF employees viewed their job as picking through garbage, rather than "recycling." The advantage of being able to collect garbage and recyclables together in one truck and one trip was far outweighed by the disadvantage of having lost much of the market value (as well as use-value) of clean, separated recyclables.

MRRF sorters then had the task of fishing out the recyclables from a sea of garbage. A single contaminated batch of recyclables could ruin an entire production batch in the remanufacturing process. Contaminated recyclables therefore had much lower market value. For example, there are over ninety varieties of paper. If they are not sorted and a remanufacturer tries to use recycled paper to make a higher-grade paper product, the resulting product will be defective. City officials nonetheless defend their decisions by claiming that the bulk of recyclable materials is low-value paper, and that a high proportion of this in blue bags was recovered. A memo from the Chicago Recycling Coalition details this problem in another way:

> The system mixes all recyclable materials together in one bag. Recycling industry representatives say that much of the material will be poor quality and difficult to recycle. FSC Paper, the area's main newsprint buyer, has said that newspaper contaminated with glass shards will damage its machinery. If the city is unable to sell the materials, they will have to be landfilled or incinerated, which defeats the whole purpose of the program. The city and Waste Management will not be able to sell these low grade materials for top dollar, so the overall cost to taxpayers is likely to be higher. (Chicago Recycling Coalition 1997)

A worker at the MRRF in its early years of operation noted:

> If something wasn't pulled out, it would contaminate the other stuff, then you would have a bunch of garbage. I mean compounded situations. Say for instance, there were different grades of paper. If the paper was all dirty and screwed up, you throw it into a bin, but if it was clean and fluffy you put it in another bin. That paper that was clean brought a higher price on the stock markets. Same with plastics; they only wanted a certain type of milk jug, because all of that plastic had a certain content of other materials in it. So if you contaminated it with something of a lesser quality, they would reject the load.

To overcome this problem, the recyclables had to be sorted in far more detail by hand. Waste Management's MRRFs were designed as a high-volume process, with profitability dependent upon the retention of a high proportion of recyclable materials. Large volumes of recyclables were thus being left unsorted because the commingled stream required much higher levels of hand sorting. Blue bags that were broken permitted their contents to mix with substantial volumes of raw garbage traversing the line at a rapid speed. The process of extracting blue bag materials was thus more dependent upon workers doing a careful job of sorting, so highly productive workers were needed to separate the items in this mess of a waste stream.

But the MRRF system was built around keeping processing costs low, and this was accomplished in a number of ways. Waste Management used a temporary job service, Remedial Environmental Management (REM), which operated much like a day labor exchange. In recent years, a powerful lobbying force in Washington, D.C., for temporary employer firms has emerged and fundamentally weakened labor legislation. As a result, workers at the Waste Management MRRFs were not formally employees of Waste Management or REM. Because of the recent changes in labor laws, they were initially classified instead as "consumers" of REM's service (Gonos 1997). They had no legal rights as workers and no legal relationship to Waste Management. REM was able to pay the workers very low wages and treat them poorly without technically violating labor laws. Waste Management was also able to mistreat these workers without fear of lawsuits. This situation was in sharp contrast to early lures offered by Waste Management. They encouraged community organizations to recruit reliable workers for the MRRFs, with the promise of a unionized status and fringe benefits after only ninety days probation.

REM "employees" were initially routinely overworked and underpaid, and both REM and Waste Management appeared to profit from this. Moreover, these workers had no benefits, no upward mobility, no pay raises, and no union representation. Through REM, workers were initially (1) paid a low wage; (2) frequently fired, and new people were rehired, with no time to learn jobs; and (3) alienated by an oppressive managerial force. These shop floor problems were compounded by the MRRF design itself. Having overspent on sorting technologies, Waste Management wanted to keep construction and operating costs low by eliminating most heating and air conditioning. In Chicago's climate, this means the facility was typically unbearably cold or overwhelmingly hot. Raw garbage, especially in the warm summer months, generates sufficient odors to make many employees nauseous. Under these conditions, workers are not highly productive. Nor are they loyal to a firm that offers them no security.

These factors and the associated low recycling and recovery rates eventually raised the ire of alderpersons in several wards. This was especially so in those wards that had previously enjoyed highly satisfactory recycling contracts with the community-based Resource Center and Up-town Recycling, Incorporated's services. For example, alderperson Toni Preckwinkle of the city's fourth ward wrote in a local newspaper that

> Hyde Parkers have had access to quality recycling programs for nearly thirty years. Ken Dunn's [of the Resource Center] pioneering efforts allowed many of us to feel that we got in on the ground floor of an exciting movement. . . . After a year and a half of operation, it seems appropriate to consider how effective the blue bag program is in Chicago. That isn't as easy as it sounds. A great deal of money has gone into promoting the blue bag program. My office has special blue plastic containers, provided by the city, in place by each desk. City employees haul a giant inflatable blue bag from festival to festival. The official message about the blue bag program is advertised in every medium. However, while I can tell you the reading scores of sixth graders at every school in my ward, I don't have a lot of facts about the blue bag program readily at hand. The official statistic is that ten percent of the city's house-holds participate. We don't know what percent of Chicago's refuse stream is impacted by the program. By way of comparison, in Beverly-Morgan Park, the Resource Center reached recycling 26 percent of the refuse stream with a local participation rate of 70 percent. If it takes 70 percent of the citizens to recycle 26 percent of the refuse stream, then ten percent of the citizens are probably recycling a very small percentage of Chicago's refuse stream. Given the official blessing of the blue bag program and the dollars allotted to pro-motion, this is troubling. Even more troubling is the fact that the City of Chicago Department of Environment held up a $482,196 payment due to Waste Management earlier this year, because the company failed to recycle paper, plastic and glass as promised. (Preckwinkle 1997)

What disturbed progressive elected officials, concerned citizens, and environmentalists even more was the city's early reluctance to release the recycling figures. Several deadlines passed before the city Depart-ment of Environment made the numbers public. At that time, they were presented in a format that was confusing and full of errors. Seabron Morgan, a former manager of a Waste Management MRRF, informed us that he had witnessed managers deliberately inflating recycling num-bers in several of the MRRFs. "They started off from day one padding and changing the numbers that were being reported to the city. I would question anything they submit. I really would."

Many of the leading U.S. recycling trade journals were already carry-ing stories about the difficulties of Chicago's blue bag program. Chi-cago's two leading newspapers, the *Sun-Times* and the *Chicago Tribune* (along with several neighborhood and weekly papers) further exposed the system's flaws. At a press conference in July of 1997, the Chicago Recycling Coalition issued a "report card" on the city's five-year-old

Solid Waste Management Plan. Recycling and composting grades were "incomplete," landfilling earned a C, and the source reduction grade was a dismal F.

The "incomplete" grade for recycling reflected the fact that neither Chicago nor Waste Management had yet released reliable data on the blue bag program, more than a year and a half after its implementation. In December 1995, when the program went on-line, the city had already indicated it would provide little data on the program. They barred news reporters (and researchers like ourselves) from the plants. They would allow outsiders in only after hours, when workers were gone and no machines were running. Criticizing this strategy, the *Chicago Tribune* wrote: "Here's a complimentary public-relations tip for Chicago officials, especially those coordinating the city's new residential recycling program: The surest way to get bad publicity is to act like you're trying to hide from bad publicity" ("Silly Blue-Bag Mystery" 1995).

In September 1997, the city and Waste Management proudly claimed they had reached their goal of a 25 percent recycling rate. It turned out, however, that "exactly half of the recycled material was screened yard waste destined for the top of Disposal Unit 1" (Kendall 1997). "Disposal Unit 1" is another name for the landfill next to the Waste Management MRRF. Another hidden issue in the numbers game was the amount of liquid that is normally contained in trash and recyclable waste that evaporates during processing. Waste Management counted the preevaporation weight of this liquid toward their recycling rate. This means that fully 6 percent of the total 25 percent recycling rate was liquid weight that later evaporated into thin air. Subtracting the yard waste and the evaporated liquid, then, we have at best a recycling rate of 6.5 percent. Furthermore, the vast majority of that material was extracted from regular trash bags, *not* the blue bags.

According to the city's own numbers (released only after repeated Freedom of Information Act requests by the Chicago Recycling Coalition), the percentage of waste recycled during December 1995 and January 1996 that originated from regular trash bags was 4.19 percent and the percentage recycled that came from blue bags was 1.80 percent. This rate could be described only as abysmal. State director of Citizens for a Better Environment, Joanna Hoelscher, declared, "If people knew [cans, bottles, and paper] were being recycled at a 5-percent rate, they would say the program is a miserable failure" (Daniels 1996).

Low participation rates among city residents was another concern raised about the blue bag program. In order to shed some light on this issue, the Chicago Recycling Coalition conducted a nonrandom survey of blue bag usage among the garbage cans of 477 households in ten

Chicago neighborhoods. While the overall participation rate was between 15 and 20 percent, it varied greatly by neighborhood and particularly by socioeconomic class. A CRC organizer commented, "The lack of participation by low-income residents is especially worrisome and may show a reluctance to buy blue bags" (Ritter 1996). Specifically, only 1.4 percent of households in the largely low-income and African American Seventh Ward's South Deering and Jeffrey Manor neighborhoods were making use of the blue bags.

In contrast, the more affluent Beverly, West Rogers Park, and Edgewater neighborhoods had participation rates of 23.6 percent, 29 percent, and 43 percent, respectively. While we have every reason to agree with the argument that social class was a determinant in producing this disparity, there is an equally interesting point that neither the media nor the CRC noticed. It turns out that those neighborhoods with highest participation rates were the very same communities in which the Resource Center and Uptown Recycling had organized recycling systems prior to the blue bag's introduction.

To the city's credit, however, the blue bag program was removing more waste for recycling than before the blue bag program came online. During the months of September and October 1997, the blue bag program recycled thirty-seven thousand tons of waste from the city of Chicago's waste stream. Most of this was waste that would otherwise have gone directly to the landfill (except the tons that would have gone through the Resource Center and Uptown Recycling's services). Moreover, as we note later, there have been considerable recent efforts (1997–99) by the city to improve on this dismal record, in response to both public criticism and to the low recovery rates at the MRRFs.

In response to its critics, the city's Department of the Environment has noted that public criticism of the blue bag system serves to further depress the participation rates of citizens, thereby exacerbating the problems of the MRRFs. However, the fixation with participation and recovery rates has also been overshadowed by an equally important problem deeply embedded in the blue bag system—the health and safety hazards within the MRRFs.

Occupational Safety Issues: Challenges and Responses

Occupational health and safety at the MRRFs was an issue to which Waste Management had paid little attention. The city and Waste Management failed to anticipate the hazardous working conditions laborers faced in the MRRFs. This is ironic, given that recycling was publicly touted as a socially responsible initiative. Most materials recovery facilities, or MRFs, are plants that sort source-separate recyclables, as typified by Evanston's MRF, outlined in chapter 5. However, there are a growing number of "dirty MRFs," such as Chicago's blue bag facilities, that sort both recyclables and municipal solid waste (MSW) in waste streams whose largest volume is household garbage. Because these facilities include both recycling and MSW recovery, Waste Management refers to them as Materials Recovery and Recycling Facilities, or MRRFs. MSW is material that one inspection service ruled "a very high health hazard, and must not be sorted by hand" (Ritter 1996).

In the first two years of the recycling program, we spoke to more than two dozen workers and managers who were employed by Waste Management in the blue bag system. Their stories resembled those of laborers in the sweatshops, steel mills, coal mines, textile mills, and meat factories of the nineteenth century United States, as well as in the contemporary Third World. Health and safety hazards at the MRRFs included a number of threats to worker well-being.

Recycling sorting centers are not normally thought of as workplaces that process chemical toxins. Yet workers at the Waste Management MRRFs routinely handle toxic substances. And because household hazardous waste is unregulated, the plastic and metal containers that recycling centers collect often contain residues of these toxic wastes. As one worker explained, he came into close contact with "anything and everything that people just normally throw out in their garbage" — bleach, battery acid, paint and paint thinner, inks, dyes, razor blades, and homemade explosives. Recycling facilities were also not intended for processing medical wastes. Yet MRRF workers also routinely handled these materials. Darnell, one Waste Management employee, explained: "They say that there is no medical waste from the garbage. But I find that totally impossible to believe, because if someone is sick at home and they regurgitate in their garbage can or use tissues or whatever, that's medical waste."

Workers punctured by syringes and hypodermic needles or sprayed with battery acid were some of the most common and potentially lethal accidents in these materials recovery facilities (Horowitz 1994; Powell 1992; Ritter 1996), a situation exacerbated by workers' widespread fear of contracting HIV. A former Waste Management manager, later turned whistle-blower, offered the following institutional analysis of the rise of medical wastes in household garbage streams:

Let's take for example, the medical waste issue alone . . . in terms of the whole medical field, it now has changed. Fewer and fewer people are allowed to stay in hospitals. Most, practically every, procedure that they can think of that they could put into an outpatient basis — they're doing it. Which means that people are taking all kinds of hypodermic needles, colostomy bags, and all this stuff home and disposing of it in the garbage. Just say, for example, all the people who are diabetics, all of the people who are forced out of the hospital because their insurance will not allow them to stay any longer, they feel like they can be better taken care of at home. Now they're sending in nurses; there's a whole network that they send out to people's houses. The reason I know this is because my dad just had serious surgery not too long ago. And he was taking all different kinds of injectables and . . . he had a colostomy bag for a while. . . . My point is just think of all the people who have a legitimate use for hypodermic needles, who have a legitimate — a hospital-prescribed — use for all of these items that are normally disposed of in a hospital setting.

Later discussions with a health professional confirmed that these practices are indeed widespread among hospitals, particularly given the continuing restructuring of the health care industry. These environmental hazards added a new and disturbing dimension to the discourse around the "health care crisis" in this nation.

Waste Management's MRRF workers also have experienced shock and stress on a routine basis. For example, Edward, a former employee, told of a grisly incident that occurred during an evening shift: "I worked in the primary department. That's where the trucks dump raw garbage right there. One time a dead lady was dumped on the floor in front of me. . . . One woman [employee] fainted and everybody else was screaming. A couple of guys were just wandering around on the catwalk [a forty-foot structure] looking like they was dazed."

Later, at the same MRRF, two deceased human infants were discovered on the recycling line on subsequent days. Thus, psychological and physical hazards intermingled as people desperate for gainful employment and job security were pressured to continue working in the face of gross health and safety violations. As Chicago is a city where the African American unemployment rate is greater than 50 percent in some neighborhoods (Wilson 1996), it is not difficult to understand one worker's explanation: "You never turn down work when you're looking for it. [But] you also have to think of your safety because that job might be there next year, but if you contracted some disease, *you* might not be there next year."

Thus, the city of Chicago misspecified the types of jobs its recycling program would create. While the blue bag program had created at least four hundred jobs in the city, these jobs were highly problematic, in four respects.

First, they paid below a living wage. The average worker at the facility made $6 an hour. Without a vacation, the worker might earn a gross income of $12,500 a year (assuming periodic overtime earnings) — about half of what a Chicago sanitation worker took home in 1988. In Chicago, this was not enough money to support a family. It is socially stressful when somebody works a full-time job and cannot support their family, which condemns the family to poverty. It sends a message to the children of these workers that work is not valuable: your parent can work full-time and your family can still live in poverty. Each of the four hundred recycling jobs thus relegated a family to poverty and created few incentives for children to seek employment in the formal economy.

Such crucial issues of job *quality* and remuneration are often ignored by poverty policy experts (see Wilson 1996). Recent research nonetheless reported an alarming increase in the number of Americans who are *working poor* (Levitan and Shapiro 1987; Schwarz and Volgy 1992). Urban areas suffer from unemployment and *under*employment, but even the working citizenry often experience deplorable employment conditions and a very low quality of life. So the usual call for "job creation" without a thoughtful plan for employment that is meaningful and safe at a livable wage will repeat the same mistakes the blue bag's administrators' made.

The second reason the MRRF jobs were problematic is that they were initially short-term jobs. The REM temporary firm's involvement seemed to ensure that most of the workers would be at the facility for only a brief period of time. Even if the pay were good, the worker was not employed long enough to get his or her family back on its feet.

The third problem is that these were deskilled jobs. Even though the facility was a high-tech structure, most of the jobs were low-tech (Wellin 1997). This is a trend we see occurring in many industries that on the outside appear to be high paying and high skilled. On the inside, these industries (including microchip makers, telecommunications services, and banks — see Pellow 1999) offer mostly low-paid, low-skilled employment. At the Chicago MRRFs, workers were not acquiring skills through their recycling employment. Even if the jobs did not pay well and were short-term, they could still have been good jobs if workers acquired new skills and became more marketable (see chapter 5 for Evanston's approach to this). Hence, these recycling jobs supported neither the community (through wages for families) nor the future prospects of workers (by increasing human capital).

Fourth and finally, the MRRF jobs created ill will in low-income ethnic communities. The MRRFs initially used strong-arm coercive management styles to maintain production schedules. Several workers spoke to journalists about the deplorable health and safety conditions in the plants. In response, REM issued a memo to its employees "strictly prohibiting" any communication with the media. Workers were explicitly instructed to respond with "no comment" to any inquiries about working conditions in the MRRFs. They were warned that "violation of this work rule may result in disciplinary action, up to and including immediate termination of employment."

Unfortunately, this was only the surface of a systematic pattern of exploitation by management in these early years. Workers regularly complained of being harassed by foremen and managers who rarely let them leave the sorting lines to use the bathrooms. Moreover, managers arbitrarily instituted mandatory overtime. One whistle-blowing former manager recalled, that the managers' "philosophy was to 'keep your foot in their ass.' That was their verbal philosophy, as communicated to us. That is bound to fail. Nothing new about that." He went on to describe the extent of the coercive conditions in his the plant:

> Yeah, you know that anybody working in those places needs a tetanus shot. You know with all of the dust and bacteria floating around in the air. If you bump your leg on a piece of metal and prick yourself . . . anything can happen [they weren't given the shots]. . . . Well it's because of the costs. The thing is that an enormous amount of money changed hands, but all of the workers were circumvented from all that. They were the last-thought-of part of the puzzle. They had all of these specifications as to how the plant should be built, but they had nothing in regards to workers' safety, training, employee retention, none of that. . . . [Man's name] was the site supervisor for REM and when things took a turn for the worse when everybody started to riot at the Medill plant and all the [pay]checks were coming in bad [underpaid, miscalculated], we had armed guards. I don't know if they were policemen or not, but they looked like street thugs. They were sitting around the dining room making sure that workers weren't going to bust any windows out or anything.

Thus workers at Waste Management were treated poorly and often had to concentrate their efforts on resisting conditions, rather than on simply working productively. There were other barriers facing employees who sought job security. The following quote was from a college course paper written by another former manager of Waste Management's MRRFs:

> At the rate of hours we are expected to work, using the hourly scale to estimate pay, moneys not paid range between $18,000 and $23,000 annually. My check stubs indicate a 40-hour workweek; however, my actual average workweek is closer to 68–70 hours per week. The conditions under which we work include lack of heat, lack of hot or cold water as well as lack of hand washing facilities after using portable toilets. . . . The majority of female employees have school-age children and are single parents. They seemingly fit the

stereotype seen and portrayed in our media as inner-city blacks who only want something for nothing. Although I have found this not to be true, our superiors believe this to be so; consequently, the way upper management treats them is colored by management's personal biases. Our plant is somewhat difficult to reach, even by car. Half of our workers walk 1.5 miles or more through open fields to get to work. There is no public transportation in the area. When hourly workers have to pick up their children from elementary schools, our supervisors get angry and want to fire or terminate them.

Like many marginalized workers in the current political economy, REM employees faced few opportunities for secure employment. Even middle managers of large corporations have no immunity from downsizing (Ehrenreich 1990; Rifkin 1995). Recycling workers are especially vulnerable in the labor market because they are low-skilled and have no collective bargaining power. Without postsecondary education or union representation, they face few opportunities for meaningful or adequately compensated work. Even though they add value to the discarded recyclables, they themselves rarely gain any real value (human capital, skills). (By contrast, in chapter 5, we outline a parallel MRF in Evanston, which dealt directly with these problems by recruiting workers to a recycling center, where they were provided with on-site employment training and placement in better positions after they had completed their stint in recycling.)

Not only was the work at the MRRF alienating because of its dead-end nature, but it was also physically hazardous. Most MRFs are non-union shops, as were the Chicago MRRFs. However, by law, employers had to follow a number of safety procedures to ensure worker well-being. These regulations were often ignored in the waste management field. For example, in 1994, thousands of waste industry employers failed to comply with the following regulations (Vogel 1995:80):

1. keep a log of injuries and illness;
2. provide proper protective gear and equipment to workers;
3. post signs and notices detailing safety procedures and workers' rights; and
4. communicate all possible work-related hazards to each employee.

On January 1, 1998, new safety standards for commingled (i.e., "dirty") MRRFs in the United States went into effect. These are voluntary performance standards, proposed by the American National Standards Institute (ANSI), and are expected to produce major changes in MRF design and operation. The new standard targets several safety and health areas, including adequate machine guarding, collisions, ergonomics, and hazardous materials such as blood-borne pathogens.

While this standard's intention might be laudable, it was limited in its scope, and as a voluntary initiative has no legal bearing on MRF operators.

More broadly, dangerous and exploitative working conditions made news headlines during 1996 and 1997, when the scourge of sweatshops received media attention. In response, President Clinton's Task Force on Sweatshops released a Workplace Code of Conduct for all corporations. This code prohibits harassment or abuse of employees, the use of child labor, and forced labor. It also encourages health and safety, collective bargaining, prevailing wages, reasonable work hours, and overtime compensation. Based on the data we had amassed, in 1995–97 Waste Management violated six of the nine points on this code of conduct in their Chicago MRRFs. Secondly, we note that this code was designed for the apparel industry, where it is known that sweatshops predominate. The problem we find is that sweatshoplike, exploitative conditions can and do exist in all industries, even "green" industries such as recycling (Pellow 1996b, 1998 a, b).

Reclaiming the MRRFs: Chicago's Attempt to Regain Control

In our interviews with Chicago officials and Waste Management managers following the completion of our field research, we discovered that city inspectors had also begun to provide feedback to city officials that the program was not adequately functioning. Reflecting on this history, a former senior official of Chicago city government indicated that he was not surprised. In his experience, every public-private partnership succeeded only when the public officials exerted firm sanctions over the private sector. By 1997, Chicago officials were beginning to do that. On the basis that recovery and diversion rates were far below the contractual goals, they refused contract payment to Waste Management. By that time, managers at the MRRFs had been replaced several times as Waste Management sought to recover profits from a losing proposition. When prices for recyclables decreased, in fact, they had essentially passed most of the waste stream through the MRRFs, and collected their waste-hauling fees.

Chicago escalated its control over WMI managers through retaining an independent consulting firm to advise on improvements in the sorting centers. In its efforts to tame and redirect this organization, it initiated a variety of changes in the MRRFs aimed at improving both recovery rates and working conditions. Generally, these tended to raise the operating costs at the MRRFs, and Waste Management officials reacted negatively. According to a former senior Chicago official, Waste Management initially attempted to use its political connections to offset the new controls. This official indicated that Waste Management "never expected to have its contract actually enforced by Chicago." But Chicago's political leaders firmly indicated that they expected such compliance, and the city staff pushed forward their proposals.

After much foot-dragging, Waste Management brought in a new manager for the MRRFs, someone with a history of turning around failing operations. This seemed to augur a new era for Chicago, as there was for the first time an actual partnership between the city and its contractor. Our interviews with the manager indicated that he saw improvement of working conditions as a key component of raising productivity levels in diverting materials at the sorting centers. Under his leadership, a variety of work changes were initiated. Improvements included new heating and cooling of the MRRFs, to enhance worker comfort; establishment through REM of union status for the sorting workers; and sustained attention to reducing turnover rates (which approached 30 percent per month in the early years).

According to this official, sorting workers, city staff, and managers began to work collaboratively for the first time. The sorting line was slowed down and the height of materials on the line reduced so that workers had more access to recyclable materials. City staff and managers engaged in line sorting so they could understand some of the sorting problems. Managers sought insights from workers about how to improve sorting productivity. As these suggestions were followed and productivity was raised, a new bonus scheme was introduced. Workers' pay bonuses ranged as high as $1.60 to $2.13 an hour, in addition to their base rates of $6.50 to $8.00 per hour. These bonuses were paid to an entire shift of workers, based on the volumes of materials that they successfully extracted from the sorting line.

In addition, some mechanical sorters for metals were added and new procedures for sorting yard wastes were added to the sorting line. As a result of all these changes, in 1998–99 the MRRFs achieved their contractual goals for the first time in the system's history. Additionally, the plant experienced reduced turnover rates for sorting workers, which dropped from 25–28 percent per month in the MRRFs' early years to less than 10 percent currently (reported by the present manager). In addition, safety meetings were scheduled regularly at all the MRRFs. According to the new manager, recycling has ranked close to mining occupations in its safety record. But he has introduced improvements both on the line and between line workers and mechanical vehicles in the plants. Among other techniques, he has instituted a program of reporting and analyzing "near misses," as well as actual accidents involving worker injuries. In addition, there are more staff positions with stable incumbents monitoring work conditions to spot hazardous work situations.

Nonetheless, none of the managers or officials have any delusion about recycling work. The current manager noted that "no one ever wanted to grow up to be a garbage sorter," but he has acted nonetheless to improve financial rewards and safety for sorters on the line. Despite the fact that the MRRFs are still losing money for Waste Management, they are now losing *less* money than in the early years. And the work improvements and other efficiency gains in diverting materials have been paid for by higher productivity in the sorting centers. For example, in its earlier operations, sorters averaged 140 pounds of recyclable materials per hour, but now have achieved rates of 310 pounds per hour, reported by WMI's current manager. The manager of the sorting centers acknowledges that Chicago's design for recycling is far from ideal, but that he is working with the system as he inherited it. City officials remain optimistic about the overall system, perhaps because they claim it has achieved most of their major economic and waste management goals.

Although criticism of the system continues (e.g., Killian 1999), city staff see recycling as now operating within their broad goals for a solid waste management system. Among the remaining problems of the system is a relatively low residential participation rate. The tensions remain, despite attention to some of the early problems of recycling that we described above, in part because of the "fully only" differences between critics and defenders of the system. Critics view the performance of the city as "only" partly achieving the ideal goals of the three Es, while defenders from the city staff see it as "fully" accomplishing much more than earlier systems in Chicago had (Schnaiberg and Gould 1994: 228–31).

Conclusion: The Blue Bag Program and the Three Es of Sustainable Community Development

Firms typically resist reforms or proposals that challenge their market share or position in the political economy. Waste Management and the city of Chicago have repeatedly defended the blue bag program on each of the three Es — economic, ecological, and equity dimensions — of sustainable community development. They also defended the program when challenged with evidence that working conditions were unsafe.

The poor performance of the MRRFs somewhat mirrored the blue bag's track record in other states, according to the Chicago Recycling Coalition:

Attempts to implement similar programs in other cities have run into problems. Houston decided to dump the blue bag after a 10–month pilot test. In Omaha, Nebraska, the contractor separating the blue bags went bankrupt a few weeks after the program was implemented. Waste Management, Inc. now sorts the blue bags in Omaha but at a much higher cost than Chicago [officials] estimated its blue bag program would cost. In Brown County, Wisconsin, the Solid Waste Department conducted a test mixing plastic bags of recyclables in with garbage and deemed it a failure. (Chicago Recycling Coalition 1997)

The manager of a Browning-Ferris, Incorporated, MRF near downtown Chicago also argued that: "the blue bag program is a farce. It hasn't worked anywhere else. We expect it to fail in two years at the most. They're not committed to recycling at all. In fact, an assistant to the commissioner of the Chicago Department of Environment says that if the program does fail, at least the MRRFs will make good waste transfer stations!"

Despite this evidence and ill will, both Waste Management and the city dismissed these stories. They claimed that the other blue bag systems were not as "comprehensive" or as "well planned" and "test piloted" as Chicago's program. City officials and Waste Management spokespersons also fought back with salvos aimed at the Chicago Recycling Coalition (CRC), for example. William Abolt, Chicago's former deputy environment commissioner (and current acting commissioner), came close to blaming CRC for the blue bag's failure: "Chicken Little has found a job as spokesperson for the CRC. . . . It's almost like it's an effort to destroy public confidence. . . . The recycling coalition is basically being a wet blanket" (Daniels 1996). Ironically, despite these rejections of external criticisms of the program, the city itself quietly determined that the initial operations were dismally below target and set out to reform the program. The former commissioner of the city's Department of the Environment, Henry Henderson, noted that "anyone who expects that a private firm will eagerly undertake public business" is naive, and that the initial failures of Waste Management were not unusual in such "partnerships."

The blue bag program nonetheless does not seem to be a step in the direction of sustainable community development. Rather, it is a program where profitability was gained by squeezing low-wage labor and producing questionable environmental impacts. Later improvements may have enhanced the working conditions and diversion rates at the four sorting centers. However, recycling in Chicago is deeply embedded within the broader goals of affordable solid waste management. Because of this, recycling activities do not afford substantial occupational opportunities. Rather, the continuing low status of recycling sorters approximates what Bennett Harrison (1994) refers to as the "low road" to economic growth. We refer to this model as the "corporate-centered" approach to development.

The corporate-centered approach stands in sharp contrast to sustainable community development. Generally, it is premised on first asking what the community can do to support private capital, rather than on the reverse. Ironically, Chicago achieved somewhat of an inversion of this approach. City officials did try to negotiate what Waste Management could do for the city. But their goals were primarily protective of the city budget, and they did not proactively seek recycling as an alternative source for creating value for the city. Indeed, it deferred these issues initially to Waste Management, encouraging the corporation to be creative in finding financial resources from recycled waste and in protecting the city from the losses or gains from this value-creating activity. Even today, recycling sorters are not city workers (or employees of Waste Management—they remain REM employees).

In this as in many other cases of corporate-centered development, the result is often a poor use of human, natural, and economic resources. In the case of the blue bag, for example, the city, workers, and the ecosystem were all taxed more than is necessary. The program's initial failures included:

1. low recovery rates and poor quality materials produced;
2. low wages and poor working conditions for laborers;
3. increased ecological disruption in low-income neighborhoods as facilities attracted rodents and produced noxious odors; and,
4. an expensive program with contracts that inhibited restructuring, and one where city investments in infrastructure might be lost.

The reformulated blue bag system today has made some small improvements. It does achieve some increase in ecological protection, because some larger share (between 5–25 percent) of solid wastes is recycled. However, the program explicitly ignores the social goals that originally drove recycling's development. Even the reformed blue bag program directly ties workers' wages into a productivity scheme that benefits Waste Management more than it does most of its sorting workers. We are reminded that even with the improved recycling operations in Chicago, its program echoes Kacandes's (1991: 53) view of recycling:

Recycling is manufacturing, and manufacturing is business, not disposal. . . . Some practitioners think of market development simply as local business promotion. Others see it as the progressive restructuring of the world economy to fully accommodate recycling. It is, of course, both. . . . The ultimate goal in market development is to increase investment in industry's capacity to recycle. Goals such as getting municipal suppliers together with reliable consumers end up becoming secondary to questions like "did companies financially commit to building new plants?"

Chicago sought out corporate agents to protect its recycling budget from the hidden hand of the treadmill of production. It made efforts to defend itself against the direct influences of national and global economic forces (Longworth 1998). However, its decision has placed it in the hands of another treadmill organization — Waste Management International — which *is* directly subjected to these forces (since it must still sell its recyclables on the market). Furthermore, WMI has sought to buffer itself by undermining the public goals of the city. In achieving this standoff with the treadmill, however, Chicago ignored the possibilities of other kinds of recycling programs that might have produced more sustainable community development. We take up this theme in the following three chapters.

Four

Community-Based Recycling:
The Struggles of a Social Movement

Community-Based Recycling Centers

Community-based recycling centers have long functioned at the margins of depressed urban communities. They were places where struggling urban populations — the homeless, new immigrants, people of color, the poor, the mentally ill — could find community and a meager income. They were additionally places where political activists could create nonprofit organizations and develop and prepare agendas for social change. Thus, community-based recycling facilities embodied three overlapping goals:

1. to offer recycling services to communities and individuals;
2. to offer recycling and environmental education to these constituencies in ways that would mobilize people to push for broader social change; and
3. to provide jobs for low-income urban populations.

In the following sections, we take the reader into the world of the struggling community-based recyclers. We provide ethnographic detail on how these pioneers have fought to create progressive spaces in the urban milieu, and why their battles have achieved at best only mixed Outcomes.[1]

The Model for Community-Based Recycling Centers:
The Resource Center

The Resource Center is a buyback recycling center in Chicago's Grand Crossing neighborhood, a community that is 99 percent African Ameri-

---

[1] The ethnographic data we present were collected over a period of four years and included intensive fieldwork, observations, personal interviews, and archival research. Much of the data gleaned from the Uptown Recycling and Resource Centers were reciprocated with volunteer work at the recycling yards. This often meant standing and working in recycling yards during rain, blistering heat, and subfreezing winter cold. It also included riding in recycling collection trucks during the early morning hours. Supplemental data were gathered through content analyses of several organizational documents, newspaper articles, and a half-dozen recycling trade journals.

can, with a third of its residents living in poverty. Grand Crossing hosts several public housing projects and still bears the wounds urban renewal left during the 1950s. Like many Chicago neighborhoods, Grand Crossing became all-black almost overnight (Massey and Denton 1993; Taub 1994). During one decade—from 1950 to 1959—fifty thousand African Americans moved in and fifty thousand whites moved out, many to the suburbs. Today this community is what William Julius Wilson (1996:19) terms a "new poverty area," where "a substantial majority of individual adults are either unemployed or have dropped out of the labor force altogether." In spite of these odds, the Grand Crossing community has considerable social potential. Local hope for stability and rejuvenation centers on the community's prime location near railroads, commuter trains, the University of Chicago, and Lake Michigan's shore.

One other reason for hope in the neighborhood is that its major promoter, The Resource Center, is still going strong. The Resource Center serves mostly low-income people who scavenge recyclables out of alleys and garbage cans and bring them to the center, in return for cash. The Resource Center is run by Ken Dunn, a legend in Chicago's environmental movement and community development circles. Dunn came to Chicago in the late 1960s as a University of Chicago graduate student in philosophy. He had been a Vietnam War protester, counterculture activist, and Peace Corps participant. As he put it, "I wanted to do something of value to the community, and being a graduate student at the U. of C. was about as far from that vision as you could get!" In 1968, he started Hyde Park Enterprise with these objectives in mind.

Initially, the Enterprise functioned as a countercultural center for people who needed to make a little money. They scavenged through garbage bins for cans, bottles, and scrap metal that could be sold on the marketplace. In addition to providing a way to earn cash, Hyde Park Enterprise was also a place to engage in political dialogue and participate in Chicago's progressive community. In 1975, Dunn incorporated the Enterprise, renaming it the Resource Center. He began to form collection routes, where residents would leave materials on the corner or next to garbage bins. This growing business drew low-income minority men into the Center. As Chicago was deindustrializing, many of these individuals had become socially, economically, and politically disenfranchised and marginalized.

Today the Resource Center has recycling and composting contracts with several neighborhoods and businesses around the Chicago area and operates a large recycling "yard" where a dozen workers process the waste for end markets. It also has a contract with the city of Chicago to operate buyback centers in the public housing operated by the

Chicago Housing Authority. The yard has a simple layout. The main recycling yard is a large outdoor property bounded by a vacant lot and a railroad track on the south and west sides, and a junkyard to the east. The property is two acres in size and is marked by several piles of newspaper, collections of plastic bottles, and aluminum cans, and a small mountain of composting yard waste. Recycling trucks come and go every half hour while workers sort through these piles of materials or exchange money for cans or paper at the drop-off station. A typical scene at the Resource Center is outlined below:

> There is a lot of hustling and bustling going on today, as there is on any given day. Most of the traffic is African American men and families bringing in goods in shopping carts or in plastic garbage bags thrown over their backs. A white guy drives in with a Chevy station wagon and goes over to unload them at the barge. Juan (a Guatemalan worker in charge of weighing materials) takes a copy of today's paper off the pile and offers it to me. I notice that they are neatly stacked and figure this guy must be a delivery person or has extras from the *Chicago Tribune*'s offices. A Chevy with two African Americans drives in and they empty cans from it. Four other African American men are coming in here with cans and various other materials. These men are some of the most marginalized people in the nation, particularly with regard to the workforce, and are just trying to make ends meet here. It's 1:55 P.M.

The above description reveals that like a library, grocery store, or a bank in a more affluent community, the Resource Center is an institution where local citizens conduct their daily "business." In the early 1980s, Kenn Dunn began to expand the organization's principal emphasis on recycling postconsumer waste by "recycling" land. In an interview with the authors, he stated: "There are seventy thousand [vacant] lots in Chicago and we're trying to redevelop all of them. Twenty to fifty years of bad policies drive down people and render them incapable of getting up in the morning and getting to work on time. . . . We think of community organizing as community empowerment. . . . After we take out the rubble, we let nature take over. If man has meaning, it is learning to work in tune with nature. It develops human character." By recycling land, the Resource Center turns vacant lots and abandoned buildings into playgrounds, parks, and gardens. The construction materials — mainly bricks and wood they extract from abandoned buildings — are used to build new products, a process Dunn calls "green demolition."

Community-based recycling is a product of social movement organizing.[2] As with many other social movements, the Chicago recycling

---

[2] By social movements we mean "a collectivity acting with some degree of organization and continuity outside of institutional channels for the purpose of promoting or resisting

movement set out to challenge conventional thinking that decoupled economic goals from social programs. History had demonstrated to these urban activists that the market supports communities and workers only when there is direct political pressure from these stakeholders to plan for how the jobs and revenue generated from economic activity will be distributed (Castells 1983; Logan and Molotch 1987). Dunn and his group saw themselves as applying pressure to ensure that economic development in Chicago would create an economy that supported the local community. "The range of our programs comprises a new way of viewing resources and thus presents a novel way of being in the world. We view resources more broadly than just cash or real estate" (Resource Center 1996). None of these practices is very lucrative. Still, Dunn is quite proud of them because they meet a range of social and ecological goals.

The Resource Center has operated under sustainable community development principles for thirty years. One guiding principle has been to keep the recycling process labor-intensive. This is a joint decision made with the workers. Dunn recounted some of this history to us as follows:

AUTHORS: *[pointing to a rusted, out-of-use conveyor belt on the periphery of the yard]* What's the story behind this thing and why don't you have a new one here?

DUNN: Well, first let me relate to you what this thing does, or did. See, the material comes in this pile you see in the foreground. There is steel, aluminum, and plastic all together. So we set this up, which works quite nice. The front end loader picks it [recyclable waste] up and dumps it in this hopper, which is elevated here. The magnet pulls out the steel and puts that in the pile, and then the aluminum and plastic comes along this conveyor and the workers would toss the aluminum in one bin and the plastic in the other bin.

AUTHORS: So this is a sorting belt?

DUNN: Yeah, it really worked fast and really worked great but everybody [his employees] hated it, and so I actually started working on it for a while, and there is something about a monotonous activity being all the same. The worst of it is that the stuff is coming along the conveyer at you and you have to kind of spot it there and follow it a little bit, and it gives you a headache to have to keep adjusting the eyes like that. It's standard that that's what everybody [in the industry] does is have everybody sort on a conveyor. So . . . what you have to do is sort of choose your spot here and

---

change in the group, society, or world order of which it is a part" (McAdam and Snow 1997).

just what comes there, rather than keep your eyes adjusting that way, so the result is that you don't pick it as cleanly.[3]

AUTHORS: So in business terms, quality control actually suffers in MRFs that use this.

DUNN: Yeah, and when I saw they [his employees] didn't like it and I sensed why they didn't like it, they said, "Could we go back to what we were doing before?" This is what they were doing before [*he motions toward several employees manually sorting through piles of newspaper and cans*]. So what they do is sort at their own rate, wading through the piles, picking up things. And it's much more labor, but I don't know how much more expensive because there is no machine maintenance, no electricity [and he doesn't exactly keep strict accounting]. See I haven't maintained this machine in five years. It's just been sitting there and rusting. . . . It's a sorting conveyor.

While the process is laudable, decision making at the Resource Center is not without conflict. Some former Resource Center employees refer to Dunn as someone "ruling with an iron hand." Others note that the conditions at the Resource Center are generally physically taxing and low paying. On the other hand, unlike most managers, Dunn himself is well known for "getting his own hands dirty" by frequently doing the work that his sorters perform. Overall, this makes the Resource Center a meaningful place to Work.

---

[3] Dunn is referring to the Fordist system of production, which entailed the mass production of homogeneous products, inflexible technologies, the adoption of standardized work routines, and increases in productivity from economies of scale (Rifkin 1995; Thompson 1989; Ritzer 1995b). The organizational goal was to displace the need for the skilled craftsmen. Workers were seen as too unpredictable: they could not work around the clock; they went on strike for increased pay; and they often got sick, quit, or died, creating a constant need for replacement, training, and costly supervision. By decreasing the number of workers needed and the basic skill level, managers minimized uncertainty. The factory worker could be replaced more easily. Managers gained tremendous control as they needed fewer workers who could be attracted from a larger pool. From an organizational perspective, "such workers could resist managerial pressures less easily and cost employers less money" (Westrum 1991:33). The assembly line was an important component of this system of production. For example, while Ford's Model T was built faster than any competitor's automobile, this was largely because the assembly line functioned as a labor control device as much as a part of the physical production apparatus. Control over the speed of the production line has been one of the key struggles between workers and managers since its invention (Clawson 1980). For workers, the assembly line has mostly been a deskilling and disempowering technology. Occupational safety advocates have also argued that the repetitive motion and the eye strain of assembly line work produced myriad hazards for laborers. Ken Dunn eschews the assembly line as a conscious strategy to construct a different system that provides a more empowering and safer working environment.

Replicating the Resource Center:
Uptown Recycling, Incorporated

A Brief History

The success of the Resource Center has been replicated on the North Side of Chicago by Uptown Recycling, Incorporated, another community-based nonprofit recycler. There are no manufacturing or industrial firms in Chicago's North Side neighborhood of Uptown, now dominated by retail stores offering general merchandise. The Uptown Chamber of Commerce boasts that it has the highest increase in retail employment in the city, at 56 percent. Uptown has a district that has become known as a "Second Chinatown" because there are several Asian restaurants and banks in the area. Uptown is one of the most ethnically diverse neighborhoods anywhere in the nation. In order to serve these various populations, many social service organizations have sprung up. Most are housed in a single building two doors down from the Uptown Recycling center.[4] There are also efforts underway to revitalize the cultural and entertainment sector in Uptown.

However, while activists celebrate Uptown's diversity, they must also fight continuously against its poverty. Fully one-fourth of the community's residents are below the poverty line, and many of those are homeless. The homeless population has two principal origins. The first wave migrated to Uptown after being displaced by urban renewal occurring on the city's Near West Side during the 1960s. The second influx arrived after the deinstitutionalization of Illinois's mental patients in the 1970s. The neighborhood hosts several forces coexisting in tension. On one side are the developers who promote commercial development and gentrification. On the other side are a variety of community groups who advocate affordable housing and jobs for the community's many low-income denizens.[5] Uptown Recycling, Inc. was, until its 1997 demise, a member of this coalition as well.

---

[4] During a visit to the Mutual Insurance Building in the Uptown Neighborhood, we saw the following organizations listed on the directory: Korean American Senior Center, Institute of Cultural Affairs, Travelers and Immigrants Aid, Anawim Center (Native American), Bosnian Refugee Center, Philippine American Social Services, Tibetan Alliance of Chicago, Refugee Services, Sarah's Circle (domestic violence advocates), Lao American Service Center, and the Ethiopian Association. Other organizations in the neighborhood housed in other buildings include the American Indian Economic Development Association, Cambodian Association of Illinois, Chinese Mutual Aid Association, and the Vietnamese Association of Illinois. We note that members of most of these ethnic groups frequent the URI buyback site.

[5] These groups include Organization of the Northeast, Voice of the People, and the Heart-of-Uptown Coalition.

Uptown Recycling, Incorporated (URI), was one of the most successful programs modeled after the Resource Center. In 1981, a local Cath-
olic parish priest, a group of Southeast Asian immigrants and refugees,
and other local residents started scavenging alleys on the North Side of
Chicago. Calling themselves "alley entrepreneurs," they dug through
garbage dumpsters, seeking recyclable materials. After some time, they
began to establish routines. But they had a difficult time finding places
to sell the materials. The only place to sell materials was the Resource
Center, which was located on the Far South Side of Chicago. URI could
not raise the capital needed to purchase and maintain trucks that could
reliably reach the Resource Center every day. Given their meager resources, a local operation was the only option. Accordingly, the Resource Center helped them set up a buyback center. Executive director
Jim Burris states the history and goals as follows:

> Uptown Recycling Station was first formed as a drop-off/buyback station for
> recyclable materials by a group of environmental activists and several Uptown
> neighborhood social service development agencies during 1982–83 [during a
> major recession when many private and public organizations were contract-
> ing], in conjunction with the Resource Center, a recycling organization lo-
> cated near the University of Chicago on the South Side. With much volunteer
> energy and a part-time paid staff funded at first by several foundation grants,
> URI's recycling programs grew, enabling it to incorporate in 1985 as an Illi-
> nois not-for-profit corporation, with its own board of directors, financial re-
> cord keeping, and tax-exempt charitable status under federal and state law.
> Over the years, collection programs expanded to include curbside residential
> collection programs and, more recently, multifamily and commercial collec-
> tions. In 1989 we changed our name to Uptown Recycling, Incorporated, to
> reflect that URI was more than a "recycling station."

By 1987, the City of Chicago recognized URI and the Resource Center as beneficial to many city neighborhoods. Both organizations were
generating jobs and money in areas increasingly depressed and rocked
with the associated social problems of crime, family violence, deindustrialization, and physical decay.[6] The Department of Streets and San-

---

[6] Job losses in Chicago's manufacturing sector were especially deep. A 1987 study
found that between 1977 and 1981, 203,700 manufacturing jobs were lost through clo-
sures and contractions in Chicago. Another 132,000 jobs were lost due to corporate decisions to shift investments outside the region. The result was that Chicago lost one-sixth of
its factories in the 1970s: 4,500 of a previous total of 30,000. Like many older industrial
cities, Chicago's lifeblood had been manufacturing employment. While deindustrialization
led to losses of backbreaking, oppressive employment, it also bled much of the city dry.
Squires et al. noted, "In a sense a transfusion has taken place; the metropolitan area is
moving from an economy heavily based on manufacturing to one increasingly oriented to

itation awarded Uptown a modest "diversion credit" for its collection routes. The diversion credit was a small amount of money paid to URI for diverting garbage from the waste stream and landfills. The credits were meant to give URI the money that the city otherwise would had paid for landfill usage. Through this "shadow pricing" arrangement, URI was allowed to stay afloat during tough times.

From 1988 onward, URI was a fairly stable small organization where the most marginal citizen-workers could informally earn income.[7] The organization had its ups and downs, as prices for recyclable materials fluctuated widely, but it continued to generate a small income for people who otherwise had little or no money. In order to maintain these jobs through the tough times, Uptown eschewed new technology that might have displaced human labor. As one manager put it, URI used a "low-tech" labor process because it "provided a few more jobs."

Uptown was run by a volunteer board, comprised of local community members. Board members came from a variety of walks of life, but they were united in viewing URI as a recycling enterprise and a social movement organization that was beneficial for the community, the local economy, and the environment. One board member noted:

> It got started with a bunch of volunteers. June Schilling and Leslie Ladd, who was also on our board. Tongue in cheek, I would say "just a couple of ladies" — but they are people, human beings, who have the power to get things going. What I'm hinting at is that when Uptown Recycling was getting started, it was very definitely still a [social] movement for these folks because their motivation was based upon a sense of the good, not upon a sense of a cost-benefit analysis or is it cheaper for them to have recycling than to have a larger dumpster. It was a sense of meaning. A qualitative evaluation rather than a quantitative calculation.

Thus the social value of recycling was much more important than the fiscal gains that might eventually accrue from this activity. This ideology was welcomed by many in the local liberal white community who quickly joined the ranks of steadfast URI supporters and customers. The executive director stated in an interview, "People began to bring in bags of recyclables not so much for the two to three dollars they could get from bringing their materials in, but because it was the right thing to do."

---

non-manufacturing sectors, for example, banking, finance, retail sales, insurance and transportation" (1987:28–29).

[7] This is very consistent with the larger international urban literature. Many scholars have argued that the increasing polarization of the labor force in major urban areas has created pressure on the poor to supplement their meager incomes through informal economic activity (see Sassen 1991).

The URI Board of Directors employed a full-time executive director, Jim Burris, to oversee the operation. Burris also embodied the recycling movement's belief in harnessing the market to meet clear social goals. He continued to live with what he calls a "community-focused orientation to life." In 1979, he moved to Chicago with his church group. They created a communally run, multiracial residential community in the largely African American Woodlawn area. This neighborhood has historically given birth to progressive settlements, organizations, and leaders (including Saul Alinsky, the legendary community organizer).

Burris had a law degree and was trying to finish a doctorate at the University of Chicago. But a professor from the Divinity School convinced him that "I wanted to be more about praxis rather than a theoretical person." Jim dropped out of the program and joined the Resource Center, which was a good complement to his planned residential community. Both "seemed to be very grass-roots oriented," attempting to transcend class, racial, and generational barriers. He later moved on to become URI's executive director.[8]

As the head of this organization, Burris oversaw a staff of twelve, who worked either in the office or in the recycling yard. Uptown typically hired people, to quote a manager, "who would otherwise be considered unemployable." Many of the workers had criminal records or substance abuse problems, or they lived on the fringes of homelessness. URI accepted referrals from churches, friends, and community organizations for job candidates who were struggling and needed a helping hand. Increasingly, they were also hiring people who had been victims of downsizing by private sector organizations. Burris used the following as an example: "I just hired a fellow from Laos yesterday . . . and this fellow told me that he was earning about thirteen dollars an hour in Minneapolis, making hearing aids. But the hearing aid industry in this country has all but collapsed; it's gone overseas. So now he's looking for five- and six-dollar-per-hour jobs, so he's come back to Chicago. So yes, we hire at the fringes."

At the other end of the spectrum, Uptown also hired idealistic college graduates who brought important accounting, organizational, and technical skills to their jobs. Like Burris and Dunn, these persons were middle-class social progressives looking for communities and organizations that offered them meaningful work. Both the Resource Center and URI employed young students representing the Volunteers in Service to America (VISTA) and the Lutheran Volunteer Corps (LVC) in an arrangement that might be characterized as a domestic Peace Corps.

[8] We should point out that URI's first executive director, Dale Alekel-Carlson, was instrumental in the organization's initial success.

Following in the tradition of the Resource Center, URI also became a vocal advocate for progressive community development programs. It consciously undertook campaigns to raise awareness among constituents, including the disenfranchised individuals who often worked for them. Thus, Uptown came to embody many of the Resource Center's goals. They sought to divert recyclable materials from the waste stream, thereby reducing Chicago's dependence on landfills and incinerators. They tried to provide entry-level jobs and a source of income for people in the Uptown community. Finally, they led aggressive education campaigns aimed at informing the public about recycling's environmental and economic benefits, as part of a strategy to create broader political awareness and social change.

Uptown Recycling: A Progressive Approach

URI operated four weekly residential collection routes in three Chicago neighborhoods: one in Lakeview, two in Rogers Park, and one in Ravenswood. Residents placed recyclables in boxes or plastic bags in alleyways or on the curbside for pickup. The center also provided glass recycling programs for bars and restaurants and office paper collection for area businesses. The weekly household collection programs grew from collecting around nine to ten tons per month in 1986 to fifty-six tons per month in 1990. URI collected recyclables from approximately nineteen thousand households with a resident participation rate that reached 80 percent at one time. This high participation rate was attributed largely to the cooperation of other community organizations. URI staff members attended several community-related events every month to maintain connections to neighborhood groups, movement organizers, and the business community. Many of the collection programs began as a direct result of presentations made to community groups or businesses. URI also published a newsletter with a circulation of two thousand. The staff was usually overwhelmed with the ever-growing requests for speaking engagements, tours of the facility, and general information on residential recycling options in the area. By any measure, this part of the program was a success and owes its achievements to URI's roots in community organizing and social movement activity.

Once the URI employees collected the recyclable materials, they were taken to the recycling yard. The recycling yard was a 50-foot by 150-foot open space, cramped between a Vietnamese restaurant and a church that doubled as a soup kitchen. It was a lot that otherwise would have sat vacant, and become strewn with garbage and overgrown with weeds. Uptown Recycling owned the property and secured it with a locked gate every night after closing time. Workers at the site performed several different jobs. Some were involved in sorting the materials into large piles at workstations around the yard. Workers at the facility typically sorted the recyclables into large piles by hand. Materials had to be carefully separated and cleaned to avoid attracting pests and rodents. Workers also interacted with customers at the buyback and the drop-off areas, negotiating prices for people who were bringing recyclables to the yard. They were URI's public relations ambassadors. Their task was to keep both the alley entrepreneurs and the middle-class clients coming back so that URI could maintain its material flows and local political support.

The actual work was structured but not routinized (Leidner 1993; Braverman 1974). Employees were encouraged to be flexible and creative. There was a strong emphasis on finding better ways of doing things. This continuous improvement effort was driven by organizational needs. Uptown existed on a marginal profit, and every worker was encouraged to find any improvement that would save URI money. The creativity was also ideological: the emphasis was on doing things in ways that empowered the workers and the organization.

URI's facility was the site of commerce, exchange, and reuse of all manner of materials. These included postconsumer waste and postindustrial metal, paper, and plastic objects that scavengers gathered from this North Side Chicago neighborhood. The following is an excerpt from our field notes at the site:

> We are standing in an aluminum shed at the Uptown yard, surrounded by a can crushing machine, weigh scale, a coffee machine, and a wooden sign leaning up against the wall displaying the prices for a great variety of materials from scrap metal to kitchen sinks. Every couple of minutes very rough-looking people (possibly homeless, definitely under- and unemployed and over thirty years of age) with grocery carts, garbage bags, and children's wagons bring pounds of materials to sell. The site manager, Souma Phosaraj, is Southeast Asian and looks about fifty. Souma oversees all monetary transactions. It is important to understand that a recycling "yard" is just that. It's an outside, open air yard. It has the best ventilation system possible, really. Ventilation is often cited as one of the chief contributors to poor working conditions in MRFs. Here this isn't a problem. However, you are then left at the mercy of the elements.

As in the Resource Center site, the Uptown yard was a place where the poor of the North Side, using their survival strategies, eked out a living. Like the organization itself, they existed on the margins of the economy and society.

One morning we took a break from sorting recyclables from the collection van to speak to the site manager, Souma Phosaaj. He filled us in on his biography and his experience with Uptown:

> I have been involved since 1984 with recycling. From 1984 to 1986 with the Resource Center and from 1986 to now with Uptown. I am the manager of the yard. I supervise, buy back . . . everything. Here is my responsibility. Rain or cold, we stay open. All year long. Last year we closed one or two days because it was so cold. We start working from eight to four. We have some pickup, and we have three vans [in incredibly bad shape]. Monday through Saturday we collect from the routes, different directions on each day. Monday we do Ravenswood; Tuesday, Rogers Park; Friday Andersenville; Saturday, East Rogers Park.

As the site manager makes clear, URI survived largely because it was almost always open and the workers put in long weeks. URI has also survived by building relationships with community organizations and customers that have endured the bad times as well as the good. Toast, a worker at the yard, stated, "Some of them [alley entrepreneurs] you get to know and others you don't. I have never gotten more "have a nice day's" than I have gotten here. The stereotype doesn't fit — they are not all mean and pissed off. Between 50 and 70 percent are regulars. Each one has a different strategy — one big load per week and others do a lot of small loads per week on a bike or some other equipment. The other day a guy brought in a pile he had been working on for three years."

These relationships stretched out into the community, involving large organizations and the city, upon which URI was dependent for the steady supply of materials. By carefully managing these relationships, Uptown and the Resource Center were both able to stay afloat. While URI usually had a negative balance, the Resource Center often made a profit from its diversified operations. Uptown was able to stay open until 1997 by taking losses on its market returns while supplementing, with some dignity and meaning, low-wage workers. The wages were important to people struggling to move out of the informal economy. Jim Burris candidly noted: "We are a small organization. We have in no way been able to compete with for-profit organizations which are into salaries, wages, and benefits. We *do* compete in terms of nonmonetary remuneration because people have more involvement in the meaning of the work. . . . We still try to make a profit in the literal, ordinary, everyday sense of the term. We have to have more income coming in than going out. What we do with that is different. We reinvest it. I have a goal of having people who have a living wage."

Thus, like the Resource Center, URI continued to operate from a hand to mouth basis, relying partially on volunteer activist-organizers continually looking to harvest "urban ore" for social and ecological value. In contrast, some observers and institutions viewed URI and the Resource Centers as "trash dealers" working with undeserving inner-city poor residents. These centers were unique among early recycling organizations. They were started in Chicago, a place where white flight, urban renewal, and central city deindustrialization were taking place on a massive scale. Other early nonprofit centers were started in college towns, where the supply of "hippie" volunteers was plentiful and the symbol of the decaying inner city was largely unknown.

Indeed, both URI and the Resource Center have become anchors in their respective communities. Businesses, residents, homeless people, underemployed citizens, and undocumented persons have come to depend on the centers for sustenance and renewal. In the Grand Crossing neighborhood, where the Resource Center is based, the only other businesses nearby are a currency exchange, a liquor store, and a small grocery that sells day-old goods at high prices. Furthermore, these businesses are absentee-owned and -staffed. The Resource Center is the only organization that employs local residents and — through materials buyback — brings dollars into the communities in which it operates. It is also one of the only institutions with origins at the University of Chicago that grew along with, rather than taking over, the surrounding community (cf. Taub 1994).

Limitations of the Community-Based Model

Uptown, Resource Centers and other community-based model of recycling are dependent upon two factors: (1) a continuous supply of high-quality materials being removed from the waste stream by low-tech scavenging and (2) a steady or rising demand for the materials, which allows the centers to sell goods at a high price. There are substantial barriers to these conditions being met in the present political economy in most urban places. We note some of these below.

The Supply-Side Problem

In Chicago, scavengers, or "alley entrepreneurs," face a number of problems when they try to remove high-quality materials from the waste stream. The most basic problem originates with the way residents dispose of waste. Rather than traditionally separating materials and leaving high-quality goods by the bin for scavengers, residents place goods in trash receptacles. This practice is partially attributable to the fact that residents do not know if there are scavengers in the area.

Upon reflection, however, there is a particular history associated with residential waste disposal. We can imagine systems where residents would actually leave higher-quality goods near the trash receptacles. Since garbage routes are predictable, scavengers presumably know when the materials would be picked up. Waste haulers could be instructed to pick up only the material left in the garbage bins. This type of system would make it easy for scavengers to locate materials in an efficient manner. Of course, it would somewhat complicate the waste hauler's job.

But we never really question our "preferences." Under the current system, then, we have little choice but to place all materials into waste bins. In fact, this practice is institutionalized through municipal ordinances that prohibit scavenging and fine people for leaving materials besides the bins.[9] Scavengers are thus forced into a system in which they have to dig through garbage bins to locate recyclable waste. This poses three barriers to the efficient removal of recyclables.

First, it is a slow process. Opening up cans and digging through all the waste takes time. Scavengers are thus restricted as to how much territory can be covered within a given period of time.

Second, technological changes have made it increasingly difficult for scavengers to locate the materials. The introduction of petroleum-based, nontransparent plastic garbage bags began in the post—World War II era. Since scavengers could no longer see into garbage cans and had to rip the bags open instead, the process slowed down. Scavengers are also placed in a confrontational relationship with residents and commercial waste haulers, who resent the intrusion into the garbage bags. Waste haulers need to be able to grab bags and throw them into trucks. They are expected to be able to cover a certain territory within a given period of time, and ripped bags make this difficult. These inefficiencies raise labor and capital costs for private waste haulers, costs that ultimately get passed on to municipal taxpayers. Residents are often angered at scavengers because having one's trash inspected represents an invasion of privacy. Based on a casual venture into any trash can, an average scavenger can discern what the resident's drinking, eating, and reading habits are (Perry 1978; Rathje and Murphy 1992). Residents are also resentful because they are left with spilled trash, which waste haulers often ignore. The trash leaves an unsightly mess, and odors remain that require immediate attention. Residents take it upon themselves to clean

---

[9] One of the authors lives in a rural community where it is commonplace for people to leave reusable materials (tires, furniture, toys) in the front yard for scavengers. The same author served on a condominium association board in Chicago where the major concern was to keep "the alley clean" from garbage by locking garbage bins from scavengers and fining people who did not use the bins "properly."

up this mess. But they still have to wait another week for the next pickup, and may face even more intrusions by scavengers in the interim.

Third, the proliferation of household chemical usage drastically reduces the availability of high-quality materials and makes scavenging more hazardous. Due to the composition of the modern waste stream (Rathje and Murphy 1992), the scavenger is often confronted with myriad hazards such as sharp metal, needles, and cleaning chemicals (Pellow 1998a, b). Noxious household cleaners often leak onto potential recyclables, making them too contaminated to be salvaged. Likewise, synthetics and other recently developed materials contaminate products, making it hard to extract potential recyclables from nonrecyclables. For example, earlier in history, Jewish peddlers in Chicago often dealt in junk; they gathered old mattresses, pillows, and other sleeping equipment for reuse by soft goods remanufacturers. When synthetics replaced natural fibers such as wool, cotton, and jute, "the scrap from the soft goods could no longer be effectively reprocessed" (Eastwood 1992:28; cf. Gould, Schnaiberg, and Weinberg 1996:140).

In combination, these factors severely limit the collection of high-quality materials by low-skilled scavengers. Community-based centers thus receive a smaller, unpredictable stream of materials from such agents. And scavengers need a higher price per item because the process of collection and sorting is inefficient. Unfortunately, the supply problem is further compounded by demand problems.

The Demand Dilemma

The rise of a high-volume economy after World War II fueled a mass consumption culture averse to purchasing reused goods. The story of the emergence and evolution of mass consumption is a complicated one (Frank 1999; Rifkin 1995; Reich 1991) that has created difficulties for community-based recycling. The United States economy has thrived, at least since World War II, based partially on the steady consumption of new goods produced by American manufacturers (Thurow 1996). Systematic efforts to shape personal consumption habits in the United States date at least as far back as the 1920s. Leaders of private industry first became concerned that many workers appeared content laboring just enough to provide for their basic needs and a few luxuries. In other words, they would prefer to "trade additional hours of work for additional hours of leisure time" (Rifkin 1995:19). This was problematic in two ways.

First, industry investors and managers craved growth in productivity, to achieve greater profit margins and market shares. A culture of work that frowned upon excessive laboring was anathema to this goal. Second, industry needed market growth, or increases in consumer demand. Firms were therefore reliant upon workers' willingness to labor longer hours. This ensured workers' ability to continually create sufficient demand for the rapidly escalating supply deriving from production (i.e., the more hours one worked, the more disposable income one could earn, with which to purchase consumer goods).

As routine overproduction created huge backlogs of product inventories, businesses sought to jump-start consumer spending, much the same way the state makes policy today. With the help of consulting psychologists, commercial marketing and advertising campaigns became efforts to deride homemade products and redirect consumers toward "new and improved," factory-made, synthetic, disposable, and modern store-bought items. After World War II, more and more Americans experienced a marked rise in disposable income and greater upward mobility. The mass consumption strategy required new supporting ideologies and structures. American firms could remain profitable only by creating massive amounts of goods. To ensure adequate demand, industry also enlisted the help of the government. The state took three steps: (1) developing a public education system capable of turning out productive workers who could earn a high wage and thus be able to consume; (2) making low-interest loans available to consumers so they could finance major purchases like homes and cars; and (3) developing an implicit agreement to allow for massive advertisement across major media (television, radio, print) that encouraged consumption of new goods.

In turn, industry tacitly agreed to cost-of-living adjustments to wages, pension plans, and productivity bargaining that ensured peace with unions. They thus guaranteed the availability of a quiescent work force needed to produce high volumes. Finally, the American family assimilated the culture of consumption (B. Rubin 1996). As Harry Braverman (1974:276) later stated, "The source of status [was] no longer the ability to make things but simply the ability to purchase them." In a recent look at American consumption patterns, the economist Robert Frank describes a new variation of American mass consumption as "luxury fever" (Frank 1999; see also Schor 1998). Frank argues that Americans measure self-worth based on their ability to consume. But now they strive to consume "luxury items," which are defined as superior goods like the overly priced big-screen television or ultrapowerful computer. Frank states, "The runaway spending at the top has been a virus, one that's spawned a luxury fever that, to one degree or another, has all of us in its grip" (1999:5).

Mass consumption and luxury fever are both directed toward new goods. Americans are barraged with messages to devalue older and used goods. The increase in consumption has gone hand in hand with the decline in waste reuse by both consumers and businesses. Frank notes that a gas grill costs moderate-income Americans twice what they need to spend. Consumers want grills that are bigger and fancier than one could ever possibly need; the grill has now become a status symbol. If buying a cheap gas grill at the local Home Depot is considered low status, purchasing a used one from the local recycling center would be out of the question.[10]

In this culture, community-based recycling centers are not only peripheral to the economy, they are a potential drain on the new-goods economy. Imagine a middle-class urban consumer culture enthralled with reused materials. This economic orientation would provide political and economic support for community-based recycling. There would be high demand for products scavenged. Like college students, families would partially achieve status based upon "finds" at local centers. This tension was high in Chicago. The city had a large manufacturing base, which was hostile to reuse. It also had large multiethnic populations who demonstrated their upward mobility in their homes by the visible consumption of new goods. Finally, the city's large suburban populations followed cultural mores even more, and their practices were especially reflected in the mass media.

Social Movement Struggles in a Global Marketplace: The Demise of Community-Based Recycling?

Despite these barriers, the two community-based centers managed to survive for some period. Their decline was initiated by the macrostructural organizational changes occurring in the waste industry. The primary change, of course, has been the rise of waste management services that compete directly with community-based recycling centers. Historically, this conflict did not exist. The waste firms hauled trash, leaving recycling to scavengers and community-based centers. The manager of Resource Management, a private suburban Chicago recycling firm, commented on this transition "There's real value in the material. So now it's a competitive thing where businesses have jumped in, they are interested in it and they are really going to do it much cheaper, more efficiently than nonprofits. So that's the transition that's occurred, unfortunately for those folks [the nonprofit recyclers]." As large private

---

[10] One exception was, of course, high-end antiques. However, even this market is remarkably small compared to the market for expensive new furniture with its limited life span. Access to antiques is also skewed toward the upper income distribution in this society, which defines these scarce items as "luxuries" because others cannot afford them.

sector organizations have recognized the economic value in recyclable materials, the future of many community-based recycling operations has been jeopardized.

As we noted in chapter 1, changes in the national and state political climate also contributed to this transformation, prompting many of the traditional waste firms to venture into recycling. In Chicago, it was apparent by the late 1980s that federal minimum content legislation would be passed soon. New efforts mandated that many industries and institutions "buy recycled" or "close the loop." This market growth signaled to corporate actors that recycling might eventually provide a substantial profit with reduced risk. As Jim Burris put it, "Cynically or otherwise, we have to realize that there is a certain ironic, wry success in that nonprofits all over the country have test-piloted it [recycling] so successfully that big capital has come in and taken over."[11]

In Chicago, the movement of private firms into recycling brought advanced technological systems that may spell doom for community-based recycling efforts. Large waste haulers use sophisticated trucking technologies that allow them to collect and transport large quantities of materials.[12] Such improvements have made waste hauling more profita-

---

[11] This is an issue of growing concern in the sustainable development arena. One reviewer of this manuscript noted, "This is a hot issue in some recent discussions that I have been having with community-based organizations around sustainable development issues. Do CBOs or other non-profits need to always be thinking of how their small ideas will play in the 'big game'—the for-profit world—if they are to succeed? Does a success invariably mean that their ideas get taken away from them and used by others for a profit without any benefit to their original communities/constituencies? Is this a 'positive function of non-profits'—they develop good ideas, they try them out on a small scale, they get used/taken over by for-profits, and the non-profits go along struggling to stay alive and develop the next idea to be given away to for-profits?" (anonymous reviewer).

[12] This starts with the invention of the Dempster Dumpster in 1934, which was really nothing more than a "large steel container fully enclosed with a curved steel top, entry doors, and dump release bottom, . . . designed to be hoisted mechanically onto a truck for transport to the dump site" (Jacobson 1993:55). This simple technology allowed carriers to double the amount of materials that could be transported and to move faster without threat of spilling materials onto the road. This advancement was shortly followed by the use of hydraulic crushers on waste trucks. Hydraulics increased carrying capacity by reducing the volume of materials. From a strict exchange-value interest, they made trash pickup and hauling more efficient by allowing fewer men in fewer trucks to haul more trash in less time than before. From an occupational safety standpoint, technology has been a mixed blessing. The Dempster Dumpster eased the strain many waste haulers regularly experienced when lifting trash cans into trucks, but the blades in the hydraulic mechanism have been notorious for crushing workers' limbs and spitting out harmful substances that may be concealed in the trash (Jacobson 1993; Russell 1996:5). From an ecological and social perspective, the hydraulics were problematic because they crushed any potentially recoverable materials, effectively putting an end to reuse activities and the income they brought in.

ble. Labor costs can be minimized by the use of a single truck that can transport massive amounts of waste, and uses fewer workers. Modern recycling trucks have progressed even farther beyond these improvements. In keeping with the information revolution, the solid waste industry has also wholeheartedly adopted new, computer-based technologies in recent years. From billing and accounting to micro–decision making, collection, processing, labeling, and shipping, the solid waste and recycling industries have begun to use labor-saving, time-saving robotics and expert systems (McAdams and McAdams 1995:125–30).

Some programs in France outfit collection bins with silicon chips that the computer on collection trucks can recognize for automated pickup and deposit. From the operation of conveyor belts to air classifiers and semiautomated sorting, the manual labor "on the line" continues to be rationalized and reduced. As one recent trade journal article ominously pointed out, "This efficient separation [process] . . . reduces the amount of manual sorting required, which is still essential as a final stage" (Larane 1995:76). These trends allow waste haulers to displace and deskill human labor to achieve greater efficiencies and profits. To some extent, they redistribute productivity gains from moderately skilled and experienced blue-collar workers to technologically trained white-collar workers in engineering and other departments, which exist far from the shop floor (Wellin 1997).

These improvements have ramifications at several levels. Once the hauling was cheaper, it became profitable for large waste haulers to enter the recycling market. Even if the margin of profit on an individual item was small, increased carrying capacity now led to substantial economies of scale. Large waste haulers entered into this domain, which led to a more global market for recycling materials, making it harder for community-based recyclers to survive. It also had devastating impacts on local scrap dealers who were the primary customer for the community-based centers. For example, Nancy Burhop, the recycling coordinator for the Evanston Recycling Center (see chapter 5), told us of one such dealer's demise: "We used to sell to Valley Scrap. We had a contract with them for two years. . . . And he's out of business; they left Evanston. We had a lot of problems with them not being able to accommodate the amount of material that we had, which was one of the reasons why the decision was made to go into recycling. This was done extremely quickly, and we all know that when things are done that way sometimes we don't do everything correctly. But we've made changes, things have improved."

The loss of the scrap dealers meant that URI and the Resource Center lost a large portion of their customer base. It also went hand in hand with a round of mergers and acquisitions in the solid waste and recycling industries. This served to further consolidate and narrow the playing field. *Business Week* magazine recorded 251 acquisitions in 1989 alone (Carless 1992), and in the first three quarters of 1995 one firm, United Waste Systems, acquired 41 companies (*Solid Waste Technologies* 1996:45). The five largest waste companies continue to capture the markets of once independent, family-owned waste haulers and processors around the nation (see table 1.3). BFI's downtown Chicago facility still bears the name of a Dutch family-owned business it recently acquired — Hoving and Sons.

Essentially, the community-based centers are becoming squeezed out of their markets. In Chicago, the city's support for the blue bag program gradually led it to withdraw support for the nonprofits. This became exacerbated as it became clear that the blue bag system was becoming more expensive. Beginning January 1, 1996, the city cut the diversion credits, providing only 25 percent of its previous support to the nonprofits. One year later, the city withdrew all of its remaining support. This effectively crippled the nonprofits as far as postconsumer recycling was concerned. Our conversations with Jim Burris of Uptown Recycling took place in this increasingly constrained context for URI. He was struggling then to ensure the survival of the organization and its efforts to create value and meaning in the local community. Burris explained URI's travails in this period: "[Although we cannot compete economically with private recyclers,] we certainly compete in the quality of the service offered — we think we offer the best. In terms of industrial processes we are low tech, "appropriate tech" at the highest. But frankly, it's hard to provide a living wage with hand sorting materials, given the fact that we are now essentially in a competitive industry as opposed to a social movement."

Burris was also honest about the changes he had to make at URI for it to survive in Chicago's increasingly competitive business climate. These changes included downsizing his workforce at times and rationalizing his accounting system. Nonetheless, he maintained a defiant stance against the ideology of profit maximization: "I hired a professional accountant for office management and bookkeeping — Jackie [an African American women] — because I know that we really have to keep those information systems effective in order to have the information to be competitive, even as we try to hold on to our mission and not let the dollar bottom line drive us." Speaking more specifically to the recent changes in the recycling industry, in a 1996 executive director's report to URI's board of directors, Burris stated:

> Throughout its first 12 years of operations, URI focused its energies on postconsumer solid waste recycling in its operations, advocacy and education.[13]

---

[13] URI successfully partnered with the following North Side neighborhood organizations: Ravenswood Manor Improvement Association, East Andersenville Residents Coun-

During the winter of 1996, through a series of Board/Staff retreats, URI reas-
sessed its mission and its program areas. A major assumption of the retreat
process was that post-consumer solid waste recycling had moved from being a
type of social movement driven by a set of environmental ideals/assumptions
and grounded in a concern for local neighborhoods, to becoming a commer-
cially-driven industry, grounded essentially in competition and profit maximization by well-capitalized corporations and local governments working
closely with those corporations. As environmental activists, we found this
premise to be, at the same time, factual; a sign of a certain type of "success"
of the recycling movement during the prior 12 years; and a recognition of the
limits of the movement to make fundamental changes in how our society
treats the environment and its wastes. (Uptown Recycling, Incorporated, Director's Report 1996)

This statement supports the thesis that nonprofit recyclers not only
identify themselves as social movement organizations, but also that they
take credit for "test-piloting" recycling for the private sector.

We obtained an even more dramatic and statistical portrait of this
struggle from one of Burris's employees, Toast. He worked in the recycling yard on the forklift, in sorting areas, and in the buyback station.
He was a member of the Lutheran Volunteer Corps (LVC), a nationwide
program that places college students in social justice–oriented organizations. In a café up the street from the recycling yard, after a day of
heavy work, Toast spoke to us:

Taking a look at the figures, I was in the office the other day and for the first
time really realized how much money we are losing. We have very little machinery, volume, and economies of scale. The recycling business is just not
working for Uptown. Look at Irving, who makes $5 an hour, Mayo, who
makes $6, and me, who makes $450/month through my LVC stipend. It takes
Irving two weeks to do a whole truck of newspaper, in which time they pay
him $480. But we only get $15 a ton for news for a 3.5 ton truck, so at most
we get $50 for the truck, for what is around $500 worth of labor. For Mayo,
who does cardboard, you get very little for cardboard. Just adding the labor — forget the fuel, capital depreciation, collection costs, and labor et ce-
tera — we're not making it. I think recycling is necessary but it's not going to
save the world and it doesn't challenge consumption. It's really business as
usual. I agree with Jim who'll tell you that recycling is and has become an
industry. It's all about the dollar; the bottom line is making money. For people
who are out here to do good, there is just no room for 'em. We're just getting
wiped out.

cil, Lakewood Balmoral Improvement Association, Rogers Park Community Action
Neighbors, and the Lakeview Citizens' Council.

The accounting figures Toast provided reveal that URI was never even "breaking even" on most dimensions.

At a February 1997 board meeting of the Chicago Recycling Coalition, Jim Burris of Uptown Recycling and Christine Kordiuk of the Resource Center announced changes that would be occurring at their respective organizations as a result of the blue bag program's monopoly over the Chicago recycling market. Since they could no longer compete for the larger contracts, they would go after smaller niches. For example, the Resource Center signed a supplemental agreement with the city to provide recycling services in Chicago Housing Authority (CHA) developments (i.e., public housing). This is an initiative that provides recycling under the assumption that public housing residents will opt not to purchase and properly use blue bags.

The authors spent a day with the Resource Center staff as they traveled from corner to corner in several CHA developments. The results were impressive, by comparison to the residential blue bag system. At each stop, dozens of residents — children, teens, parents, and grandparents — would bring cardboard, paper, bottles, and cans to the pickup truck to have them weighed and paid for. Several residents proudly informed us that "this program puts a little change into our pockets and has helped keep the streets and sidewalks in this community cleaner than they've been in a long time." Ironically, though part of the larger blue bag program, this project is the only component that is source separated and does not use blue bags. This system consequently produces the highest quality products that enter the blue bag MRFs. The buyback model of recycling is the oldest and most enduring practice, largely because of its relevance to poor citizen-workers. As the Resource Center's Christine Kordiuk explains, "Local folks don't support us because their money is going toward 'saving the environment' or anything like that; [they support us because] it's [the money] being parlayed right back into the community into tangible changes." Thus the Resource Center and Uptown Recycling worked with the Chicago Recycling Coalition, a social movement organization that advocated recycling, reuse, and composting. However, they were no match for Waste Management's political and economic muscle.

The city's blue bag program required that one organization would have the exclusive right to recycling in Chicago's neighborhoods — Waste Management. This meant that Uptown Recycling's residential customers were forced by the city to support its new blue bag program. URI was ultimately forced to close its doors. As Jim Burris explained, "The political decision by the city to invest in single family recycling with the blue bag had the single greatest impact on our program." In 1997, after ceasing all recycling collection operations, URI sold its buyback facility to the Resource Center because it could no longer compete with Waste Management's recycling program. It is some consolation to residents in the Uptown neighborhood that the buyback center will remain open for an unspecified period of time under the management of the Resource Center. The impact of a complete shutdown of that operation would have been disastrous, particularly in the Uptown and Edgewater communities, where recent reform of welfare and immigration laws already have damaged the social organization. To quote one community activist in Uptown, "If the center closes, people will literally starve to death. This buyback center is where people get money to eat. If this is gone, they will do whatever it takes to survive, even kill each other, Maybe."

Moving toward the Three Es: Assessing the Achievements of the Community-Based Centers

The act of recycling by community groups is intended to provide environmental and social benefits. It is but one component in the social movement agenda to provide the larger community with some education that might eventually lead to progressive, critical thinking about wastefulness in the operations of the treadmill. Below is a list of related projects of the community-based groups, all of which attempt to contribute to the three Es of sustainable community development.

Creative Reuse Efforts

In 1995, the Resource Center decided to provide a way of taking "junk" from individuals and institutions who would normally send it to landfills and, instead, to refurbish it for reuse: "The Creative Reuse Warehouse in Chicago's Maxwell Street neighborhood was born of a need to develop an appropriate plan of action so that resources can be reused to their fullest potential. By reaching beyond household recyclables, resources such as . . . used office furniture and supplies, salvaged lumber, and broken bikes are turned into valuable assets for communities, schools, and the general public" (Ken Dunn, "Letter from the Director," Resource Center Newsletter 1996).

The Creative Reuse Warehouse accepted everything from aquariums to wood scraps. In a system where exchange value was a small but necessary component, the warehouse accepted a three dollars donation for every "bag" of materials visitors take, or visitors could swap a bag of their own materials for a bag from the warehouse in a "creative exchange." One of the major motivations for the creation of a reuse center was to offer schoolteachers affordable materials for creative classroom instruction. Other clients and customers included artists, parents, social service agencies, and curious individuals.

Before it closed down, Uptown Recycling had actively pursued the possibility of establishing a similar reuse center on Chicago's North Side. Jim Burris was then thinking of focusing more on "white goods" — home appliances — and furniture refurbishing. He was pursuing agreements with local housing agencies and advocates such as Habitat for Humanity. URI would provide collection and refurbishing services for affordable-housing agencies. The tentative plans for the center included rehabbing an old warehouse using ecological design techniques and recycled parts; creating a small-business incubator; and building a job training and apprenticeship program for youth and adults. Local citizen-workers and area businesses would have reaped numerous benefits. With the demise of URI, however, the future of this plan is uncertain.

Big Fish Furniture

Part of the Resource Center's reuse efforts include a wood salvaging operation. Ken Dunn initiated this program after meeting the driver of a large semitrailer hauling wood from a demolished building to a landfill. He made a deal with the driver to deliver the wood to Big Fish Furniture, a wood shop in Hyde Park, thus diverting these loads from the landfill. This type of wood was perfect for building shelves and dining-room tables. In return, Big Fish donates 10 percent of their profits to the Resource Center.

The Resource Center is now actively seeking materials from building and construction sites for reuse purposes, in what they are calling "green demolition." We note that while the Resource Center is losing money on its curbside and buyback/drop-off recycling, the reuse end is actually profitable. The Creative Reuse Warehouse coordinator, Christine Kordiuk, informed us that "we're making money in reuse and we're very surprised too! It's a year-and-a-half old project, although Ken's been doing it on a small scale for twenty-five years."

The Big Fish shop is located on a site the Resource Center has used for over twenty years. This is also the location of community gardens, an earthen stove for community cookouts, apple trees, truck farms, an artist studio, and a bicycle repair shop. Dunn explains the logic behind the Big Fish furniture shop:

> Our woodworking shop is producing a few nice lines of furniture out of this old material, with a marketing edge. And we're going to need a marketing

edge because the trend is Scandinavian furniture. . . . So the marketing niche is that many of us like quality things. I think everybody does. Why would you deal with something rickety, falling down and ugly when you can have fine things? I think a lot of us have given up on having fine things, knowing that it often means participating in this global economy, which we think is harmful to our community and to the South Side. Well, if you can salvage wood from the waste stream, prevent it from going to the landfill, give it another life — in fact, give it a really long 'nother life, because there's real craftsmanship put into the making of this furniture, so that it will actually become like an heirloom and be passed on and on. It's well made out of quality materials. Instead of buying another couple of years by having it being used as a fence post in some garden, we're buying another hundred years of use out of the crime we committed by tearing down that tree in the first place.

Thus, the Resource Center harvests the urban ore to harness the power of the marketplace for the good of the local community. In a way, the Resource Center is bringing the Grand Crossing/Hyde Park area back full circle, since it was the site of a strong furniture-making sector earlier in the twentieth century.

The Blackstone Bike Co-op

Out of concern for the children in the poor neighborhoods around Hyde Park who needed safe recreational outlets and experience with skill-building activities, the Resource Center devised the following plan: "In April of 1994, the Resource Center staff decided to provide a productive outlet for neighborhood children in need of bicycles. Since that time, the Bicycle Co-op has repaired several hundred used and discarded bikes. The shop is stocked with recycled and donated bicycles and parts. This is a place where neighborhood children can customize and repair their own bikes under adult supervision. The essential spirit of the bike shop is to engage children's curiosity and to match their energy and enthusiasm with worthwhile projects while teaching them new skills" (Resource Center 1996). Through this program the Resource Center again mobilized all available resources toward the end of improving the lot of another often voiceless group of people — children.

Turn a Lot Around

The Resource Center views "recycling" more broadly than the process of postconsumer waste remanufacturing. Dunn has always sought to revitalize communities through recycling's many forms. One way to do this is by recycling land—specifically, blighted and vacant city lots that proliferate in poor and minority communities. The Turn a Lot Around project was developed to "clean and reclaim neglected vacant lots as gardens or community spaces" (Resource Center 1996) and has created attractive plots in neighborhoods all across Chicago's South Side, including spaces in public housing projects. Many of the individuals who manage these gardens sell the produce locally. As we drove through the Grand Crossing neighborhood with Ken Dunn, we observed professionally landscaped lots with evergreens and colorful flowers growing in compost, bordered by reused railroad ties. Dunn views the decline and rise of neighborhoods as being driven more by perception than empirical reality. Racial segregation, white flight, and economic disinvestment all occur largely because of perceptions about urban neighborhoods, which are often inaccurate—though they are self-fulfilling prophecies (Taub 1994). Dunn connects the Turn a Lot Around program to this theory: "This is all the theory of decline being perception. And there's a lot of progress. We bring in compost, railroad ties, take away the rubble, bring in plants. So this [lot] has just had a couple weeks work on it. Let's go around the block and see some of the lots we've finished. Take a right turn at the fire hydrant there. So in the areas where we work we try to get all the vacant buildings boarded up that way, which instead of saying, 'This place is going down," it says, 'Here's some value in this building: doesn't this look attractive?' So it kind of turns the psychology around." Ken Dunn informed us that in some cases, the sight of reclaimed lots has indeed inspired developers to build new homes in these neighborhoods.

Windows to the Future

In addition to vacant lots, thousands of abandoned buildings and condemned homes dot the landscape of Chicago's South Side. These buildings drive more affluent residents away, reduce property tax bases, and create eyesores and potential havens for criminals. The Resource Center's Windows to the Future initiative attempts to manage this problem by boarding up and painting artwork on the windows of these buildings. Dunn recounts a successful effort to oust drug dealers from one such property: "This [property] had gotten to be a major gang hangout and a place for drug selling—these three vacant lots. And so the community—we talked to them—they decided that they were going to spend time on these three lots. And the gang and drug dealing has actually gone elsewhere. They got the gang out of here and the perception has been that this community is on the way back."

One building the authors saw was a home with pictures of children and their families painted on the boarded windows. The Resource Center's goal here is to secure buildings that are structurally sound and provide a sense of caring for them in hopes that they will be rehabilitated to provide low-income housing. The Department of Housing and Urban Development (HUD) recently sold one such home to an owner who then renovated it. Similar efforts are underway in other cities. The Heidelberg Project in Detroit, for example, is run by an artist who reuses housing materials to create art in front of abandoned homes in that city. This project has attracted the attention of developers, artists, and community activists nationally and internationally. Of more immediate importance to the residents of this community, the Resource Center's work has removed areas of Grand Crossing and other neighborhoods from the unofficial "off-limits" status by which they were stigmatized. Dunn explains: "There is still the stamp of care and that's maybe what's needed to turn things around. And if you are building housing in the City, what better place than here? We're right along the Illinois Central [railroad] tracks here [and] near the lake [Michigan]. This is a prime place to live. What you need to do is watch the community. As long as it's going down, stay out. But as soon as it starts coming back you'd better get in there and build the housing." Windows to the Future therefore has symbolic meaning. The word *window* indicates opportunity and the word *future* underscores the focus on the long-term viability of the Neighborhood.

Community-Based Sustainable Development Enterprises: "Doing Good but Not Doing Well"

Community-based recycling has a dual status as an economic enterprise on one hand and a social movement on the other. The relative emphasis on the two dimensions of this type of recycling organization has varied over time and space. Their struggles and the eventual closing of Uptown Recycling warrant a brief assessment of the achievements of nonprofit, community-based recycling centers.

URI's survival for over a decade was testimony that a social movement organization could create a community-based recycling center. In contrast, a former official of the city of Chicago labeled these organizations as "boutiques" that could never serve the entire Chicago area. Yet by allowing marginalized social groups operating in the informal economy to bring scavenged materials to the recycling yard where the materials could be sold in bulk to larger for-profit firms, both the Resource Center and URI served as "mediating institutions" (Lamphere 1992) between the larger political economy and the local community and also as intermediaries between the formal and informal economies. As such, they provided a modicum of social and economic stability that local residents could depend on over time. An alley entrepreneur, carting up several pounds of scrap metal and aluminum to the Resource Cener's buyback site, told us: "Well it's a blessing. You know what I'm saying? Because a lot of brothers are on General Assistance. They [the government] cut that out. And then they don't want to give you no work. So I got to fall back on this and then a lot of people ain't got nothing to fall back on, man. And everybody's in the street." This entrepreneur offered a searing critique of welfare reform and its impact on persons who have to live hand-to-mouth.

Phil Foster, an alley entrepreneur who describes himself as "the homeless man on Fifty-third street," has frequented the Resource Center's buyback site since 1986. He had a lot of positive things to say about Ken Dunn and the center:

> I think I'm very good friends with Ken on an employer-employee basis. I'm a scavenger and I go to him for my livelihood. If this place closed it would be a big hardship on me. . . . I don't want to be on public aid unless it's absolutely necessary. But that's the reason why I want to recycle, because it keeps me free from public assistance. And it's a little money, not much, but I'd rather have this than be on the public aid all the time.

> AUTHORS: Did you know that just yesterday President Clinton signed a welfare reform bill that some people think will throw a lot of folks out onto the street? What do you think about that?
> PHIL: Public aid should be for those who really need it. And that's all I got to say.

This is a surprising comment because this man looked as if he had not had new clothes, a bath, a haircut, a square meal, or a tooth brushing in years! He also wore no shoes.

Damon, an Uptown Recycling employee, told us that he had been addicted to drugs, living on the street, and in prison over several years. He found difficult to "go straight" with odd jobs and day labor his only employment options. His work at Uptown Recycling, however, was his first steady, reliable employment in years.

These are just a few of the stories we heard from alley entrepreneurs and employees who eked out a living through URI and the Resource Center. These "mediating institutions" (Lamphere 1992) also pushed for positive political change. Both organizations were represented on the Chicago Recycling Coalition's board of directors. They were instrumental in helping pass the Burke-Hanson Ordinance, mandating recycling in the city of Chicago. Both organizations also worked in the public schools to educate youth and the general public about materials recycling, composting, and reuse. These campaigns were as much about political education as they were about environmental education. Both URI and the Resource Center stayed close to their social movement roots in this respect. They saw education as a long-term effort to change the way citizen-workers view the world, in order to impact social behavior.

The centers also constructed a strong political community by creating networks of politically mobilized groups within the neighborhoods. For example: URI provided a place where the local liberal community could volunteer time for the organization. URI and the Resource Center were aided by a substantial cadre of volunteers who engaged in much of the work that the "rank-and-file" laborers did, as a demonstration of their commitment to the social movement. Volunteerism is a core foundation of most social causes, despite the tendency for "social movement industries" to develop. URI's staff and volunteers canvassed the neighborhood, mobilizing resources in a classic community organizing strategy (McCarthy and Zald 1977). They recruited local associations to marshal support for curbside pickup programs. Over time, the connections with local neighborhood networks increased, creating strong political support for a population that was otherwise hidden and forgotten — the poor, the homeless, people of color, and immigrants.

Yet, while there is much to celebrate about community-based recycling, its future seems bleak. This uncertainty in Chicago is of course most readily observable in the failure of Uptown Recycling to survive in the blue bag era. This has brought about a substantial job loss for people like Phil and Damon. It has also left the neighborhood without a centering force for the political networks. As we noted above, while still operating today, the Resource Center has also found the emerging recycling marketplace a hostile terrain that threatens its survival.

Thus, the blue bag program is an example of a municipal program that was well funded but socially uncreative. The Resource Center and Uptown Recycling are examples of two major recycling operations that were very innovative at organizing around socially creative ideas and practices. The failure of the community-based centers cannot be attributed to programmatic miscalculations by the organizations. Rather, the community-based centers failed because they could not overcome the challenges posed by the existing political-economic structure, which had led to a powerful group of larger waste-hauling organizations expanding their interests into recycling. Community-based centers were resisted by a combination of municipal officials and private-sector waste haulers and overpowered by the substantial influence of these large firms in their market decisions, and by these same firms' influence on municipal officials and agencies.

Five

Industrial Recycling Zones and Parks: Creating Alternative Recycling Models

Environmental Movements and Industrial Ecology: The Logic of Recycling Parks and Recycling Zones

In this chapter, we outline some recent attempts to create recycling industrial parks or zones and innovative MRFs. Recycling industrial parks or zones modify production processes in order to "reduce, reuse, and recycle" their feedstocks and waste products. The impetus arises from the work of ecologists, systems theorists, and business leaders who have developed the concept of industrial ecology (Tibbs 1992, 1993; Ayres 1989; Graedel and Allenby 1995; Socolow et al. 1995). Industrial ecology emphasizes a new paradigm under which firms would operate. Environmental standards and regulations are seen as business opportunities under this paradigm, rather than as obstacles to be dodged (Bell 1998). The National Academy of Sciences has defined industrial ecology as "a new approach to the industrial design of products and processes and the implementation of sustainable manufacturing strategies. It is a concept in which an industrial system is viewed, not in isolation from its surrounding systems, but in concert with them. Industrial ecology seeks to optimize the total material cycle from virgin material to finished material, to component, to product, to waste product, and to ultimate disposal" (Jelewski et al 1992). Thus, industrial ecology calls for a more holistic examination of production, where wastes generated from one part of a production process may actually become feedstocks for another part of production.

Proponents of industrial ecology have developed designs for industrial systems that are powered with few inputs, except solar power, and that produce few wastes. A much-cited example is the industrial ecosystem in Kalundborg, Denmark, which contains a host of linked industrial facilities, including a refinery, power plant, pharmaceutical company, fish farm, greenhouse, wallboard factory, and a district heating plant. The facilities are linked to each other through a system design that allows them to share and exchange energy and wastes. Thus, the entire system is a network of interrelated processes. Every waste produced is used as a feedstock in another process. Hardin Tibbs refers to the project as an "industrial ecosystem" (1992). As in a natural ecosystem, industrial ecology projects are premised on three central assumptions: (1) an industrial system should be able to function within its means; (2) an industrial system should feature diversity and interconnection of constituents and (3) there should be no waste. By-products of every metabolic process should be the inputs for another process. In a sense, the linkages create a kind of industrial "food chain." Marstrander's (1996: 200) depiction notes that limited resources are required as inputs, and limited wastes are produced. Instead of simply using resources, firms share energy and "all sorts of activities related to the recycling of used products."[1]

The cases offered in this chapter raise a number of doubts about the feasibility of industrial ecology as a pragmatic strategy for sustainable community development. The political space for industrial ecology advocacy has arisen mostly because contemporary environmental movements have challenged the logic of modern corporate practices. Such social movements have increased the transaction costs of many multinational firms. Among other activities, environmental groups have filed lawsuits and engaged in publicity campaigns, documenting environmental degradation generated by these corporations. Additional pressure from these movements has been stimulated by new scientific evidence of widespread ecological problems, including global warming, the growing ozone hole, and habitat destruction.[2]

More recently, political and economic space for industrial ecology has arisen as the publicity about global environmental issues has energized national governments to consider new policies to regulate national and multinational firms operating in their countries. A major task force of the President's Council on Sustainable Development presented a series

[1] Early precursors of this logic included the idea of earth as a "spaceship," which must husband and reuse its resources in order to survive in a hostile galaxy. Moreover, techniques derived from these concepts were actually modeled in various spacecrafts conducting missions in the earth's orbit. Biological wastes of the crew were recycled and reused, for example, in order to minimize the need for a larger weight of support systems on long space voyages. And with regard to solid waste more broadly, space vehicles could not merely dispose of these in space, since the solid materials would continue to orbit the earth and present potential hazards for spacecraft.

[2] Small-scale environmental movement groups, even in "developing" countries, have increasing access to information on both these environmental problems and anticorporate campaigns through the Internet and other means of rapid and cost-effective communication. Thus, a variety of such movements can raise the cost of "business as usual" for corporate leaders and managers by publicizing their firm's problems, even to the extent that such groups have been raising these issues at annual shareholder meetings. An even newer strategy used by some social and environmental organizations is to purchase blocks of shares in the polluting/depleting firms. They then use their voting position to gain seats on the boards of trustees of these firms or to propose shareholder resolutions in order to place pressures directly onto senior officers of the firms (Gedicks 1993).

of recommendations to Vice President Gore's office. These would suc-
cessively raise standards for energy use and resulting emission for firms
in order to reduce global warming (PCSD 1999). Again, this can be
traced to efforts by the environmental movement to raise awareness and
even fund research. It follows on international conferences in Rio de
Janeiro and Kyoto seeking international agreements to reduce global
warming. U.S. environmental movements have pressured the President's
Council to adopt some American responses because the United States
has been relatively unresponsive to the international pressures at these
conferences.

It is important to note that the earliest impetus for industrial ecology
actually arose from within the environmental research community itself.
The basic design, engineering apparatus, work, and management techniques have largely been developed by environmentalists working in a
variety of academic fields. This context is important to recognize. Industrial ecology did not arise from within mainstream firms or dominant
political channels. Rather, it arose as a challenge to the existing system
by various elements from within the *environmental* community. As a
challenger to the system, industrial ecology faces two problems.

First, it is a small movement representing a few firms, academic departments, and think tanks. Its small scale means that industrial ecology
advocates have not been able to fund pilot projects needed to attract
attention from major financial institutions or venture capitalists. IE advocates also do not enjoy any substantial public presence in the mainstream media. While some foundations are interested, they lack the capital it would take to fund the quantity and quality of pilot projects to
give industrial ecology a national presence. As a result, it is difficult for
local groups to obtain the financial support needed to implement local
industrial ecology projects.

The second obstacle industrial ecology confronts is the active organizational hostility that is typically directed against any challenge movement (Gamson 1975). The movement is not large enough to successfully
organize a major campaign. By contrast, the oil/gas and auto industries
have effectively lobbied against solar power and other alternative energy sources and public transit systems for decades. Yet alternative local
projects still raise enough uneasiness among larger established industrial
actors for the latter to engage in local campaigns designed to undermine
these organizations. Recycling-arena projects are labeled by other waste
firms and mainstream political organizations as unproven, risky, and
futuristic. These negative labels exacerbate the financial problems of
community-based alternative organizations. They also intimidate local
politicians who do not want to risk their political capital on "unproven" projects. Simultaneously, these mainstream firms attempt to

capture local political support by repackaging their own efforts as being "green." Thus, they argue that *they* can better provide the ecological benefits without the economic risks associated with "pie-in-the-sky" technologies.

Some environmentalists nonetheless argue that even these resistant firms will come around to industrial ecology once they recognize its economic potential. They also argue that local or national governments need only offer clear economic signals to firms in order to get them to recognize and incorporate ecological values. An early argument by economists (e.g., Mishan 1967; Boulding 1971, 1973) was that once firms obtained a proper evaluation of environmental harms, they would "internalize" these costs in their planning. Western economics argued that such internalization would be in the firms' long-term interests. If they avoided exacerbating environmental problems, it would ultimately (and often in the near term) prove cheaper and more profitable for them to do so.[3]

The examples in this chapter suggest that this scenario has often not been much realized. In the following sections we present some case studies. We then use these case to generate some broader theoretical interpretations.

Promises in Maywood

Maywood, Illinois, is a Near West suburb of Chicago that has become a deindustrialized community of color. In the early 1970s, Maywood was a prospering industrial community where citizen-workers had jobs and their families had homes. The American Can Company alone employed

---

[3] It is also important to note that a key component of this argument is that regulatory bodies and environmental activists must actively guard against corporate violations. Once the political and economic pressures exerted by these two protesting entities diminishes, then the firm's managers often realize that it is cheaper once more to pollute and deplete, since "no one is watching." Even where the firm has installed costly new physical technologies to reduce environmental additions and withdrawals, we argue that it may nonetheless be more profitable not to retrofit other facilities with them or not to apply these same technologies in plants engaged in new manufacturing lines.

Some of this pattern has been observed by David Sonnenfeld (1998). He notes that the practices of Southeast Asian forest product companies have often involved technologies that reduce the use of chlorine in the pulp and paper process. In part, these technologies have become cheaper because western European countries have done the research and development costs in order to protect their own waterways. Yet despite this "industrial ecology" step, other types of practices in these companies have become more environmentally pernicious. This is often a pattern where additions can be relatively cheaply reduced by firms, but these same firms expand their withdrawals from ecosystems (thereby depleting habitats) in order to sustain high profits.

over twenty-five hundred local residents. This bustling economy was matched by the local culture. Maywood was known for its vibrant downtown retail district, complete with playhouses and movie theaters. For many years, Maywood had been known as the "Village of Eternal Light."

If Maywood in 1970 represented everything that was right about American society, Maywood in the 1990s represented everything that had gone wrong since then in urban America. As in many marginalized urban communities, the decline of Maywood can actually be traced to race baiting that began in the 1960s. Small numbers of African Americans moved into Maywood in search of social stability and jobs. Unscrupulous realtors began panic-peddling the housing market. Realtors pitted whites against blacks, block busting neighborhoods by driving whites out of Maywood and admitting blacks, depressing the local housing market. Maywood's housing market collapsed at the same time the broader deindustrialization of urban America was accelerating.

Maywood's own industrial base disappeared by the end of the 1970s. Closings started with the American Can and Canada Dry companies. After these facilities shut down, wages declined, inducing next a collapse of the local retail sector. The central business district then lost its major retail stores, including Sears, Montgomery Ward, and Florsheim Shoes. These closings further depressed the local wage base. Thus began the vicious cycle of social and economic decline. In the 1980s, Maywood's depression was typical of many Chicago areas (see Wilson 1996 for a thorough review). With no industrial tax base, real estate taxes increased. People with economic resources fled to escape the high taxes. Maywood was left with those residents who were unable to leave. High local unemployment created considerable increases in the need for social services, but the Reagan administration had cut such federal programs.

Maywood was stuck: to revitalize their economy they needed an infusion of revenue. The federal government would not help, and the local residents *could* not help. By 1990, Maywood was beset by a high crime rate, high unemployment, and higher taxes. At the same time, it had lower revenues for all services (including police). It also had growing homelessness, a rapid rise in drug abuse and teenage pregnancies, and increased youth gang activity. As happened in many other marginalized urban communities, Maywood refused to simply give up. Instead the community turned inward, with local leaders seeking new ideas for community development.

The response, known as the "Maywood Strategic Plan," concluded that the village faced three intersecting dilemmas: (1) the flight of private industry, (2) the withdrawal of the federal government, and (3) the

loss of local residents with resources. Left with fewer resources, Maywood responded by seeking ways to "maximize the coordination of all
existing resources in the neighborhood planning units" (Resource Conversion Systems 1994: 6). The architect of the Maywood vision described the problem and response:

> Maywood is ideally located near the business core of the Midwest. It is situ-
> ated within 15 miles of Chicago's Central Business District, the Loop. The
> greater metropolitan area is home to a population base of approximately six
> million. The work-force pool is recognized for its "hard work" ethic in indus-
> try. Unfortunately here, as elsewhere, there has existed a complete lack of
> local or regional planning for reuse of its vast urban waste resource. For
> years, the only classical disposition considered had been landfilling and incin-
> eration (Resource Conversion Systems 1994).

At a time when other urban areas were simply scrambling for economic
development at all costs, the Maywood Plan made an unprecedented
link between its urban decline and opportunities for environmental restoration that could provide social, economic, and ecological benefits.

In the late 1980s, two urban planners, Ralph O'Conner, Maywood's
director of community development, and Bill Connerty, conducted a
"community visioning plan" for Maywood. From their inventory of local human and natural resources, it became apparent to them that Maywood had two primary resources: a proven productive labor force that
was desperate for jobs, and garbage. Linking the two assets, they devised a unique plan to put people back to work through remanufacturing. The local workforce was going to turn garbage into marketable
products. This idea was buttressed by the availability of cheap land in
Maywood. Many of the old industrial sites were not marketable. Industrial properties located in such declining communities—especially
brownfield sites contaminated from previous users—attracted few buyers.
It seemed reasonable that Maywood could procure such a piece of land
on which to place an innovative recycling mill. Ralph O'Conner stated,
"So you ask yourself, 'What is my son going to do? Is he going to run
around mad at the world as a victim because of something that happened five hundred years ago?' In the end, it's going to boil down to: if
the street is not safe enough to walk on, then how am I going to get
business to come in? So what resource do I have? Waste and idle people.
You put those together and it's the future: recycling people. It'll be a
rebirth of people's minds."

Placing mini-mills in the urban core was not a new idea. Others had
talked about the "urban forest"—a metaphor for the plentiful supply of
discarded paper products—to be used as secondary fiber in remanufac-

turing operations. Maywood's challenge was even greater. They had to transform what many observers saw as an urban *wasteland* into a plentiful urban *forest*. To grow that forest, an innovative plan was necessary. O'Conner and Connerty therefore envisioned a recycling industrial park. Basic to the plan was the establishment of an advanced Integrated Materials Recovery Facility (I-MRF).

The I-MRF would take both presorted recyclables from curbside pickups and mixed solid waste from trash receptacles. Both materials would then be taken to the I-MRF, where new sorting, screening, pneumatics, impulse, and magnetic technologies would be used to extract paper, metals, plastics, and glass. Every material recovered from the waste stream would flow directly into an adjacent industrial plant, which would convert the materials into new products. The idea was to have as many of these converting plants as possible. These would either be on-site or located nearby in Maywood. Chart 5.1 is a representation of the envisioned facility.

Both presorted and mixed waste deliveries would be brought to the loading dock of the I-MRF. Waste paper removed would first be redirected to a mini–pulp mill located in the recycling park. The mill would repulp the paper directly for sales on the open market. Revenue from these sales would help support the industrial park through the minimill's rent payments. Organics (i.e., food and yard wastes) would next be removed from the waste stream. They would be fed directly into an ethanol plant, which would work in conjunction with a utility plant on-site to generate power to run the I-MRF. Excess power and ethanol would be sold, bring still more income for the industrial park. Originally, other recyclables were to be sold on the open market via brokers, creating revenue for the park. Over time, more of these converted materials would be used in the facility by new manufacturing tenants. Initially, 60–70 percent of the locally generated waste would be recycled into energy and paper. An additional 10–15 percent would be recovered recyclables to be baled on site and sold in commercial markets.

The Village of Maywood would benefit in a number of other ways. First, the industrial park would initially provide 275 permanent jobs. These would be filled by local residents, thus providing an influx of revenue into the village. Wages would likely be spent in local stores and banks. This would inject more money into local circulation and revitalize the old central business district.

Second, the Industrial Park would generate more revenue as the local tax base increased. The village could then expand much-needed social services. Maywood would levy taxes against the facility based on its advancing capital improvements. A portion of these taxes would be

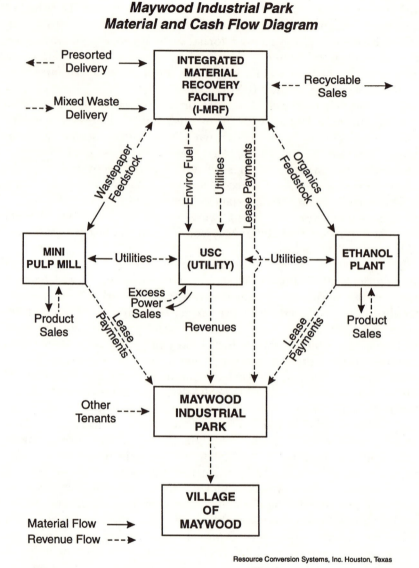

5.1 Proposed Maywood Recycling Industrial Park (Resource Conversion Systems, Inc. 1994)

used in part to retire Maywood bonds previously issued to provide financing for public improvements designed to support the I-MRF. The rest could then be used for other public needs.

Third, the facility would increase outside traffic into the village.

Truck drivers would deliver garbage and remove products. This increased traffic, in combination with a revitalized local workforce, would support a variety of new small businesses, which could include gas stations, diners, pharmacies, and other service enterprises. And fourth, Maywood could then supply the I-MRF with water and waste-water services on a metered fee basis, creating even more revenue for the city.

The planners purposely selected paper as one of the initial products the park would produce because it seemed to fit well within the emerging political economy. The state of Illinois had earlier mandated that at least 25 percent of Illinois's total purchases of paper and paper products be remanufactured (i.e., recycled) products. This was to increase to 40 percent by 1996. Such requirements, combined with the emergence of local markets, suggested that paper would be a readily marketable product. There also seemed to be a related growing demand for cardboard products, and there were a number of companies interested in moving to Maywood in the near future to use their cardboard.

Ethanol, the I-MRF's second product, also seemed to command another growing market. Organic wastes removed from the waste stream could not be directly marketed. Instead of paying tipping fees to landfill them, the I-MRF would use these organics to generate energy and to be converted into ethanol. This process would keep the I-MRF operational costs low. Converted ethanol would also tap into a growing market, since it had the additional appeal as a fuel regarded as somewhat environmentally friendly. Moreover, it was politically attractive as a secure resource, especially by contrast with petroleum. This plan was proposed just after the Gulf War, which had stimulated new fears of disrupted oil imports for the first time since the 1970s energy crisis.

The I-MRF facility would be located on nineteen acres of consolidated industrial property where the American Can Company (ACC) once stood. This location provided O'Conner and Connerty with the symbolism of Maywood's rebirth from the "ashes" of ACC. The facility was bounded by working rails on one side and major roads on other sides. Moreover, the site was not likely to be used otherwise. Ironically, the city of Maywood was founded in 1869 by a group of wealthy industrialists from Vermont. They founded the Maywood Company, which attempted to build the "ideal community" next to an expanding city of Chicago. Maywood would once again serve as a site for another revolutionary way to combine commerce and community, the I-MRF, and as a place that escaped the social problems associated with Chicago. But how could Maywood implement this impressive idea after the village had foundered?

Initially, Maywood contracted out with a small Texas firm called Resource Conversion Systems (RCS). RCS seemed to be on the verge of

securing the capital needed to start the industrial park. At the sugges-
tion of RCS, Maywood sent out a Request for Proposals (RFP) in the
fall of 1990. It required, said Bill Connerty, "something innovative and
creative in a manufacturing process, where they used feedstock from the
area's recycling program." It also stipulated that the facility must contain no incineration. Reaching this stage was an expensive and time-
consuming process: Maywood had spent thirty thousand dollars and six
months just preparing for the RFP.

It soon became apparent that although Maywood had the science and
politics right, they were not going to be able to come up with financing.
Large economic actors did not want to invest money and time in a
project that was so different from conventional practices. This paralleled Chicago's experience with Waste Management, which was primarily interested in recycling programs built on preexisting practices and in
the city's willingness to put up much of the risk capital. Maywood
could not meet either of these two conditions. Developing a very different type of production system required creativity, flexibility, and faith.
Large players were opposed to these risky conditions. And Maywood
needed their help because it lacked indigenous resources.

Conversely, smaller companies with new technologies were not big
enough to pay for the full program. Of one company that did want to
take part in the recycling park, O'Conner noted:

> It's basically small guys that are getting capitalized, and most of them just
> want to license their technology and let you know it's available. A lot of them
> don't want to put that much in from an equity standpoint. . . . . We've got
> one tire [recycling] guy who will put together the plant. You buy the equip-
> ment — they don't want to run it and they don't want any equity in it — all
> they want is to give you a license agreement and sell you their equipment and
> they're out — a turnkey operation. They'll train you and they'll set it up, but
> they don't really want to own it.

A growing sociological literature confirms the widespread existence
of this dilemma of financing innovations (e.g., Harrison 1994). Large
players in the marketplace tend to develop technologies that fit within
their these production patterns. Their goal is to take preexisting processes and lines and make them operate more efficiently. Revolutionary
technologies tend to come from the outside. They are generated by
more entrepreneurial firms. Yet these innovative firms often run into
difficult capital outlay problems. It takes an average of seven years to
get a new technology from idea to market (Timmons 1994). Somebody
has to float a startup company of highly experienced personnel for a
significant period of time. This means that the firm is often nearly cash-
dry by the time the product gets to market and has great difficulty ad-

vertising or setting up new marketing networks. Many good technologies never succeed because their creators lack the necessary funds.

Many such companies could have done quite well had they been able to locate in Maywood. With such close proximity to Chicago, media coverage would have been guaranteed, thus widening their customer base. But the firms did not have the funds to do this. What emerged was a plan for a small city with innovative ideas and firms, and a range of innovative technologies that could put the ideas into practice. But a paucity of funds to link the two eventually undermined the project, a common paradox and market failure. Large cities do not have the incentive to search out small innovative players, while the large market players are only seeking markets for conventional products in these large municipalities. The latter effectively lock out innovative smaller players, who cannot match offers in terms of either cost or size. This was indeed the case in Chicago with respect to the community-based recycling centers, which were displaced by Waste Management. More depressed municipalities also have the incentive, but lack the financial base. As O'Conner stated: "No one has that much faith in the marketplace for recycled products and emerging technologies. That's why it's going to take places like Maywood that are biting on the concept of sustainability to keep pushing for that type of thing."

Absent players include local banks. Community reinvestment studies demonstrate that depressed communities can be a windfall for large urban banks (Taub 1994). For the vast majority of communities, however, these banks have been absent. As O'Conner noted, the problem for "eco-preneurs" like himself and Connerty was quite simple: "They were not able to develop the technology to convince the capital markets that there was something pending here. Everybody [we] talked with looked at it with the mind that it was unproven technology . . . [and] there was no sense in throwing away risk capital in something that didn't have a proven track record."

Another useful and related political-economic model is the emerging practice of "micro-lending" to small business entrepreneurs (Derber 1995). Micro-lending has also caught on in the Third World, with Bangladesh's Grameen Bank being the hallmark. Founded and managed by Professor Muhammad Yunus, the Grameen Bank has provided thousands of village entrepreneurs with small business loans. One of the bank's missions is to help "raise families out of poverty" (Cabral 1998) through funding self-employment ventures. The Ford Foundation, the Aspen Institute, and others have also recently become active in micro-lending. Yet micro-credit proponents often ignore the alarmingly high rate of failure among small businesses. At the very least, though, micro-lending offers one alternative investment model. Innovative and risky

proposals like Maywood's recycling industrial park might have had
some chance if such progressive banks had been involved (cf. Taub
1994). Unfortunately, the plan for a Recycling Industrial Park in Maywood was put on indefinite hold. O'Conner and Connerty were dismissed, but still retained enough faith in their ideas to set up a consulting firm, Ersatz, to try to market their concept to other communities.

Reviving West Garfield Park: The Bethel New Life Story

A variation on the Recycling Industrial Park proposal in Maywood was
a Recycling Industrial Zone proposed by Bethel New Life. Bethel is a
nonprofit community development corporation (CDC) located in the
poor African American community of West Garfield Park, on Chicago's
West Side. Community development practitioners at Bethel New Life
faced obstacles similar to those confronting the Maywood planners.
They had the challenge of trying to be socially and environmentally
responsible *and* fiscally solvent from within an economically hollowed-
out community. Bethel's social mission was also a part of its religious
mission, as it was affiliated with the Lutheran Church. Since the five
riots occurring between 1965 and 1969 in West Garfield Park, Bethel
New Life's president, Mary Nelson, struggled to revitalize this blighted,
poverty-stricken, and polluted community.

West Garfield Park was crippled by the flight of banks, investors,
grocery stores, and other businesses during the 1970s. It suffered the
pain of white flight during the late 1960s and early 1970s. Between
1970 and 1990, the community also lost about 40 percent of its housing stock. West Garfield Park in 1994 was nearly 100 percent African
American and the unemployment rate was "close to 27%" (Bethel New
Life 1994). Nelson notes that the neighborhood was haunted by "dete-
riorating apartment buildings. Drug pushers are visible on the streets
day and night [in] a ghost town of an industrial area."

Mary Nelson explained that West Garfield Park "looks like Germany
after the second world war" (Bethel New Life 1994). In a five-block
area on Lake Street, the main industrial area, there were thirteen empty
buildings. Many of them had "for sale" signs posted. Toxic waste was
recently discovered inside and around a large building where children
played. But this "brownfield" had yet to be cleaned because of developers' fears of cleanup liability and costs. There were forty known
brownfields in West Garfield Park alone, making it a classic urban
wasteland.

Bethel New Life was one of a growing number of CDCs that aimed
to move beyond a "bricks and mortar" approach to community devel-

opment. They were seeking new ways to build up the social infrastructure as well as the physical infrastructure (H. Rubin 1994; Stoecker
1994). Bethel's mission was to create a viable and sustainable community by providing living wage jobs. Bethel had a proven track record in
this area. The organization was a multitiered, complex CDC that had
leveraged resources to build several single and multifamily homes in the
community. It also maintained an employment agency, a small business
institute, and a performing arts center and engaged in land redevelopment and waste recycling.

The story of Bethel New Life is instructive because they were a few
steps ahead of the Maywood planners. Since 1984, Bethel had operated
a buyback recycling center that had paid out over one million dollars in
cash to residents. Deciding to take the next step, in 1992 they opened a
full-sized materials recovery facility that created thirty-five new jobs.
But once they realized such jobs were dead-end positions, they closed
the MRF and started work on the concept of a recycling industrial zone
instead.

Similar to O'Conner and Connerty's ideas for Maywood, Bethel then
saw a partial solution to their community's problems by connecting two
resources: unemployed residents and the abundance of municipal waste
in the area. Mary Nelson envisioned the MRF as just one component of
a recycling industrial zone. She had plans to attract industrial recyclers
of construction and demolition debris and tires to the area. Like O'Conner and Connerty's plans, these were largely new and untested technologies. Nelson also stirred up anger among several Chicago-based environmentalists by seeking an agreement from the city of Chicago to buy
steam from its large (and polluting) municipal incinerator to heat
Bethel's recycling plant (this was the Northwest Incinerator, which was
later shut down).

Although that agreement never materialized, two years later, Bethel
turned over the MRF ownership to a for-profit company under a lease
agreement. This was a minority-owned company specializing in commercial paper recycling. Bethel made the pragmatic decision to partner
with Fiber Source because the latter had the greater capacity, capital
resources, and expertise needed to survive in a volatile business climate.
True to its social service roots, Bethel had Fiber Source sign a hiring
agreement to the effect that they would, to quote a Bethel employee,
"first hire from applicants that we refer from our employment center."
This was where Bethel ran into problems. As Steve Steinhoff, Bethel's
director of industrial development, explained it: "Unfortunately, the
partnership with Fiber Source didn't really work out from the standpoint of (1) their living up to any commitment to hire people who the
employment office referred to them, or even develop any type of work-

ing relationship with our employment office and (2) our effort to either lease or sell them the equipment that was in the building or sell them the property — all those negotiations for a long period of time never went anywhere."

When asked, "Is it possible that Fiber Source was concerned with the quality of the local labor pool?" Steinhoff replied, "I'm sure that was part of it, but in my opinion they never made any reasonable or sincere attempt to address that. After a lot of hounding and badgering, they placed a call to our office and hired one person and a month later they fired him. They were not sincere [and] it was clear that they did not have any goal or desire to make that part of their objective. They saw that as a kind of pain that they had to deal with."

In accordance with the "low road" to development that many firms are taking, the desire for limited corporate liability for their employees is becoming popular (Gonos 1997). By signing a hiring agreement with Bethel, Fiber Source was able to secure the development of a new site and new markets. But they had little intention of hiring locally. Bethel sought a relationship or a partnership, while Fiber Source viewed the deal as simply another transaction. They may have decided that agreeing to locate a business in the blighted neighborhood of West Garfield Park was sufficient to satisfy Bethel and local citizen-workers. It is likely that they did not anticipate Bethel's aggressive efforts to enforce this agreement.

In a real sense, both Bethel and Maywood were trying to build "something out of nothing," to pull their communities up by their bootstraps (an impossible act, according to the laws of physics). Both organizations were concerned with attracting new technologies to areas that were characterized by high unemployment, degraded housing stock, and a lack of the basic institutions needed to make their communities function smoothly. Maywood and West Garfield Park are in many ways hyperrepresentations of the ills facing neighborhoods of poor urban citizen-workers. Thus, it is not surprising that officials in Maywood and West Garfield Park were desperate enough to consider unproven technologies that might eventually provide net economic and social benefits. These dilemmas are not unique to Maywood and West Garfield Park: in the next section, we outline similar dynamics in two other regional communities — DuPage County, Illinois, and Gary, Indiana.

Resistance to Innovations: DuPage County and Gary, Indiana

In other cities and counties located in the Chicagoland area, recycling advocates are also struggling to create new development linkages from recycling. We briefly turn to two areas near Chicago where these trends are also apparent.

DuPage County

In DuPage County, Illinois, a public-private MRF was built in 1991 to meet the state of Illinois's waste recycling requirements. This was the first publicly owned, privately operated MRF in the Midwest (Evanston's Center was built in 1992). A number of similar centers had been in operation in New England and California. DuPage County is home to the two largest landfills in Illinois — Green Valley (Waste Management–operated, owned by DuPage County Forest District) and Mallard Lake (Browning Ferris Industries–operated).

A 1988 Illinois law established a surcharge on all landfills. It mandated that 40 percent of this surcharge would go to the host county, and 60 percent would go to fund a solid waste plan and recycling programs. When the DuPage MRF was built in 1991, it was one of the most modern facilities in the world. It was designed to run for one shift — eight hours — at 155 tons per day (tpd). As Eric Keeley, the manager of the MRF at that time, remembers it, "We did a capacity test, and it had a capacity rating of greater than 210 tons per day with peaks over 300!"

Unfortunately for Keeley and his prized MRF, the DuPage County political and economic elite were not interested in supporting public-private recycling partnerships. During the early-to-mid 1990s, the prevailing political climate was hostile to the idea of "big government." Social service–oriented programs, even those with minimal state support, were often viewed as fiscal drains. This was especially so in DuPage County, the third richest county per capita in the United States and a bastion of fiscal conservatism. The twenty-five-member county board was all Republican, and the members were vocal supporters of free-market policies.

To make matters worse for Keeley, Waste Management was also headquartered in the county and was a highly respected business presence. As if that were not enough, Keeley told us about the difficulties he had competing in the same county with another medium-sized private recycler, Resource Management:

> The county wanted us to fail because of severe pressures from local corporations and outlying MRFs in other counties. Any action I took to upgrade and support our facility was viewed as a direct attack on other facilities. We spent $10 million for the intermediate processing facility [another term for a MRF] — $5 million went to the building, $1.5 million went to the land, and the $3 million or so left over went to equipment. The reason for this was the

zoning laws. Zoning is harsh—we need so many sprinklers, and they don't want trash around. Cal's [the manager of Resource Management, Naperville's private MRF] facility is different. Go there and I dare you to look for a sprinkler there. In ours, in DuPage, a fire isn't a concern because workers can drown (because we have so many sprinklers)!

The political ascendancy of a "small government" ideology and the presence of nearby influential private firms both created a hostile environment for this MRF.

Aside from the favoritism that Keeley alleges Resource Management received from county officials, local commodification of recycling soon displaced its social and ecological dimensions. This commodification led to the regressive policy we have termed "getting the materials right" (Weinberg, Pellow, and Schnaiberg 1996:278). In Keeley's words,

> Other things were happening. I like to call it a number of things, like the "Recycling is good, therefore more recycling is better, right?" problem. Or "municipal materials madness." MRFs were adding materials to their list with total disregard for the hierarchy of solid waste reduction. "More is better" was the philosophy. A numerical listing of all the materials that you recycle became fashionable. Cal's facility did this with junk mail, letterhead, stationary, all mixed paper, Barbie dolls, and even pine cones! This is artificial inflation and has no measurable impact on waste reduction. Others added polystyrene packing peanuts for curbside recycling containers in Lisle, Illinois. I called them and asked, why not take it to a place that already reuses polystyrene, like UPS or Mail Boxes, Etc.? They responded, "Oh Eric, we don't want to confuse the people!" Putting aside all the ecological impacts, the sheer absurdity of doing that versus reuse is crazy.

These practices Keeley decries are firmly embedded in the "business as usual" (Stretton 1976) approach to community development. For that reason, many environmentalists have labeled the practice of "getting the materials right" an "antirecycling" practice because of its strong market value orientation (Weinberg, Pellow, and Schnaiberg 1996:278).

Gary, Indiana

Gary, Indiana, is an industrial suburb of Chicago, founded in the first decade of this century as a center of steel production that employed low-wage labor. Nearly a century later, this town epitomizes the rust-belt, postindustrial, crime- and poverty-ridden urban core with a large African American population. Places like DuPage County, not surprisingly, look far more attractive to some businesses than Gary, Indiana might. Conversely, some low-road industries might actually find Gary more attractive. In spite of its current depressed condition, some entrepreneurs, eco-preneurs, and urban planners believe that places like Gary can be revitalized in a sustainable, responsible way with a combination of older and newer business development

The two eco-preneurs initially associated with the Maywood proposals met recently with city officials in Gary to discuss the possibility of locating environmentally sound industries there. Their consulting firm, Ersatz, was given a positive reception, in large part because Gary's citizen-workers were weary of the pollution and the brownfield sites that have plagued their municipal landscape. These ecological problems are viewed as social problems that have an interactive effect with the high crime and poverty in the area. Ralph O'Conner, one of two eco-preneurs now with Ersatz described Gary's dilemma:

> The bottom line is that you're taking an area that's not producing revenue for its state. Take an area like Gary, with all the tax-delinquent steel mill property. What we're talking about [with our new environmental industry] is a net gain in new tax revenue to the state by the people that are employed and paying taxes, by the real estate taxes that are going into the school system there to decrease dependence on state funding. There's got to be a bigger picture painted for all the players at the state level where they can say it makes sense. The other contradiction is that you can go overboard being mired with the solid waste aspect of this process and lose sight of the economic development aspect of it. The Supreme Court handed down a decision that prohibited flow control. You can't demand that haulers bring their waste to you if you're a municipality or a county. They have the right to be after the most economical deal that they can find, even if it means going back to Waste Management. So you can imagine who typically wins. Waste Management is in Gary. It appears that they've enamored themselves with the local powers that be, to the extent that they are calling the shots. They have a lake/quarry shaped like a J . . . [and] they want to send waste to this site.

Like Maywood and West Garfield Park, Gary is a stark portrait of a "hollowed-out" industrial city with myriad social, economic, and environmental ills. With regard to its waste problems, it also seems to be under the influence of a large multinational corporation — Waste Management.

Through attracting Ersatz's eco-preneurs, O'Conner and Connerty, Gary is thus attempting to approach a high road to investment. Despite its current low-road strategy through the blue bag, Chicago also has a history of efforts at progressive development. Much of this history must be credited to the city's strong tradition of community organizing, which supported the community centers described in chapter 4. If Gary is to succeed with its revitalization plans, community organizations must also become major players in that process. Yet, as of this writing, the waste-based industrial proposal remains far lower on the local political agenda than the two innovative planners had hoped.

Planning for Industrial Recycling Zones: Is Ecological Modernization in Our Future?

The cases of Maywood, West Garfield Park, DuPage County, and Gary raise troubling questions about industrial ecology and the related theorizing of ecological modernization.[4] Originally, industrial ecology laid out a model for how changes in technological and scientific practices could lead to sustainable forms of production. They raised a set of serious questions about the social context as it supports efforts to implement new ecologically sound technology. In the social sciences, these ideas have been taken up in a newer literature on ecological modernization. This theory has gained increasing popularity in both the western European scholarly community (Spaargaren 1997; Mol 1995, 1996; Spaargaren and Mol 1992) and, recently, in the United States (Cohen 1998; Sonnenfeld 1998).

Ecological modernization has its roots in social theories of *reflexive modernization* in advanced industrial societies. In perhaps the most concise statement, Arthur P. J. Mol articulates the theory as focusing "on the growing independence, 'emancipation' or empowerment of the ecological perspective or sphere from the basic three analytical spheres or perspectives in modern society: political, economic, and socio-ideological or societal" (1995:64).

The core of Mol's theory is a set of six hypotheses, which are outlined in chart 5.2.

Thus, proponents of ecological modernization maintain that environmental issues have become institutionalized within corporate decision-making processes. Furthermore, they believe that new technological innovations are allowing firms to deal more effectively with tensions between economic growth and environmental sustainability. Ecological modernization is a theoretical model in which there are changes in both technological and scientific practices as well as consistent adjustments in cultural and institutional organization. Ecological modernization theor-

---

[4] The relationship between industrial ecology and ecological modernization is difficult to sort through, especially given the emergent quantity of the ecological modernization literature. To the extent that we get this relationship correct, we thank Maurie Cohen. We also thank Arthur Mol for helping us sort through our own confusion on the ecological modernization framework.

CHART 5.2
Ecological Modernization: Six Hypotheses

1. The design, performance and evaluation of processes of production and consumption are increasingly based on ecological criteria, besides economic criteria, among others;

2. Modern science and technology play a pivotal role in these ecology-induced transformations, which are no longer limited to the introduction of add-on technologies or process-integrated adaptations, but include changes in product chains, technical systems, and economic sectors/clusters;

3. Private economic actors and economic and market mechanisms play an increasingly important role in processes of ecological restructuring, while the role of state agencies changes from bureaucratic, top-down *dirigism* to 'negotiated rulemaking' and the creation of favorable conditions for such transformation processes;

4. Environmental NGO's change their ideology, and expand their traditional strategy of keeping the environment on the public and political agendas toward participation in direct negotiations with economic agents and state representatives close to the center of the decision-making process, and the development of concrete proposals for environmental reform;

5. This process of ecological restructuring is becoming increasingly interdependent with processes of globalization in the political and economic dimension and will therefore not remain confined to one nation-state;

6. Alternative de-industrialization initiatives for limiting ecological deterioration are applied only to a marginal extent due to limited economic feasibility and poor ideological support, among other factors.

     * from Mol 1995, page 64

ists refute calls by earlier environmentalists for a reduction in technology — *dematerialization* — as a strategy for preserving ecosystems. Instead, ecological modernizationists call for more advanced technological innovation — *superindustrialization* — which will lead to ecologically sustainable forms of production and consumption.

Proponents of the ecological modernization theory have been critical of other streams of environmental social science for focusing narrowly on the *capitalist* character of production, thereby missing the more robust and ecologically driven *industrial* aspects of production. Ecological modernization proponents emphasize the institutional level of analysis, which assesses the extent to which the ecological sphere has become an independent sphere. Mol (1995:63), for example, proposes that there are three analytic spheres, each of which is really a network characterized as a social system "in which actors engage in more or less permanent, institutionalized interactions." The three spheres are: (1) policy networks that concentrate on industry-government relations; (2) economic networks that concentrate on economic interactions between economic agents in and around an industrial sector; and (3) societal networks that concentrate on the relations between the economic sector and civil society organizations (Mol 1995; see also Spaargaren 1997).

The aim of ecological modernization theorists has been to demonstrate that within each network, there have been significant environmentally induced institutional transformations. This suggests that there is an *ecological sphere* that makes a difference *independently* of these other spheres. To the extent that this is true, they state that the environment has been emancipated from these other spheres and is beginning to constitute its own sphere — an initiation of ecological modernization.

We believe our examples presented over the last three chapters challenge the ecological modernization thesis in several respects. First, the examples of Maywood and Gary suggest that there are some firms acting in ways theorized by ecological modernizationist logic. But, these firms are not economically viable because they go against the logic of the larger political economy. These firms' efforts were labeled risky, futuristic, and unproven, and they were not supported by the political establishment. Eventually, the planners in the Maywood case were fired by the mayor. Likewise, the West Garfield Park efforts by Bethel New Life have received no widespread political support and were later undermined by a private firm whose promises fell far short of its deeds. Finally, conventional banking and industrial institutions were not willing to finance the projects. Thus, they never got far beyond the drawing board.

Second, the major institutional actors directing recycling exhibit few of the features that ecological modernization would suggest are essential. This was true for Waste Management in Chicago and Gary, as well as for the political establishments in each of the communities studied. Each of these actors professed a type of environmental responsibility. For example: Waste Management's proclamation became a headline in the *Financial Times*; "Raising Environmental Standards Is Not Part of Our Job. It's Our Whole Business" (May 19, 1994). Likewise, the Daley administration, the county administrator in DuPage, and officials in Gary all referred to themselves as "environmentally responsible." But they either cannot or do not treat ecological issues independently of their political and economic contexts.

From a waste management or sustainable community development standpoint, we also note the absence of attention to a large component of *ecological problems* — ecological withdrawals, or forms of depleting ecosystems. Our cases exhibit little attention to habitat destruction, which is a frequent component of production expansion within the global political economy (Schnaiberg and Gould 1994). Such ecological withdrawals have also been addressed much less frequently in environmental regulation regimes of the state. Paradoxically, they have largely been ignored even in the successful cases of ecological modernization. Indeed, in keeping with the rising tide of global capital transfers (Barnet and Cavanagh 1994; Longworth 1998), our inferences from chapters 3 and 4 are that ecological modernization may only mask increased *total* materialization of production.

Rising materialist pressures come from the growth of ever more affluent shareholders, who are able to generate profits wherever expanded production levels and contracted labor costs exist. Paradoxically, as we have noted elsewhere (Gould, Schnaiberg, and Weinberg 1996), it is far easier to regulate ecological additions (pollution) than ecological withdrawals. There are technical solutions for most additions, at least superficially, at the site of production. But the solutions for many withdrawals are the very processes of deindustrialization that ecological modernization theorists and proponents decry as unworkable. Their call for "superindustrialization," as Sonnenfeld (1998) has noted, may actually be a license for super*materialization* of production, increasing rates of natural resource extraction.

One of the ironies we have noted in the United States is that there has been growing mobilization and subsequent attention to toxic wastes from production. In part, this is because these are human health hazards whose impacts are more visible in urban areas (Brown and Mikkelsen 1997; Szasz 1994). The broad array of ecological hazards associated with deforestation and mineral extraction associated with habitat destruction has largely been ignored by the central thrust of both environmental regulation and ecological modernization. Ironically, many issues of U.S. worker health and safety have similarly been ignored (Pellow 1998a, b; Sheehan and Wedeen 1993). Firms attend more to the politically potent issues arising from more powerful communities of middle- and upper-class citizen-workers (Schnaiberg1986) who perceive that they are being exposed to toxic hazards.

This too may differ from the situation in western Europe. There, powerful and diffuse labor unions have maintained their social influence over both the production process and the state's political process, despite weaknesses arising from incursions of global capital flows. The U.S. failure to sustain the objectives of the recent Kyoto conference on global warming gases is the most visible of its failures to deal with habitat destruction and rising energy consumption. Once again, for historical reasons of community structures as well as the differences in the social contract across continents, these tendencies are less evident within western Europe—though not necessarily so in the overseas enterprises funded by European capital. For example, Daimler-Benz acquired Chrysler Corporation recently as part of its transition to lowering labor costs and reducing the role of labor in production decision-making. Likewise, European firms such as Royal Dutch Shell wreaked ecological havoc in natural and human habitats such as Nigerian oil reserve areas. And companies long associated with progressive social democratic nations, such as Sweden's Volvo corporation, have begun to move production south to the "better business climates" of Estonia and Latvia—a Scandinavian version of "maquiladorization."

Mol and others refer to ecological modernization as a theory. In contrast, we see it as more of a *vision* of what the future *might* be. Our case studies, though, suggest that the conditions for ecological modernization are rarely met. Furthermore, we note that even if the ecological dimensions of production were eventually to take on a greater priority, the ecological modernization thesis remains largely silent on the crucial questions of community, social inequality, and the role of labor. The blue bag program raised a number of these issues directly in chapter 3. In recent years social inequality within and between communities, nations, and corporations has increased dramatically, while the power of labor has receded significantly (Gordon 1996). Any model of a sustainable future must confront these issues directly. Importantly, in our two major cases in this chapter, the future of communities and the role of labor were central to the planners' visions. However, these concepts were largely ignored by the industrial and fiscal agents involved in discussions about implementing these plans. Financial institutions, seeking to minimize their fiscal risk, labeled the designs as too untested.

Furthermore, our vision is that an ecologically sound future can be achieved only through the use or threat of political mobilization and disruptive actions directed toward those powerful actors who currently resist efforts to reach such a state. This enduring conflict among labor, capital, and the state is in sharp contrast to the more peaceful future envisioned by some ecological modernization proponents. Our conflict perspective is reinforced by the difficulties encountered in the case studies outlined above. Good ideas, optimistic economic models, and concerted efforts by socially and ecologically oriented planners in several communities appear to founder in the hostile setting of investment strategies that Longworth (1998) emphasizes are built around a single value of "efficiency," the increase in shareholders' rates of return on their investment. Maximizing shareholder value is the new mantra, almost a religion, promulgated by industry consultants and managers as the penultimate example of "best practices." These cases suggest that ecological modernization may be quite limited within the United States (and elsewhere), and not necessarily a first step toward sustainable community development.

Despite the appeal of local proposals for integrated recycling-industrial zones or parks, none of the cases we followed actually developed the forms that were envisioned. Bethel New Life achieved only a very modest start. Its new industrial zone firm neither stimulated new recycling activity in West Garfield Park nor met Bethel New Life's expectations of creating substantial employment in the new "sustainable industry" zone. Perhaps the other extreme was the case of Maywood, where the proponents of the industrial zone were fired before they ever implemented any of their plans. Using Mol's criteria, these proposals have not produced "superindustrialization," with its low ecological inputs and low environmental outflows. Nor have they managed to "dematerialize" national and regional production practices. There is a potential for this, though, in the substitution of labor for ecological resources in recycling MRFs.

As the details of each case study have been presented here, we often fail to address the macrostructural social contexts in which these case histories are embedded. Longworth's (1998) analysis of "best practice" criteria for global industrial investment parallels our own model of the tempo and direction of the transnationalization of the treadmill of production (Gould, Schnaiberg, and Weinberg 1996). We use his distinctions between those actors whose interests are increasingly represented in production decisions — the shareholders who own publicly traded global companies — and the "stakeholders" whose local fates are dictated by global shareholder–based decisions.

Except in the small numbers of locally owned and largely family owned businesses (cf. Shuman 1998), Longworth's analysis suggests that there are *dialectical* tensions between the interests of shareholders and those of stakeholders. This is a central feature of the treadmill of production (see chapter 2), in that governments seek to support both stakeholder and shareholder interests in their support for treadmill expansion. What makes this a dialectical system are the tough trade-offs between support for either set of interests. Mol's and other analyses of ecological modernization see this ecological attention as emerging independently of the political and economic spheres. They also ignore the

social distributive outcomes of any ecological modernization of firms —
how any particular form of ecological planning will affect the interests
of either stakeholders or shareholders. Each of these interest groups has
its own set of political interests, and any ecological modernization path
de facto favors one or the other set of interests. Because ecological modernization focuses on the interior decision making of the firm, it eschews much consideration of the interests of stakeholders and, through
the isolated decisions of corporate managers, does not challenge the
domination of shareholders.

Longworth's work and our case studies in this chapter (as well as
chapters 3 and 4) help us understand what it would take to create a
synthesis that would truly empower stakeholders as much as shareholders in the national global economic system. The highly demarcated
social representation within political parties in western Europe as well
as the significant presence of progressive labor unions there suggest that
European stakeholders may have benefited somewhat from higher levels
of ecological modernization. Stakeholders are represented in the political sphere through the highly differentiated political parties. They are
also represented in the economic sphere, where firms have been induced
to construct some form of "co-determination." In the latter, both managers and workers have some decision-making power over the firm's
current and future economic decisions. On both of these levels of stakeholder representation, the United States offers substantially less support
than does western Europe. As a consequence, the United States has increasingly marginalized workers and local residents, generating one of
the highest levels of social stratification within the industrial countries.
Chart 5.3 lays out the logic of these dialectical decision-making systems.

Barring some political-economic shifts toward the European model,
we believe that future efforts to construct sustainable community recycling industrial zones and parks in the United States are unlikely to meet
with success. Some firms might actually improve their economic status
by investing in recycling-based industrial zones. But the modern U.S.
firm is deeply embedded in processes of *institutional isomorphism* (Di-
Maggio and Powell 1988, 1991). Simply put, this means that managers
(as well as professors in management schools) tend to follow the crowd
in making investment decisions. The modern exemplar of this is the rise
of outsourcing and downsizing, despite the fact that some analysts find
little or no evidence that firms actually enhance their shareholder values
by this process.

The failure of comprehensive ecological and social planning documented in this chapter points to the limited diffusion of ecological modernization to major firms in the United States. Moreover, even if such
diffusion were to be increased, many ecological problems remain ob-

CHART 5.3
Variations in political-economic structures that influence adoption of ecological modernization

HIGH POLITICAL
SUPPORT FOR
STAKEHOLDERS

WESTERN EUROPE
 *HIGHEST ECOLOGICAL
  MODERNIZATION LEVELS

**ORGANIZATIONAL
CONTROL BY
STAKEHOLDERS**

**ORGANIZATIONAL
CONTROL BY
SHAREHOLDERS**

UNITED STATES
 *LOWEST ECOLOGICAL
  MODERNIZATION LEVELS

HIGH POLITICAL
SUPPORT FOR
SHAREHOLDERS

scured in the focus of ecologically modern firms. Finally, even if these ecological dimensions were to be addressed, there is little linkage of ecological modernization to processes of social distribution. Sustainable community development requires attention to all these dimensions of social production, and our cases attest to the rather limited development of any political or economic support for the three Es of such types of development. Local stakeholders have often been excluded from decision-making in our cases, except where these stakeholders are powerful shareholders as well, and thus command political attention.

Six

Social Linkage Programs: Recycling Practices in Evanston

Finding Alternatives: The Road to Locating the Three Es

In this chapter, we explore the promise and contribution of recycling linkage programs. Like social linkage programs, recycling linkage programs connect private sector growth with contributions to the public good.[1] Thus, a local municipality awards a private firm with an economically favorable contract to run part of the recycling program. In exchange, the contractor agrees to make concessions by operating the program in ways that are socially beneficial for the community.

Recycling linkage programs suggest that there are alternative political-economic spaces that permit some forms of recycling that may actually contribute to sustainable community development. We first introduce the model and its promises and limits, focusing on a specific program in Evanston, Illinois. Next, we trace the very recent decision by that community to shut down this program and to privatize most of its recycling operations. Finally, we offer an analysis of the factors leading to the abandonment of what we consider the single recycling program in our study that most approaches the multiple criteria of sustainable community development.

Recycling Working as a Social Linkage: The Rise of the PIC Program in Evanston

Evanston is the first suburb north of Chicago. Founded in the 1850s, it lies on the shores of Lake Michigan, as does its hallmark institution, Northwestern University. Like Chicago, Evanston has become a city marked by great social diversity and contrasts. Described in various publications as a quaint college town with the advantages of proximity to a large metropolis and a high degree of racial integration, it also contains a widening social divide between those segments who benefit from the increasing level of development and those who are left out.

Evanston's African American community is generally segregated, with

---

[1] For example, a developer may be given a permit to construct a new building if he or she hires minority contractors.

many of these minority citizens located within a narrow space along the city's western border with the village of Skokie. This neighborhood is also located within Evanston's industrial-retail corridor. Scrap yards, gravel and concrete yards, and a sanitation canal are all operated in this area. As in the rest of the United States, poverty in on the rise in this African American community. Despite these divisions and inequalities, Evanston has long enjoyed a reputation for moral reform:

> In the twentieth century, Evanston has led in the resolution of urban controversies, including initiation of zoning to protect the residential character of its neighborhoods in the 1920s, an innovative integration plan for its schools in the 1960s, plans to preserve its architectural heritage and at the same time provide affordable housing for its low income residents in the 1970s, providing shelters and support for the homeless and plans to revitalize the downtown business district in the 1980s. (Lindstrom, Traore, and Untermeyer 1995:254)

Continuing this progressive tradition, Evanston's leaders began to use recycling to salvage both at-risk young adults and natural resources. The recycling program epitomized how small social and political steps could produce significant differences in social distributional outcomes. At first glance, Evanston's recycling program was similar to Chicago's program. Both operated with the economically conservative, mainstream type of recycling production network. Recyclables were placed on the curb by residential and commercial units. They were picked up by municipal recycling trucks and taken to a local city-owned MRF, where they were sorted and baled for resale. Sorted materials were sold on the open market through an array of brokers. Manufacturing firms who ultimately purchased these materials used the recycled materials as one feedstock in their production of new products.

Upon closer inspection, however, the programs could not have been farther apart in both process and outcome. Evanston's program differed in two ways from Chicago's. First, the program was based on the *quality* of the recyclables, not the *quantity*. Recyclables did not reach Evanston's Recycling Center via trash cans. Residents and businesses instead placed recyclable materials in distinctive orange plastic bins or specially marked dumpsters (for paper) and closed plastic cans (for glass, aluminum, and plastics). These materials were picked up by specialized recycling collection trucks. Evanston operated trucks for collections from single-family homes and small blocks of flats. Browning-Ferris Industries (BFI), second only in scale of organization to Waste Management, picked up materials from dumpsters and large garbage cans in larger residential units and commercial operations, including the recyclables from Northwestern University (negotiated separately by university recycling program officials — see Lounsbury 1997).

In neither pickup operation were recyclables commingled with trash. Recycling work in these cases was thus not as hazardous as it was in Waste Management's Chicago MRRFs. Moreover, the recovery rate for these materials that were separated at the source of the waste stream was nearly 100 percent of the volume received at the Evanston MRF. Evanston's emphasized doing things right program at every step of the process, as opposed to doing as much as possible.

The second difference between Waste Management and the Evanston program was that Evanston ran their center as a linkage program. By *linkage* we mean that the local government mandated a recycling program that would contribute to other social programs. Linkage programs have primarily been associated with municipalities controlling developers. Developers gentrifying a depressed neighborhood, for example, might be required to help pay for low-income housing in another neighborhood (Molotch 1990). Linkage programs are unique, often creating public-private agreements for a specific project that links a variety of local needs. Evanston's program took this logic one step further. It combined the job retraining needs of its low-income residents with the ecological and fiscal goals normally espoused by recycling programs.

Evanston thus developed a true partnership with the private sector, which included long-term commitments from corporate underwriters. Evanston's multitiered public-private partnership was one where the social, ecological, and economic benefits were stated up front. Then, Evanston contracted with different types of organizations for specific roles in integrating these multiple needs. Its municipal recycling center was run as a job retraining program, unlike conventional MRFs. Most MRFs are primarily market-oriented, albeit with varying levels of ecological concern (Lounsbury 1997). Retraining here was run by the Private Industry Council of Northern Cook County (PIC), later renamed the Workforce Development Council. PIC was an outgrowth of the federal PIC program, which emerged from the Job Training Partnership Act of 1982. PIC operated with donations from the private sector along with some federal money. In addition, Keep Evanston Beautiful (KEB), a local community group associated with Keep America Beautiful, ran local recycling educational programs with a small yearly grant from the city of Evanston. (Keep America Beautiful is a social lobby organization, underwritten by the packaging industries and their end-users of disposable packaging and containers.) KEB worked closely with PIC and Evanston's recycling program. Moreover, the center's recycling coordinator was the former executive director of KEB.

The centerpiece of the program was the publicly owned MRF built by the city of Evanston in 1992. Early on, it was apparent to Joan Barr, then the mayor of Evanston, that the program was best suited to provide deskilled, low-wage jobs. At the time, the city was increasingly concerned with locating job opportunities for its low-income and unemployed residents, especially older teens and young adults. City leaders acknowledged that even low-wage jobs provided badly needed opportunities for at-risk teenagers who might otherwise turn to drugs and gangs. Barr had heard about PIC and contacted them. They explored the possibility of turning the Recycling Center into a starting point for teenagers who wanted long-term, living-wage employment. As one employee recalls, "She [the mayor] made contact with them [PIC] and said, 'We're building this Recycling Center and maybe this would be a place to use some of your people.'"

In addition to the twenty PIC employees, there were two individuals who were chiefly responsible for making PIC's Futures through Recycling program work. Nancy Burhop was the center's recycling coordinator. She served also as a multitask coordinator, shifting at any given moment from businessperson to mentor to educator to carpenter. During one visit we watched her send and receive several faxes to and from brokers; answer phone calls from residents with questions or complaints about the curbside recycling pickups; arrange tours with local school administrators; advise a worker on what to do with a piece of damaged machinery; weigh in several trucks delivering and picking up recyclable materials; and bandage a worker's cut finger.

Burhop got into recycling through a background in advertising. She moved to Evanston after having spent a decade in England. At the time, she was looking for avenues out of the advertising world. The recycling coordinator position seemed to combine her business skills with her desire to engage in meaningful work (Lounsbury 1997). Burhop brought to the program a philosophy similar to that which drives many socially esponsible businesses (Weinberg 1998; Shuman 1998). Her thinking was embedded in the realities of the marketplace, but her goals were social and ecological.

The second key person was Herman Jackson, PIC's program coordinator and supervisor of worker-trainees. Jackson was an experienced specialist in worker training, retraining, and counseling. He had previously worked with youth and adults who were dealing with bouts of homelessness, drug addiction, and prison sentences. Jackson also had extensive experience counseling employees subjected to corporate downsizing. He spoke proudly of the recycling center's role in addressing social problems:

When society and the system have beaten you down so much and you've basically given up. . . . You've been through a lot of programs before, where they promised something to you and didn't deliver. . . . Now that there's something that works, people are willing to try. Once they get in here and they see that it works, or if a close friend had been in here and knows that it works, they want to try. I've got young people coming in here who are in gangs, who really don't want to be there. It is because they have nowhere else to turn. If they have something [else] that can keep them off the streets, and keep them out of the gangs, then they won't be there. I've had young guys come in here before and tell me "I don't have any work experience. I've never worked before but I don't want to be on the streets. I'm tired of being in gangs. I want something to do with my life, in my spare time." And here's a program that gives them that opportunity, and that's what attracts them to it.

Jackson's pride in the center's success is derived from his observation that neither poor, young African American males nor social programs designed to improve their lot have been successful in recent years.

Jackson always had good reason to boast about PIC's successes. But he was also a realist. When we visited the center during the fall of 1996, we asked how the much-touted "economic boom" was impacting the PIC. He commented: "I don't know what world these politicians are living in, but there certainly isn't any economic boom going on here. I've never gotten more calls for retraining downsized folks than I'm getting now." An African American male himself, Jackson provided a valuable cultural link to the mostly African American crew of MRF trainees. Moreover, he never shied away from discussions with PIC trainees about racial discrimination in the workplace, and in society in general. In fact, he actually integrated black history into the curriculum at the MRF. Jackson was also concerned with producing a quality product as well as preparing workers for a competitive job market. As one employee explained to us, "Herman is a fun person, but when it's time to get down to business, it's time to go to work."

Together, Jackson and Burhop ran the facility, providing the glue for the city and PIC's public-private partnership. Evanston was charged with bringing in recyclables and selling the baled materials. PIC was charged with the sorting and baling. Rather than hire deskilled labor and maintain them in dead-end jobs, PIC hired at-risk older teenagers and unemployed younger adults to participate in an eight-month program. Once accepted into the retraining program, the trainees worked at the MRF four-and-a-half days a week. On the fifth day, they attended a half-day job-training seminar held in a classroom built into the MRF. To be eligible for the program, prospective trainees had to be residents of the city of Evanston and be receiving some form of General Assistance. One manager stated, "We're putting the money back into the community."

Most of the trainees were African American males whose families lived in poverty. They were often former gang members who had gotten into trouble with the law. Ages ranged between fifteen and thirty-five, although most were between eighteen and twenty-five. Trainees were originally hired for a sixty-day probationary period. They were screened for drugs and put through a rigorous training period, where they were watched closely by supervisors. Early days in the program were organized to teach them good work habits and good work skills, which they would later need in order to gain and retain long-term employment. A supervisor stated that "you're going to get a lot of people with some rough edges that don't know how to be at work on time. . . . [With] a lot of these guys I end up doing parenting skills . . . helping them to know what a budget is like and know the importance of having a savings account." Nancy Burhop, Evanston's recycling coordinator, noted that, "there are a lot of benefits to the program. Some of these kids don't know how to make phone calls or to make an appointment to see somebody."

These basic "life skills" (Auletta 1982) are an integral part of many welfare-to-work training programs. Many of the participants in such programs come from communities where a significant number of adults do not hold regular jobs. This collective lack of gainful employment is thought to further impede the life chances of young adults (Wilson 1996).

PIC trainees worked from 9:00 A.M. to 5:00 P.M., standing next to conveyor belts and sorting recyclables on two work lines. One conveyor belt was for paper products, including newspapers, cardboard boxes, and magazines. The other conveyor belt was for "wet" products, including glass, plastic bottles, and aluminum and steel cans. Trainees were rotated, according to one supervisor, "so that the positions don't get so boring." Trainees stood on the lines, removing recyclable materials and throwing them down the appropriate chutes into large bunkers. The materials in the bunkers were then baled and shipped to market. There was also an emphasis on making sure that poor-quality materials — those that were too dirty or contaminated — were removed from the recycling stream.

Again, *quality*, not quantity, dominated here. Managers preferred to get a good price for the product while they taught good work habits, as opposed to accepting the common alternative of a low price and sloppy work habits (the latter being the case in Chicago's initial program operations). Discipline, patience, quality control, and teamwork were the habits inculcated in trainees and designed to help them obtain and retain future employment.

Work at the MRF was also designed to give trainees the esteem, skills, and networks needed for them to gain long-term, living-wage employment. Within the first few weeks, every trainee was put through a two-hour motivation and self-esteem class. Their Friday seminar was also seen as pivotal to the success of the MRF and its training program. Classes varied each week, although each was designed to provide a range of occupational and personal skills that would help trainees turn their lives around. Herman Jackson stated: "Cause we get people in here who have hit rock bottom, whose self-esteem is very low. And we all know that, as human beings, once your esteem goes, then you basically have no purpose for living. So this program really gives a lot of people a second chance. . . . That's what makes the program so fascinating, to see people turn themselves around like that."

Some classes were skills oriented: a professor from a local community college helped worker-trainees upgrade their math, reading, and writing skills. Other classes were more practical or life-oriented. Experts from the community lectured about personal finances, health issues, and community issues. Most job retraining programs accept only applicants who are likely to succeed, a kind of social Darwinism. But Evanston's program purposely tried to attract the "hard core." They wanted to find those trainees who were capable but not likely to find success through existing business channels. Friday classes gave them skills they needed to pass employment tests, including the way to conduct themselves during a job interview. They also imparted information that trainees needed to enable them to make better choices in their everyday lives. In one class we observed, the teacher began with the following:

> Self-esteem, building your motivation, and the job market are some things we are going to talk about today. A lot of times you are going to say to yourself, "I didn't know that about myself, I didn't know that about the job market." That's what we're doing in this session. What we want to talk about today is your strengths and weaknesses, how things that you like to do interrelate with your work environment and your personal environment. We are going to also ask you what you would do if you had one million dollars tax free money. That's a lot of money and we'll want to know what you would do with it. We're also going to do an exercise where a doctor tells you that you have six months to live and you have to decide what you would do.

For the next two hours, the instructor led the trainees through a series of exercises. They started by talking about different people's strengths and weaknesses. Jackson said, "I would like somebody to give me their definition of a weakness and your definition of a strength." The discussion was clearly geared toward instilling in the trainees the fact that everyone has weaknesses. The goal was to help trainees feel empowered by their strengths while they also acknowledged and worked on their weaknesses. Discussions quickly shifted toward job interviews.

Jackson told them, "Now when you identify your weakness in an interview, identify it in a positive sense, which means that you know you have this weakness, but you're doing something about it."

The class discussion was both practical and personal. The instructor wanted the trainees to identify personal limits that they needed to work on while they were in the PIC program. He also wanted them to feel empowered enough by their strengths so that they could talk openly and impressively at a job interview. After a break, the class began a discussion of career goals. Trainees were led to recognize some long-term worthwhile goals. They were then challenged to think how they could use the PIC program to start working toward these goals.

At some point, the lesson turned to a consideration of recent changes in U.S. labor markets. The instructor used the experiences of the trainees to talk about how to identify stable jobs. He also told them how to use short-term employment to their benefit. This led into a discussion of African American culture and history. Again the class was tuned toward the practical and personal. Trainees were led to realize their dual goals, to gain the skills and knowledge needed to master the job market, *and* to build their self-esteem and perseverance. Every exercise ended with a discussion about how they could use the next few months at the MRF to their benefit. The instructor challenged the trainees who made declarations about what they would do if they had the hypothetical million dollars or if they had just six months left to live. "It is interesting that, as we do this exercise, you are saying you would do certain things. But the question you can ask yourself is why aren't you doing these things now?"

If the trainees made it through the eight months of the program, PIC would help them locate employment. The PIC representative worked closely with area companies located in the suburban region surrounding Evanston. He spent much of his time building corporate relationships and convincing personnel managers that PIC would send them good employees. PIC had such a good reputation for producing reliable employees that employers often overlooked a trainee's poor work history. Personnel managers then agreed to interview trainees for available jobs. Job openings were posted on a bulletin board at the MRF. PIC screened the trainees for each job to make sure that they would represent the program well. PIC also set up the interview. Trainees were paid for the time it took to do the interview, including travel. Jackson stated, "Basically, I pave the way and it's up to them once they get there to take it from there. They have to actually get the job, convince the employer that they're the right person. Those are some of the tools we work on in class on Fridays."

Most trainees got jobs on the first or second interview. While the jobs were mostly in manufacturing, transportation, and city government, the pay was good. Many trainees obtained jobs and earned in the range of eighteen to twenty-five dollars per hour. PIC also funded trainees' educational opportunities for those who aimed for higher-paying jobs or long-term jobs where they could climb the career ladder. PIC would pay for them to earn their general education degree to complete high school or an associate's degree (two years at a junior college) or both. PIC paid for the books, fees, and tuition. PIC would also help trainees locate appropriate schooling programs, fill out applications, and get accepted.

The relationship between PIC and area colleges seemed to open avenues for the trainees that would have otherwise been inaccessible, given the trainees' poor work histories. One trainee, Jonathan, told us how the program fit in with his plans:

> I still want to go to school through here. I want to go to trade school. That's really what I want to do. Now you can't really just graduate from high school now and not go to college or take any kind of further education. In this day you got to have more education. I really want to take advantage of it because that way I won't have to take no grant [i.e., a loan] out. Because you're constantly paying that back, but this program gives you a job and also they pay for two years of your schooling, 100 percent of it. So with these opportunities, I really want to take advantage of it.

Recent research on social inequality and social mobility underscores the importance of intergenerational wealth in predicting the life chances of young persons in the United States (Conley 1999; Oliver and Shapiro 1995). Not surprisingly, African Americans possess only a fraction of the wealth that white Americans enjoy, reducing their life chances dramatically. Jonathan's statement reveals that the Evanston Recycling Center appeared to play a role in addressing this gap for a small number of individuals.

Relationships were the lifeblood of the Evanston MRF. Two of the most important functions of the program were based on PIC's relationships: firms seeking to recruit good workers and brokers offering decent market prices for recyclables. Most trainees heard about the program through word of mouth from friends and relatives. Every trainee we interviewed had found out about the job through some such network. Research demonstrates that "getting a job" with decent pay and mobility options usually hinges on "who you know" (Granovetter 1974). Unfortunately, such networks rarely link low-income minorities with higher-paying jobs and employers (Wilson 1987). Building those networks to provide trainees with bridges to better jobs was an important part of the PIC's mission.

Finding good prices for recyclables could also be frustrating and hard work in this volatile market. Evanston's recycling coordinator, Nancy Burhop, sought to build relationships with buyers and brokers she could trust. She told us, "I don't always sell to the same people, but I do try to establish relationships with people that I feel are honest and treating me properly." This social element of business is often lost on neoclassical assumptions of marketplace behavior (for a critique, see Granovetter 1985).

The Evanston program's success was extraordinary. First, it allowed the city to run a financially viable recycling program, even through the market slump of the early 1990s. They performed well in part by reducing labor costs—a rule of thumb by which most private sector firms operate. Rather than pay the normal seven-to-ten dollars hour, trainees were paid five dollars an hour. However, because of the training (i.e., future employment) dimension of the program, these low wages were understood as a stepping stone to a better-paying job. The city continued to save money on the program, relative to dumping solid waste in landfills. Workers understood that participation in the PIC program offered them a chance to step into higher wages.

Second, the city produced some of the highest-quality recyclables in the area. Even during market slumps, they were able to get top dollar for their product. The superior quality of the product was attributed to PIC's policy of accepting only source-separated recyclables (i.e., no garbage), a managerial emphasis on quality control, and workers trained to sort very productively on the MRF conveyors. Herman Jackson noted the financial returns on the investment in these first-rate products: "For example, with newspaper, the city of Evanston gets one hundred dollars a bale (a great price at a time when other MRFs were getting eighty to ninety dollars). And it's not because it's [from] the city of Evanston; it's because we have good trainees that are doing an outstanding job. Because if they didn't clean the stuff out like it's supposed to be, they wouldn't get that type of money for the product."

Worker productivity was directly related to trainee satisfaction. Trainees did not view this as dirty work or dead-end employment, but as an opportunity to "get out" and find a better future. Trainees were neither at the facility nor at one task there long enough to get bored. Bill, a PIC trainee, explained: "I don't mind working [here]. But I don't want to keep a job like this, making what I'm making. It's OK for now. In the long run I need to further my skills so that way I can make a good living." Every trainee we interviewed echoed Bill's sentiment.

The program also benefited the Evanston community as a whole. At-risk teenagers and young adults were taken off the street and placed where they could begin doing something productive. Trainees who finished the program were taken off General Assistance, and they then brought a wage back into the community. Ecologically, the program produced a clean product. It diverted more than 1 million pounds of recyclables from the waste stream each month. This high-quality product netted the center enough funds to pay off the $1.2 million construction cost in just three years. Because of the program's success, PIC was even awarded a $60,000 grant for capital upgrades from the Illinois Department of Commerce and Community Affairs.

Not only did the recycling part of the Evanston PIC program do well; so did its employment component. The center was proud of its high job placement rate: nearly 90 percent of the trainees acquired gainful employment in nearby businesses in Cook County. Herman Jackson pointed out in 1995 that "in this economy, to have a placement rate around 90 percent, you're doing a hell of a job." This record was especially impressive in light of the fact that many job training programs fail to achieve job placement and retention of trainees.

The Evanston/PIC program's successes were due largely to the pragmatic orientation of the Evanston city administration, which worked collaboratively with private firms in such a way that the gains were distributed to local taxpayers and workers. The city and private capital achieved gains without either being subordinate to the other. Their partnership was based on the recognition that the state and private capital interests have a great deal of interdependence (Clavel and Kleniewski 1990; Evans 1979; Evans, Reuschemeyer, and Skocpol 1985; Logan and Swanstrom 1990).

Delinking the Evanston Program: The New "Bottom Line" Orientation to Local Recycling

When we completed our first draft of this book, we were enthusiastic about the successes of the Evanston program. For a variety of political and social reasons, Evanston had chosen to use recycling as both an environmental program and one with public linkages. Alas, within a few short months, we were faced with yet another case that had failed to produce sustainable community development around its recycling program. What makes our revised analysis of the Evanston case so painful is the fact that this was not merely a promising *proposed* program such as Maywood's, but an existing and apparently successful program. As with the community-based centers of chapter 4, Evanston's program achieved some of the simultaneous environmental, equity, and economic goals of sustainable community development. Unlike the community-based programs, moreover, Evanston's recycling program represented a clear local government decision to move toward both social and ecological goals, at quite a modest economic cost to the city and its residents.

Yet within several months of our assessment, it is instructive to note how differently the program was being described to the city manager by Evanston's director of management and budget:

> The Recycling Center opened in March of 1992. At the time, municipalities across Illinois were responding to the State of Illinois mandate that required the reduction of materials in the waste stream. Recycling was new and the future of the market was unclear. The Recycling Center was built with the vision that the City could save money in three ways: by diverting material from the waste stream; by not having to transport large amounts of material to a site outside of the City thus reducing transportation and labor costs; and by the sale of processed materials. The sale of material and the recycling surcharge of $1.00 per month per household was expected to make the recycling program a self-supporting enterprise. Unfortunately, the recycling market has changed dramatically and the City can no longer compete in the market place. (Casey and Steen 1998:1)

That a management and budget officer should stress the economic factors in recycling is perhaps not surprising. What is more surprising was how this framing was widely echoed among political officials in the city and even to some extent by the director of the Recycling Center herself. In effect, we were witnessing a process in which an operating program with elements of sustainable community development had been attained in Evanston — but one that was no longer capable of being sustained politically. In April 1998 we participated in a local conference for Earth Day, with Nancy Burhop of the Evanston MRF and other community-based recycling leaders. This was the first public occasion at which we were made aware of the economic fragility of the Evanston MRF. At that meeting, Burhop reported that ever since Browning-Ferris Industries had bought out a regional recycler, Active Service, BFI had chosen to convert its new materials transfer station in Evanston into a long-haul center. This "transfer" operation is one way of segregating recyclables and landfill-destined solid wastes, the process used in Chicago's MRRFs, described in chapter 3. And it substantially lowered the sales revenue of Evanston's publicly owned recycling center.

Active Service, a local enterprise, had earlier brought many of its recyclables — especially the highly valued office paper from Northwestern University — to Evanston's MRF. Active Service achieved savings in transportation costs by not having to haul recyclables to more remote sorting and processing facilities. This local waste stream was one of the components that had permitted Nancy Burhop to achieve high sales revenues for Evanston's MRF. As she noted a month later at a committee hearing into the recycling program: "A reason our income went down was the loss of material from Active Service when they were acquired by BFI, and now that we are not operating at capacity. . . . We could get more materials without our having to pick it up, if rental units, which total over 8,000 more living units, were required to recycle. I felt *most haulers would bring recyclables from those units to Evanston's facility*, which would have given us additional materials without increased cost to the city" (Nilges 1998:1, italics ours).

The combination of a steady stream of recyclables and the desirable physical properties of office paper from Northwestern University made Evanston MRF's paper products highly marketable and profitable. Paradoxically, given the strong market component of Evanston's program, it would appear that the community's profits from paper recycling also then led BFI's managers to seek out higher corporate returns. They then began to negotiate with other recycling centers and remanufacturers for Northwestern's recyclables and other commercial recycling pickups.

Evanston's *public* loss of revenue was BFI's *private* gain of profits.[2] But even more to the point of this political drama, the timing of this shift at the Evanston recycling center was crucial. Indeed, this single act alone may have tilted Evanston officials and city council members in a rather different direction, away from the previous experiences of the recycling center as a "going concern." Ironically, what precipitated the evaluation of the program by municipal authorities was that the volume of local recyclables had risen to the point where four additional recycling trucks were needed, an expenditure estimated at about $500,000. In the April 1998 meeting, Burhop had been anticipating these critical assessments. Following a local media report about a potential change in the recycling operations, we traced the first official document—a report to the city manager (Casey and Steen 1998).

The central argument of this report was that Evanston was paying too much for recycling, compared with other North Shore suburbs. All of the other suburbs were outsourcing their collection of recyclables, and paying approximately $3.00 per household for the service, as compared with the current Evanston MRF total cost of about $5.05. The report also acknowledged that the net cost per household was "fully" $2.97, factoring in the sale of recyclables and the monthly user fee of

---

[2] At the same Earth Day meeting referenced above, Ken Dunn, the director of Chicago's Resource Center, echoed Burhop's complaint, and also confirmed our conclusions in chapter 4. He framed the demise of the Uptown Recycling Center and the growing problems of Evanston's social linkage program in a pithy statement, reminiscent of Jim Burris's assessment in chapter 4: "I suppose you can say that our [sustainable development] movements were successful, in one way. We helped to test-market the practice of recycling for the emerging recycling industry!"

$1.00 per household. They noted that other north shore suburbs had costs of "pickup and processing" ranging from "$2.16 . . . to $3.00" (Casey and Steen 1998:2).

Within two days, the "political" part of local government met, in the form of the Administration and Public Works Committee, to offer a discussion about the city manager's report (Nilges 1998). The draft minutes of that meeting on May 6, 1998, represent perhaps the most interesting municipal debate about an ongoing operation that is somewhat congruent with the principles of sustainable community development. (Schnaiberg 1993, 1997b). Present at this meeting were five Evanston alderpersons and a number of municipal staff members, including Nancy Burhop. The meeting opened with a reference to the city manager's report of two days earlier, which noted that "the Recycling Center has been operating at a loss for a number of year." (Nilges 1998:1). One of the staff noted, however, that "if one took into account the amount of money made selling the material *and also the amount saved by not hauling it to a landfill or for collection,* the Center did not look too bad" (Nilges 1998:2, italics ours). The director of management and the budget replied: "Mr. Casey noted that, whether the City or someone else handles Evanston's recycling, we are still diverting the materials from the waste stream, so 'it's a wash.' He said for us to break even, *we would have to triple the tonnage*" (Nilges 1998:2, italics ours).

Interestingly, none of the alderpersons present challenged this assertion by noting that the same argument could be used to justify continuation of the Recycling Center! Ironically, none of those present even raised the possibility of changing the behaviors of BFI, as the dominant commercial recycling collection firm in Evanston, in directions that could restore more revenue to the Recycling Center. Indeed, at this point, the alderpersons presiding over the committee meeting noted: "After reviewing the options, it's a cut and dried decision" (Nilges 1998:2).

Pointedly, the social linkage part of the Recycling Center — which is what we had noted made this operation more of a sustainable community development practice — was virtually ignored throughout the committee meeting of May 6, 1998. The only comment we found was the following:

Mr. Edwards [superintendent of streets and sanitation] brought up the retraining component of the Recycling Center, noting that the program *has value to the community: it has made a number of residents working and taxpaying citizens.* This component would need to be explored. To Alderman Rainey's question, Mr. Edwards said the budget to pay PIC for employees and two supervisors is $195,000. The pay range is minimum wage, he believed, and they work five days a week, including four hours of training on Friday. He noted that this figure has been set for several years, but we've spent more than that with the overtime needed with equipment failures, etc. (Nilges 1998:3; italics ours)

Note that the rationale for this training component is framed primarily in *economic* terms, rather than as the *social* linkage we outlined in the previous section. In some ways, this spirited defense of the training component via an economic analysis reinforces the market framing of recycling, rather than the sustainable community development framing. The following comment, in response to the quote above, indicates how this reframing of the trainee program led to its peripheralization in the debate: "Alderman Feldman said we have to fulfill our responsibility to programs like this one, though he said no one would maintain that this program *has to remain in business*. He felt it would be appropriate to examine programs like that for other activities, *but to keep doing what we're doing just for that program would be self-destructive, and said we could still pursue our obligation to support training programs*" (Nilges 1998: 3; italics ours).

Having started on this line of narrow *economic* reasoning about Evanston's PIC program, this alderperson continued to thrust aside all empirical evidence of *social* gains from PIC and its successor, the Workforce Development Council. The superintendent of streets and sanitation stated to him that there were between thirteen and fifteen trainees on the line, and that about "200 residents have gone through the program." But this was not sufficient for the alderperson. "[He] wanted information as to where those people are now, not only the number who went through. If people don't move on and get jobs in other places, he said this would be an employment program, not a training program. Mr. Edwards said we have statistics from the Workforce Development Council." (Nilges 1998:3). The statistics referred to are those we reported in the previous section, and they represent a strong record of placing PIC/WFDC trainees in the private sector. They are a powerful testimonial to what can be accomplished using a creative sustainable community development approach, rather than merely a "bottom line" approach, to city services.

Increasingly, the tone of the committee discussion shifted farther away from any accurate depiction of the history and goals of the PIC trainee program. Instead of viewing this as a program to rehabilitate young at-risk adults that used the Recycling Center as an interim training period, the alderman gradually transformed this discussion into another "bottom line" economic analysis. Consider the following two quotes by Alderperson Rainey: "Alderman Rainey pointed out that it was the responsibility of Workforce Development Council to place their participants. . . . . She noted that we should let it be known that we have recycling trainees who could be hired by recycling companies" (Nilges 1998:4–5, italics ours).

When the authors read the city manager's report and the committee minutes, it was clear to us that this model for locally based sustainable community development was in danger of being abandoned. In particular, the tenor of the discussion indicated that the city was reverting to treating them as peripheral *employees*, not trainees. Furthermore, at best, their futures were considered to lie in the recycling *industry*. In contrast, the PIC program treated recycling as a short-term training position, a springboard for its trainees to gain more human capital, in order to then find better employment elsewhere.

Similarly, the *ecological* component of the Recycling Center program rapidly declined in centrality in the city discussions. We note that in addition to achieving the laudable social goal of job training and placement, the PIC MRF also recycled thousands of tons of waste each month and produced a high-quality product. At the May 6 meeting, Nancy Burhop reported on one of the likely contractors the city would pick — Groot Recycling: "Groot's facility is what is known as a 'dirty mrf,' dealing mostly with garbage, from which only about 30 percent is recycled, 90 percent of that being curbside paper" (Nilges 1998:2).

As with the future of the PIC trainees, no one grasped this revelation, nor did anyone suggest a systematic evaluation of proposed bidders to ensure that they actually "recycled" the Evanston materials they collected. The description of Groot, a private recycler with a long history in Chicago, suggests an operation somewhat similar to Chicago's blue bag program (chapter 3). In our frustration over both the social and ecological tone of the committee discussion, we decided to send a memo to the City Council, which we distributed on July 15, 1998. During its May 6 meeting, the Administration and Public Works Committee had authorized the city manager of Evanston to put out a Request for Proposals for outside private contractors to bid for collecting and "processing" Evanston's recyclable materials.

We submitted our sharp disagreement with the committee well before the full City Council had to review the committee's proposals and the RFPs. Yet we never received any invitation to discuss this matter at any City Council or committee meeting, nor did we ever receive any inquiries asking us to clarify points in our memo. It would appear that whatever took place publicly thereafter, the city was committed to scuttling the Recycling Center and outsourcing its recycling services. On November 9, 1998, the City Council essentially voted to "privatize Evanston's recycling services." By then, the city staff had narrowed down the choices to "two Chicago-area [*sic*] recycling companies, BFI Waste Systems and Groot Recycling & Waste Services, Inc." (Demes 1998a).

Local African American politicians and business representatives made a plea for favoring BFI as a company with stronger "local" roots, since it hired more local minority employees at its Evanston waste transfer facility. At its meeting, the City Council approved a contract with Groot, arguing that its annual fees of $586,768 (Kline 1998) were $98,000 lower than BFI's for curbside and alley pickup of materials (thus, they also ignored the African American community's call for contracting with a purportedly more socially responsible firm). The meeting was long and acrimonious (Demes 1998b), and failed to consider any sustainable community development themes. The authors had earlier decided, in the absence of a response to our memo, that attending the meeting would be merely an exercise in frustration and futility for us. The fate of Evanston's recycling program had been definitively set in the committee meeting of May 6, and most policy changes from May to November were largely epiphenomenal.

In their final vote, there were no specifications about recycling processes to be used—only about pickup schedules and materials to be collected. Collectibles were, admittedly, more extensive than those from the Recycling Center, but in the absence of monitoring by Evanston, they were likely to end up in landfills, rather than as remanufactured goods. Moreover, Evanston agreed to retain the city-hired employees of the center and shift them into the Streets and Sanitation Department. But the fifteen trainee positions with the state-funded Workforce Development Council/PIC job program would be eliminated. The ultimate rationale for the outsourcing decision was, not surprisingly, primarily economic: "The action will result in savings of about 60% in the City's annual recycling budget. Evanston residents will continue to pay the same $1 per month recycling surcharge and will receive the same alley and curbside pick-up service" (Demes 1998b:1).

Interestingly, taking this course is likely to save the city as much as 3 million dollars over a five-year period. By contrast, in this era of Evanston's tight city budgets and high local property taxes, the same City Council approved an "economic development plan" that would require the city to invest about $20 million to subsidize the private developer of a new shopping mall and movie theater "multiplex." Despite sharp divisions within the city's political and business sectors, the decision was made to encourage national and multinational investors to establish commercial outlets there. The interest alone on this new Evanston city bond for this project would have more than covered the "inefficient" operations of the Recycling Center. But in these two actions taken nearly simultaneously, the city of Evanston opted to abandon its only hope for sustainable community development.

Understanding the Dimensions of Variability in Recycling Programs

In the last few chapters, we have looked at four types of programs in the Chicago area. Each type produced a very different outcome.[3] Chart 6.1 summarizes the findings of chapters 3–6.

Chart 6.1 makes it clear that any program would be socially, ecologically, and economically superior to the municipally based/privatized type of system that Evanston negotiated with Groot Recycling in November 1998. The new program would not produce good jobs. Furthermore, since the training program was largely responsible for the clean waste stream and efficiency, the economic and ecological benefits would also disappear. Ironically, the city would likely lose money over the long run, despite the short-term savings.

The blue bag (chapter 3) epitomized the municipal/privatized category, where the changes involved are "business as usual" at best and "the rich rob the poor" at worst (Stretton 1976). Business as usual generally means the low road is taken: human capital formation and improved community health are of little concern. The municipally based/privatized model thus scores low on its social outcomes. Because pollution is not curtailed and because source reduction is a low priority (and recovery rates are accordingly low), the ecological outcomes of this type of program are low. Given the taxpayer's bill and the poor market performance of the processed recyclables, the fiscal outcomes are also low. This is certainly true in Chicago's Waste Management MRRFs, and appears likely to be reproduced in Evanston's new privatized system, which will involve Groot's "dirty MRF" — a commingled or mixed waste processing facility.

The second type of recycling program is the struggling community-based, not-for-profit organization (chapter 4) rooted in social movements and neighborhoods. The type of change sought and achieved by

---

[3] Consistent with the rest of this book, outcomes are treated qualitatively. We look at the range of factors undergirding each of the outcomes. *Equity* refers to the quality of jobs produced, which is defined as a product of the wages, benefits, skills enhancement, and stability. The *ecological* category refers to the program's impact on ecosystem withdrawals and additions to the local ecosystem. With community-based centers we take into account that they lead to some reuse, which minimizes problems of ecosystem additions and withdrawals during the remanufacturing process (Geithman 1997:12). *Economy* refers to the generation of local economic revitalization, which, of course, can occur in any number of ways.

CHART 6.1
Outcomes Associated with Different Recycling Programs: The Three E's of
Sustainable Community Development

Type of Program	Type of Change	Equity	Outcomes Ecological	Economy
Municipally Based/ Privatized [Chicago, Evanston-Groot]	Little or none	Low	Low	Low
Community-Based [Uptown, The Resource Center]	Incremental/ Transformative	Medium	High	Medium
Recycling Indus-trial Zones [Maywood, Bethel New Life]	Transformative	High	High	High
Linkage [Evanston Re-cycling Center]	Incremental/ Transformative	High	Medium	High

these organizations is often transformative, but done through small in-crements, on a daily basis. There is much less capital and substantially more labor used in these models than in any other type of recycling program. And while there are great successes, there is limited mobility for workers. For this reason, the community-based centers tend to have medium social outcomes. Reuse, recycling, and composting are all suc-cessful components of URI and the Resource Center's programs. In the limited spaces within which they operate, they tend to have high ecolog-ical impacts.

And finally, because mobility is so limited for their workers and the territory in which they operate is rather small, the community-based centers often have medium fiscal outcomes. This of course is partly by design; both Jim Burris and Ken Dunn had inveighed against the reifica-tion of money for its own sake. The driving purpose of these centers was to discover and create sustainable community development that functioned largely independently of an obsession with money. And, as we noted above, both Jim Burris and Ken Dunn offered the bittersweet assessment that their operations had "test-marketed" recycling for Waste Management, BFI, and other large firms in the emerging "recy-cling industry."

The proposed recycling industrial parks and zones in West Garfield

Park and Maywood (chapter 5) sought to produce stable, sustainable communities out of urban wastelands. Because these plans were so ambitious, they were transformative in nature. Recycling parks and zones, as conceived in these cases, would transform communities marked by social disorganization into ecotopias characterized by strong kinship networks and communitarianism. This would constitute a high social outcome. The very nature of an eco-industrial park suggests that nearly all waste brought to the site and the waste produced on-site will be put back into productive, environmentally responsible use. Thus, these sites would produce high ecological outcomes. And because the potential market value from these activities is so great, the fiscal outcomes are high as well. Bethel New Life did in fact manage to create one industrial linkage with local recycling feedstock — but it failed to capture employment gains from this move, negating one of its main objectives.

Linkage programs like the Evanston/PIC partnership reported in this chapter accomplished much more with much less funding. By harnessing existing markets and labor pools to address a local, manageable problem, this six-year-long program (1992–98) achieved incremental change that bordered on the transformative. Certainly for the many individuals who were trained and able to secure stable employment, the PIC program was a major springboard. Given these retraining and linkage successes, the Evanston/PIC program receives high marks for its social outcomes. Apart from the social dimensions, this recycling program was successful at diverting tens of thousands of tons of waste from landfills every year. It thus had a medium score for ecological outcome, since it chose not to divert other less-marketable items from landfills. In terms of getting top dollar for its quality recyclables and running a near self-sustaining operation, this program also received high marks for its fiscal outcomes.

Searching for Sustainable Development:
Do Technology and Scale Matter?

We must emphasize that, in general, recycling work is tough, dirty, undesirable, often dangerous, pays low-wages, and offers limited mobility. A recent study, commissioned by the Mott Foundation, concluded: "These jobs tend to be of relatively low quality. With little attention given to job quality or job ladder issues, there is little likelihood that these new jobs will provide an effective avenue for rising out of poverty" (Siegel and Kwass 1995:35).

We agree. However, communities must begin their struggle for redevelopment somewhere. We chose to study recycling because of its symbolic and substantive value for low-income persons and struggling urban areas. Recycling is both a labor process and a production process. We can thus use it to analyze many problems confronting any number of policies targeting redevelopment in the urban core. The problems and potentials we found in recycling are mirrored in most social policies that attempt to improve the condition of cities, struggling neighborhoods, and their low-income denizens.

Paradoxically, recycling may turn out to be an even more efficient canary in the mine for proponents of local sustainable community development. As with much of the literature on sustainable community development, there is a good deal of theory emphasizing *visions* of what this might look like (e.g., Shuman 1998). Yet there are far fewer analyses of sustainable community development *practices* (cf. Schnaiberg 1997b). Recycling is one arena whose history has happened to overlap with a growing interest in sustainable community development — initially, from an ecological and later from a social-fiscal viewpoint. Because of this, recycling has drawn the interest of many creative analysts, policy makers, and community activists.

Thus chapters 3–6 have laid out quite a diverse array of practices, which we have evaluated using the three Es criteria of sustainable community development. As chart 6.1 details, the results have been quite mixed. Overall, we would argue that recycling has generally achieved only modest ecological outcomes, and not many social or fiscal gains. We note especially the rise and fall of both the community-based organizations outlined in chapter 4 and the municipal "experiment" in Evanston detailed in this chapter. Also, we note the stifling of transformative efforts in Maywood and West Garfield Park. These cases offer us rich insights into some of the problematics involved in achieving sustainable community development and in sustaining programs even once they have been developed. Hence the title of this book, "the search for sustainable community development."

Three other features of the recycling programs we studied may seem at first blush to make them less valid predictors of other sustainable community development practices:

1. Recycling materials are primarily high-volume and low-value commodities in the marketplace.

2. Most recycling programs have some linkages to market transactions, since the remanufacturing process is rarely fully done through sustainable development and/or community-based practices.

3. Recycling programs are relatively socially and politically visible (and therefore vulnerable to criticisms by local residents) because they deal with high-volume materials, on the one hand, and rely on some visible governmental assistance, on the other hand.

The fall of the Evanston/PIC program, outlined in this chapter, exemplifies all three of these elements, though the recycling practices described in chapters 3–5 also embody at least the first two of these problematics. This may seem to be a liability in our analysis as an approach to charting dead ends and possible pathways for sustainable community development. Ironically, though, even the most ardent of sustainable community development proponents note that many of these traits characterize most alternative development practices. This actually turns out to be somewhat axiomatic, as Schnaiberg and Gould (1994: chap. 8) have argued. Firms in the global economy are constantly seeking new opportunities to turn local values into commodified market value products. Thus, the field of operations for many sustainable community development programs will be initially concentrated in the "less profitable" and perhaps riskier areas of local development, since there will be less corporate interest in (and more resistance to) this alternative economic activity. But precisely because market actors are not involved in such programs, they will have to rely on some form of government assistance to get started and maintain themselves for the first years of their operations. Thus they will be operating on less-desirable material inputs (those which cannot be marketed profitably), and therefore the programs will have greater visibility because of government support and regulation.

Moreover, they will in most cases have either inputs that they must purchase from the private sector, or outputs that they must sell to the private sector. One of the hopes of some of these social entrepreneurs is that they will become successful enough to attract investment beyond initial government subsidies. In part, this is a hope for legitimacy in the larger economy, and even for greater stability than may exist in either less-developed countries' national governments or in industrial societies' local government units. Thus, these local organizations are involved in both politics *and* markets. The same situation is likely to persist well into any foreseeable period of greater sustainable community development. New practices of sustainable community development sometimes resemble the proverbial bootstrap operation, as if pulling themselves up were merely a difficult goal, rather than a physically impossible one. Progressive recycling programs in our study have had to steer a near impossible course of constant political negotiation with local government, on the one hand, and an approach-avoidance relation to major firms, on the other.[4]

[4] Indeed, many of our observations here are congruent with the arguments of Schnaiberg and Gould (1994: chapter 8) about alternative technology in less-developed countries. They found that alternative or appropriate technology (AT), stimulated by the writings and practices of E. F. Schumacher (1973) and support from his international institutes, was mostly applied where private sector capital had chosen *not* to invest. Thus,

Each of these relationships (or transactions) generally places the organizers of recycling programs in a dependent and vulnerable role, subject to political and economic pressures. Governmental and private firm "assistance" is highly contingent and unpredictable. Indeed, the greater the success, the more danger there is of cannibalization by firms with substantial funds for acquisition or for competition. Once again, this is a path most clearly seen in this chapter on the Evanston program. But it is evident as well in chapters 3–5: indeed, even Waste Management was subjected to this dynamic when it was acquired by USA Waste Services. This seems to be an underlying dialectic of the struggle toward sustainable community development, which we address in our final chapter.

In making these arguments, we have often been questioned about the issues of technology and scale. Too often, technology and scale are posed as deterministic factors of a program's success or failure. Thus, people have often asked: Does your analysis suggest that only low-technology or small-scale programs achieve sustainable community development? The problem with these questions is that by attempting to isolate these "variables," one can draw contradictory conclusions across the cases. For example; the PIC Evanston program was the most successful model at achieving each of the three Es. It was a fairly high-technology program and is of a much larger scale than the community-based centers. Contrarily, the Chicago program is the farthest from achieving the three Es. But it is also a high technology program.

One reviewer of an earlier version of this manuscript noted, "The authors talk about community-based recycling schemes as an alternative to the large scale 'blue bag program'; [but] because they operate at such different levels of scale the two programs are probably not alternatives. The real alternative would probably be a larger scale version of the Evanston program." The reality is more complicated. In our interviews with activists at the Chicago Recycling Coalition and other local organizations, they claim that it would have been possible for several organizations like the Resource Center and Uptown Recycling to handle the entire city of Chicago. These activists argue that neighborhood contracts would have given the community-based centers the financial resources to expand the scope of their programs. We are somewhat dubious of this claim. Even if they would not have been able to handle the Chicago-wide scale of operations, one could make an argument that

---

AT in these southern nations was *interstitial* and often *transitional*. AT organizations remained operating only until major firms chose to participate. The latter would either invest in takeovers of these communally based organizations or create competitive firms that drove these organizations out of the marketplace. In effect, this is remarkably parallel to Ken Dunn and Jim Burris's assessment of community-based recycling as a "test market" for an emergent recycling *industry*.

Chicago would nonetheless have been better off with a variety of smaller programs that contained some reuse components. Community-based centers could thus have had a larger ecological impact even if they captured only a partial volume of the total waste stream.

Questions of technology and scale are not social realities; they are questions of political construction. Technology can be very beneficial in terms of moving a practice toward sustainable community development. The proposed Recycling Parks in Maywood were one example. The PIC/Evanston program was another good illustration. Technology can also pose problems, as the blue bag program documented. Scale works similarly. The ability of the Evanston/PIC to achieve a citywide scale would have also been politically constructed. They needed a strong local business sector that was willing to hire the trainees. Likewise, it may be true that smaller-scale programs achieved a greater degree of environmental sustainability and social equity. Yet we can also imagine scenarios where this might not be true.

Arguments that hinge upon such determining factors as technology and scale fall short of providing a persuasive explanation. The impact of these determining factors depends upon the ever-shifting larger political and economic context. What matters more than scale or technology are the motives of different social groups, and the means that they have to push these motives.[5] As we stated in chapter 2, this is a fairly standard political economy or social conflict view of social processes. We turn to this perspective in the next chapter.

[5] Although in a different context, many of these tensions are noted in an excellent report produced by the Roberts Foundation on U.S.-based urban microlending programs (Emerson and Twersky 1996).

Seven

The Treadmill of Production:
Toward a Political-Economic Grounding of
Sustainable Community Development

Revisiting the Treadmill of Production

Throughout the last four chapters, we have provided a number of details and insights into the recent history of recycling. Our task here is to paint on a larger canvas. In chapter 2, we outlined our theoretical starting points, using a political-economy concept — the treadmill of production (Schnaiberg 1980; Schnaiberg and Gould 1994; Gould, Schnaiberg, and Weinberg 1996). We draw on this concept to outline the dynamics that shape individual, organizational, and institutional behaviors within the capitalist production process, especially as they relate to environmental decision making, particularly as it addresses recycling programs.

While the concept was originally used to discuss national level data, we have also used the treadmill to illustrate links between local (Weinberg 1997b), national (Pellow 1998b), and global processes (Gould, Weinberg, and Schnaiberg 1995). The interactions among these various levels of structures and processes ultimately help shape local political conflicts over natural resource usage (Gould, Schnaiberg, and Weinberg 1995; Weinberg 1997c). In this chapter, we apply the treadmill concept to describe how an array of local, national, and global processes actually undergirds the local recycling cases outlined in the previous chapters.

Our goal here is to develop a political-economic understanding of how recycling decisions move us toward or away from sustainable community development. Consistent with other political-economic frameworks (Logan and Swanstrom 1990), our analysis examines the ways in which different social actors adapt to the political and economic contexts in which they are embedded. We also pay close attention to the often-hidden but important role of power. This leads us to trace the conflicts resulting from actors' use of different forms of power to push their self-interested agendas into a range of public arenas — the political, economic, and cultural (Logan and Molotch 1987; Walton 1993).

At the outset, our assumption is that the underlying dynamics that have shaped recycling practices are typical of most political and economic processes in the United States. Recycling enthusiasts' rhetoric appears to be innovative and exciting to the participants. Yet the underlying motives and practices of many recycling organizations are similar from those of many "mainstream" organizations. Most of these organizations have practices that predate modern recycling, practices dictated by the political-economic infrastructure that was operational well before recycling became in vogue.

As noted in chapter 2, the concept of the treadmill of production forces us to look at sustainable community development *ideals* within a political-economic *system*. In this system, powerful market actors extract natural resources and convert them into profits through market exchanges. Their profits are then reinvested into the firm in order for it to purchase new physical capital for production processes, so that the firm will accrue increasing levels of profits. We have referred to five tendencies of this political economy, which constitute the core of this treadmill of production:

1. expand industrial production and economic development,
2. increase consumption,
3. solve social and ecological problems by speeding up the treadmill,
4. concentrate economic expansion around large-scale capital, and
5. construct a political alliance of private capital, labor, and governments.

These dynamics capture the current political economy in the United States to a greater extent than is evident in most other industrial societies (Longworth 1998). The concept of the treadmill of production is not meant to be an all-encompassing, grand-theoretical model. Rather, we use the treadmill to highlight *specific* dynamics that help shape social-environmental actions. In particular, we trace the influence of powerful market agents who are driven by a narrow set of economic values. These actors use political, legal, and cultural arenas to push their agendas over those of other actors, even those who have more socially and environmentally oriented values (Gould, Schnaiberg, and Weinberg 1996; Schnaiberg 1980; Schnaiberg and Gould 1994; Weinberg 1997b). Market interchanges have thus come to dominate almost every decision made about urban areas (Logan and Molotch 1987; Squires 1994; Zukon 1995). Even those aspects of community life that are not related to market activity, such as clean air and water, are frequently analyzed in terms of their market value.

We believe that the cases offered in the four previous chapters attest to the pervasive influence of the treadmill. In most of the cases, recycling's potential social and ecological contributions were overwhelmed by more narrowly focused market interests. Attempts to address social equity and ecological problems in the poor neighborhoods of Chicago's South Side (The Resource Center), in its North Side (Uptown Recycling, Inc.), and in the suburb of Evanston (PIC) were largely undone by political-economic forces seeking to minimize government expenditures and maximize private profits. In the process, these state actors catered to private industry. Beneficiaries included the largest multinational corporations in the waste business — USA Waste Services (which recently acquired Waste Management), Browning-Ferris Industries, and Groot Recycling Services.

The Globalizing Treadmill

One subtle but powerful influence throughout the local cases was the effect of globalization. While capitalist production has had a significant international component for the last century at least, the breadth and depth of globalization today is unprecedented. The result is that we now live in a society thoroughly embedded in a transnational treadmill of production (Longworth 1998). Recycling appears be a local practice, but it is always embedded within global processes. These processes have emerged due to substantial advances in communication and transportation technologies. Firms can now locate production in many places around the world (Barnet and Cavanagh 1994; Grieder 1997; Harrison 1994; Reich 1991). New technologies reduce the need for products to be produced close to markets. Products can also now be made in pieces, in different locales, and assembled on an "as-needed" basis. Recently, for example, journalists have exposed the practices of transnational computer manufacturers who pay their workers to assemble electronic parts in their own homes — a return to the "piecework" system (Ewell 1999)

Globalization has thus significantly reduced the bargaining capacity of communities and workers in any single nation, let alone in any single community. Workers have found that their ability to strike is less effective. Firms shut down operations and move production elsewhere. Employees of the blue bag program complained bitterly about being forced to sort through raw garbage strewn with toxic chemicals, needles, and other hazardous materials. But they were also desperate for any employment opportunity; hence, they did not collectively rebel or strike. Workers were also aware that striking would not work. Initially, there was no union organized within the MRRF facilities.

Moreover, even if these sorting workers had successfully become organized, they could have been easily replaced by other workers. Contemporary labor law permits such replacement, and the plentiful supply of desperate unemployed persons in the nearby community reduced the corporate cost of worker replacement while increasing the risks for workers seeking to engage in collective action. Likewise, communities often feel that they must do whatever it takes to attract and retain firms (Logan and Swanstrom 1990). We will note later in this chapter that this may not actually be the case. However, in the framework of symbolic interactionism, if community leaders *feel* they have no bargaining power, they help perpetuate their weakness.

Earlier in this chapter we noted the evolution in our use of the treadmill of production from national level processes to global dynamics. We see the *continuity* between the older national form and the newer transnational form of the treadmill as twofold. First, the driving force continues to be the private sector's economic search for profitability, which has been expanded to a global quest for markets and a global recruitment of labor forces around the world that can generate still-higher profits per unit of production. Second, the nation-state and the local and national labor forces of both industrial and developing countries have actually increased their political commitment to the treadmill, despite the fact that the social distributional gains from the expansion of production have become truncated for many citizens.

In sharp contrast, the *discontinuity* between the older national forms and newer transnational forms of the treadmill lies primarily along two axes. There has been an increasing domination of transnational treadmill market actors over local and national institutions of the nation-state. Likewise, these transnational market actors exert increasing dominance over community groups and other associations that more directly represent communities (including both their population and their labor forces).

These changes can be visualized as a recent increase in the "tilt" of the treadmill. When a treadmill is tilted to a greater degree, the user must expend more physical energy merely to sustain his or her initial velocity. We will also refer to this process as an "acceleration" of the treadmill, produced in large part by shifts in political power away from communities and toward capital owners, managers, and investors. In the new transnational treadmill, communities must confront four stark resistances arising from acceleration of the transnational treadmill of production.

DOWNWARD PRESSURE ON WAGES AND THE RISE OF A BI-POLAR WAGE STRUCTURE

From 1979 to 1993, the top 20 percent of wage earners' incomes rose by 18 percent, while the poorest 20 percent of the population saw a 15 percent decline in wages. As Robert Kuttner (1997:86) has documented, wealth "has now reached its point of greatest concentration since the

1920s. All of the gains to equality of the postwar boom have been wiped out."

INCREASING MARGINALIZATION OF WORKERS IN LOW-INCOME AND MINORITY COMMUNITIES

In the 1996 presidential race, both political parties ignored issues concerning the poor and marginalized. Unionization of the workforce is down to 11 percent (Kuttner 1996). The 2000 political race appears equally insensitive to class and racial inequalities, despite some rhetoric on issues of health care and retirement protection.

DEREGULATION AND AN ABANDONMENT OF THE LIBERAL ACTIVIST STATE

Under greater pressure from capital owners (Beeghley 1996), there has been a shift in the United States to "small government." The prime concern has been to decrease taxes, ostensibly to induce both new domestic investment and new domestic consumption. Instead, this has led to a greater export of manufacturing jobs, merely offering more U.S. service employment at low-wage levels, and a redistribution of income and wealth upwards (Phillips 1989, 1993).

ENVIRONMENTAL PROBLEMS

Old problems of pollution have not been addressed. The appearance of ecological improvement within the United States is often the result of our exporting dirty technologies to Third World nations. Additionally, new scientific findings have led to greater awareness of other problems, such as the effects of toxic waste on human reproductive systems and urban respiratory problems such as asthma.

These factors constitute large impediments to sustainable community development. Local governments, community development agencies, and other local nongovernmental organizations (NGOs) have struggled to find nonglobal and nontreadmill forms of control over local and non-local markets in order to avoid ceding to these unsustainability demands from global investors. Some local stakeholders have sought ways to harness the power of the globalizing marketplace to meet local needs for economic viability, social stability, and ecological sustainability (Shuman 1998). Recycling is a good example of an approach with the potential to achieve these goals of sustainable community development. Communities that recycle have sought to capture materials in the waste stream and to bundle them for resale to globalizing remanufacturing markets.

Yet, to create genuinely sustainable community development projects, a community faces many new obstacles in the globalizing economy. Markets are competitive, entry costs are high, and large firms have an array of market advantages. Some economists have begun to refer to this terrain as a *winner-takes-all market* (Frank and Cook 1995). In these markets, there tend to be larger winners, but fewer of them. Communities must compete in these markets while simultaneously addressing a host of social problems that have emerged in recent years. The latter include

1. the decline in urban employment paying living wages;
2. the stagnation or reduction in wages for most urban workers, reducing their buying power and contributions to local tax rolls;
3. growing competition among communities for business investment, resulting in a variety of tax reductions to induce corporations to locate in communities, and thus reducing future streams of revenue;
4. growing demand for public services, including health and housing, due in part to declines in personal income among the working population;
5. increasing attacks on high city taxes by all enterprises, who threaten to move to suburban or rural locations; and
6. the displacement of smaller-scale urban enterprises by large-scale national and international businesses, including franchised operations.

These factors also contextualized and shaped the nature of urban recycling in each of our cases. Both Chicago and its inner ring of suburbs have confronted a loss of employment, particularly for unskilled workers. In order to address this glut of unemployed and underemployed workers, each municipal entity has sought to induce new businesses to relocate within their boundaries, to raise both employment potential and "tax bases." The latter has become a central feature of municipal planning. The decline in corporate benefits for a large regional population of citizen-workers has led to an increase in their demands for public health and other services.

This has meant that Chicago, as well as Evanston and other older inner-ring suburbs, has been forced to offer taxpayer-based inducements to businesses in order to generate new employment and taxes. This was also true to some extent in Maywood, Uptown, and other poor Chicago neighborhoods. Each of these recycling programs was in part designed for the purpose of addressing multiple pressing social problems. But in each case, the promise of the redress of social and economic problems was sidelined by the "need" to use city funds to attract corporate investors and operators.

The city of Evanston had been successful at attracting new business investments in entertainment, retail shopping districts, grocery stores, and high-rent housing. Even here, though, the forces listed above have widened a two-tiered quality of life in this city on the northern border of Chicago. There remains a significant pocket of poverty, high crime, and joblessness, especially among the Evanston's African American residents. The recycling program agreement with PIC was constructed specifically to address this problem.

Small businesses in each of these towns were failing at an alarming rate, which lowered opportunities for local workers and reduced the local tax base. The taxpayers have paid a heavy price as well. Collectively, each of these cities has given millions of taxpayer dollars to businesses willing to locate in the area, with no enforceable commitment from these firms to stay for any specified length of time. Why do cities give such large breaks to private enterprise? In the next sections, we consider the roots of the state's behavior.

The State's Ambivalent Role in Managing the Treadmill

We also note that the role of the state in recycling was one of ambivalence in all the previous chapters. As we noted in chapter 1, the state's role is both to facilitate capital accumulation and to legitimate the socioeconomic structure for the citizenry (O'Connor 1973, 1988). In its role as facilitator of a prosperous economy, the state, to ensure continuous economic growth, protects unlimited access to natural resources. In its role as distributive justice legitimator, it must maintain resource levels for noneconomic community uses, such as clean water and spaces for recreational activities. Sustainable community development is, therefore, attractive to communities when local problems arise. Yet most of these ideas never get beyond the discussion stage, due to resistance from private sector actors and their political allies, who are both following the rules of the treadmill game.

Changing urban constituencies have created a number of political and economic constraints on the state in recent years. Urban governments have increasingly felt squeezed: both central cities and older suburban communities are confronting an increase in demands for city services, while their capacities to provide such services are declining. This is largely the direct result of patterns of capital allocation, which support national and international shareholders at the expense of local stakeholders (Longworth 1998). It is also an outcome of the political influence of large-scale capital investors on the federal government.

Since the Reagan era, there has been a consistent push for less regulation, lower taxes, and more state subsidization for large capital-intensive projects. The criterion of sustainability for private capital owners and managers has been *corporate* sustainability. Their central concern has been to ensure rising profitability and stock price increases. This is not necessarily bad. A depressed economy with low stock prices would not be ripe for urban reform. But it is also true that corporate sustainability does not *automatically* lead to community sustainability. Indeed, a community's difficulty achieving sustainable forms of development is often precisely what maintains corporate sustainability. Communities that offer investors access to natural resources below market costs, cheap labor, and noncompetitive markets are often seen by corporate actors as fertile grounds for corporate sustainability. This dynamic indicates that the needs of communities and corporations are often fundamentally at odds.

This arrangement also makes it harder for nongovernmental organizations and social advocates to raise money, to gain access to public officials, or to convince local politicians to consider plans for sustainable community development. As we noted in chapter 3, recycling programs in Chicago were shaped behind closed doors by large-scale capital owners and the Daley political machine. Paradoxically, the Daley machine, seeking to avoid increasing local taxes to pay for recycling programs actually enticed Waste Management into recycling operations as a means of protecting Chicago's financial security. As we documented in chapters 4, 5, and 6, proponents of innovative recycling programs confronted a hostile political climate. Uptown Recycling, the Resource Center, and the Maywood Recycling Park were stymied by their lack of access to government officials. Their political disempowerment was paralleled by a lack of economic access to private investors.

These sustainable recycling advocates were also powerless to influence federal regulatory patterns, which supported private capital projects that were decreasingly oriented to the needs of local stakeholders. This last point is important. With strong OSHA enforcement of worker safety regulations or EPA enforcement of environmental practices, the blue bag program would have been much more expensive for Waste Management and the city of Chicago to operate. It would either never have been implemented or would have been changed sooner after implementation, rather than after several years of exploiting vulnerable workers.

Why did Chicago in particular and other cities more generally find themselves in this unenviable position? Probably the greatest contributing factor is the transformation of basic industry vis-à-vis the inner city. Responding to emerging global challenges, private firms have created myriad social crises. Many firms have left the inner city, thus creating a rising demand for services (welfare payments, unemployment, retraining, and environmental cleanup). Moreover, their lobbyists have urged the federal government to reduce corporate and personal taxes, thereby decreasing available public revenues to provide these services. Finally, in their campaign contributions, they have helped put forward an ideology and practice that has led to a decrease in federally supported social services as a poverty reduction strategy (Longworth 1998).

In this climate, smaller scale community-based recycling programs that could have created integrated programs to deal with ecological, equity, and economic needs appeared less attractive to state agents. Instead, the latter opted for the "more efficient" large-scale, economically driven programs that touted their potential for revenue generation and job creation. At most, though, these firms generated low-wage and dead-end jobs. The Daley administration certainly had some concerns about equity issues, as did the Evanston City Council. Likewise, OSHA officials had concerns about worker safety issues. The EPA was also aware of the potential impact these recycling programs might have had on environmental quality. But each of these state actors was also under substantial political pressure to accommodate large capital interests (Lowi 1979). We will return to this issue in the next section (see trend 2 below).

Grounding Sustainable Community Development in the Treadmill of Production

The treadmill of production is often inaccurately perceived as a mono-lithic concept. The treadmill changes over time, as noted in the histories of Chicago and Evanston and outlined in chapter 2. There are also variations within the treadmill at any particular place, as evidenced by the diversity of programs descrobed in chapters 3–6. Generally, though, the treadmill is not a favorable context for creating and maintaining sustainable community development projects. The diversity of programs we studied is gradually converging into several nonsustainable forms of recycling. The globalizing treadmill is currently creating two trends that make for formidable difficulties for sustainable community development projects. In the rest of this chapter, we explore these trends. In the next chapter, we explore some contexts where limited subversion of these trends may be possible.

Trend 1: The Perceived Role of Firms in the Global Economy: The Resistance to Supporting the Three Es

One reframing of our arguments in chapters 3–6 is that by the 1980s, most private sector firms had become largely alienated from equity and environmental concerns (Longworth 1998). Citizens were primarily concerned with obtaining a fair share of local economic development. They sought to maintain enough fiscal solvency of their communities to address local social needs. And they also desired to reduce their health hazards from landfills and incinerators (Stoecker 1994). At the same time, though, firms became even more focused on their own bottom lines — increasing profitability and share values for their investors (Korten 1996; Shuman 1998; Useem 1993). Because of this tension, firms and their managers were becoming more and more alienated from the concerns of local populations.

In the formal language of economics, citizen concerns of social equity and environmental quality were heightened by the rising visible negative externalities of private capital during the 1970s and 1980s. During the 1980s, increasing unemployment and environmental pollution were plaguing urban communities around the country. These were major concerns of many workers and citizen activists. However, firms were increasingly resistant to internalizing the costs of dealing with these local problems. Their calculated removal from such concerns was rationalized by their argument that they faced fiercer competition in the global marketplace (Harrison 1994; Korten 1996). Others have suggested that this argument was partly a smokescreen designed to mask a campaign to increase managers' share of profits by reducing the share distributed to workers and local communities (Gordon 1996).

Increasingly, even where firms have remained active in local philanthropic activities, they have been practicing more "strategic philanthropy" than a genuine mutualism with the community (Kanter 1995; Silver 1998). Firms tend to donate to community organizations in ways that enhance their public relations, facilitating their greater market and ideological penetration of the community and improving their profitability. As "philanthropic" actors, they tend to "give back" only a small share of what they have extracted from increased downsizing and hardball negotiations for "deals" with community leaders. For example, Waste Management has been providing funds for "environmental education" in the city of Chicago's public schools. However, this program is nothing more than an effort to persuade schoolchildren and their parents of the "benefits" of Waste Management's blue bag recycling system.

As more and more large firms have become engaged in mergers and acquisitions, their "philanthropic" spirit has been increasingly redirected to the headquarter's city of the newly merged company. If the headquarters is in a city other than where the acquired or merged firm was centered, then donations to local nonprofit organizations will be reduced. There is simply no longer a corporate need to maintain a local presence. Thus, there is little corporate pressure to express any loyalty to such local potential beneficiaries. Unfortunately, it is difficult for foundations and other philanthropic concerns to fill this void. In Chicago, for example, after the blue bag program went on-line, the executive director of Citizens for a Better Environment complained that "no one's funding solid waste issues anymore. It's not like the issue has gone away, because we still have trash being landfilled and very little of it actually being recycled, reused, or composted. But the foundations are supporting advocacy work in this area, so our focus has had to shift in order to keep the organization alive."

Economic factors thus seem to dominate even the world of "giving" for "good causes." But the theory of the firm has always used such narrow criteria to define success for the business. When firms had more enduring dependencies on localities, they more frequently shared *some* concerns about the habitability and quality of life of their host communities (Shuman 1998). Owners and managers often lived locally, and thus shared some of the fates of their communities of operation. Even in this period, though, owners and managers were always careful to live upwind and upstream from their polluting industries (Hurley 1995).

In Evanston, part of the financial problems stemmed from a loss of major employers, who moved to other communities. Paradoxically, one of the major new investors in a downtown Evanston housing development is an insurance company that moved from that site, taking over two hundred well-paying jobs with them. The most ironic occurrence in Evanston's recycling history is perhaps in the recent competition over the privatization of the city's Recycling Center. The most active competitor to the winner, Groot Recycling, was Browning-Ferris Industries. BFI had claimed to be a "good citizen" of Evanston because it had located a waste transfer station there when it bought out the local firm, Active Service Recycling. Yet it was BFI's withdrawal from hauling office paper wastes to Evanston's MRF that changed the economics of the Recycling Center and led to the eventual abandonment of both the center and its social retraining program. It was Northwestern University, which provided fellowship support for this book's authors, that both underwrote our research *and* permitted BFI to unilaterally take its "local" waste and sell it extralocally.

Likewise, the village of Maywood reaped national publicity through its proposed industrial park. This was so much the case that when we first visited the planners, we fully believed that the park was up and running. Yet the only reward the two planners received was being fired by the village. They were also strung along by private investors who claimed that *their* technologies were "imminently" on-line.

By 1980, then, it was becoming clear to most Chicago-area decision makers involved in economic and community development that the technological, organizational, and political dimensions of Chicago's economy were changing. Contemporary post-Fordist (Lipietz 1987) forms of production technology allowed firms to produce more goods with fewer workers. In turn, this led to downsizing many long-established manufacturing firms, especially on the City's South and West sides (Gordon 1996; Harrison 1994; Logan and Swanstrom 1990; *Economist* 1991). This anticommunity stance was exacerbated by the fact that more firms had become publicly owned, and thus more vulnerable to stockholder rebellions and pressures for managers to return to more profitable ventures. Budros (1997:230) puts it well: "Central to the new U.S. economy are 'institutional investors' (especially pension funds), which have pushed non-owning managers to increase shareholder value (stock prices and dividends), often dismissing unresponsive managerial teams."

In his book documenting the rise of institutional investing, Useem (1993:1) argues similarly: "During the late 1980s and early 1990s . . . large shareholders rebelled, pressing companies to build organizational forms more suited to their purposes. . . . A driving principle behind this transformation was that the organization's architecture should be aligned more closely around what shareholders sought from their ownership stake."

In our earlier work, we noted some of the same tendencies:

Unlike the fantasy of *It's a Wonderful Life*, the level of investment in most larger firms is sufficiently high that a handful of local, friendly, community investors no longer constitutes the core of investors. The firms' relations to ecosystems thus change, because the expansionary impulses for investors under their goal of maximizing share values is perfectly open-ended. No longer do more localized investors have as a primary goal the provision of local services or local employment (including employment for family members), or the improvement of the community's economy. Instead, when investors (or potential investors) believe that their investments/shares can earn more under other managerial conditions, the managers in place have to struggle to run even faster on the treadmill of production. (Schnaiberg and Gould 1994:51)

Useem offers the following quotes from interviews with corporate officers of Fortune 500 companies:

Central management repeatedly focused attention on the singular importance of this one measure of performance. "Stakeholder value is our internal corporate driving force," one company's president commented. (1993:76–77)

"We want the employees to learn that the company is being managed for the benefit of the shareholders, and that decisions we make with regard to facilities and operations have that at their root." (1993:72)

Many of these issues have been playing themselves out in Chicago region. Despite their initial dismissal of recycling's ecological and social goals in favor of narrow economic and market interests, Waste Management nonetheless incurred the wrath of its shareholders. In this era of globalization, where capital can flow to profitable enterprises virtually anywhere in the world, shareholders attacked Waste Management for not being "efficient" enough to generate higher dividends and increased stock values. As low as Waste Management's road to profits had been (Harrison 1994), the shareholders defined it as "not low enough." In their estimation, too much of the potential profit had been drained by "unproductive" activities such as recycling.

What this means is that Waste Management's profit margin for recycling, while substantially higher than that of the community-based programs, has simply been socially defined as "not high enough" by an organized group of shareholders. (Indeed, current managers have reported to us a continuing loss rather than a profit for the Chicago MRRFs). Paradoxically, the central figure in this corporate drama has been George Soros, whose investment funds have included a block of Waste Management. Soros also runs a "humanitarian" foundation that supports research and development for "social justice in the city." But his philanthropic actions were painfully dwarfed by his economic actions in socially unjust operations such as Waste Management's.

The eventual outcome of these pressures may be the dismantling of the blue bag program. Unwilling to pay larger contract fees, the city of Chicago will be under pressure to abandon recycling, although it will continue to have to follow Illinois state mandates for recycling a substantial portion of their solid waste stream. Waste Management will likely convert its MRRF into a waste transfer station, leaving Chicago to juggle its agenda in the other three MRRFs owned by the city. Chicago has a heavy capital investment in the MRRFs, but has also protected its operating budget by passing on problems to Waste Management. If Chicago cannot get another corporation to take over its recycling/waste-hauling contract, it may seek to avoid shutting down the blue bag program by operating it with city staff.

It is unlikely that Chicago would consider shifting its program to community-based organizations, since most of their centers and personnel have already been put out of business. Likewise, the city will have missed an opportunity to develop innovative recycling parks like those proposed in Maywood and West Garfield Park that could have produced hundreds of well-paying jobs. The closings and missed opportunities are pernicious, particularly in areas where welfare and immigration reform have already weakened the social and economic foundations of the impoverished immigrant and native communities. The Uptown Recycling Center has already closed and the Resource Center continues to shift its focus away from traditional postconsumer waste recycling. As those populations previously served by these programs are left without options, we have no way to gauge the effects. The people who used the center remain socially invisible. They exist in regions of the city that have become abandoned (Squires et al. 1987; Wilson 1996). If they are starving, few people will notice and it will likely go unreported in either media accounts or census numbers.

Thus the role of the city and Waste Management in Chicago's recycling history reveals an unflattering and dim portrait that has done great damage to the prospect of sustainable community development in this metropolis. The good news is that there is nothing natural or inevitable about this process. What is disarming, however, is that much of the problem is rooted not only in the battles against multinational corporations, but also in a myth that plagues even the most powerful political bodies in this nation's largest cities.

Trend 2: The Growing Myth of Urban Disempowerment

Why did Chicago's community developers come to create a recycling system as wasteful of human and natural resources as the blue bag program? The answer: like most city administrations, the Daley regime assumed that the city was marginalized and powerless vis-à-vis private capital on the issue of the sale of recyclable materials. Ironically, Chicago acted powerfully to use Waste Management as a corporate buffer to offset this vulnerability. The "urban disempowerment myth" that afflicts cities such as Chicago is consistent with the argument of Paul Peterson (1981:45), who has maintained: "In the global economy private capital is freed of many of the limitations of place. Cities are rendered obsolete. Industry can come and go as it pleases. Forced to adapt to this changed market place, cities have no choice but to participate in the market for mobile capital. The only other choice is to face economic decline."

Urban governments have come to believe that they are in a disempowered position. Given the current dynamics of the treadmill, they are largely correct (Longworth 1998). Certainly globalization has shifted the power balance toward firms. But Peterson and others have gone one step further by arguing that the *only* viable response is reduced taxes and regulations to create a "good business environment." This "bidding down" is intended to attract new investors. Some urban sociologists have called this "mainstream" economic development policy (Clavel and Kleniewski 1990) the "corporate-centered" development approach (see Logan and Swanstrom 1990). Its starting question is "What are the needs of the corporation?" rather than asking "What are the needs in different parts of the community?" This led to substantial economic, social, and environmental concessions, as noted in chapter 3. As the initial blue bag program and the abandonment of the PIC program in Evanston demonstrated, a "good business climate" often includes non-union jobs, lower wages, reduced or no unemployment benefits, subsidized financing, land giveaways, relaxed regulations, and various tax breaks.

Corporate-centered development stresses that growth should be pursued as the panacea for all urban distributive gaps. This "monocultural" approach to redevelopment has two inherent difficulties. First, growth is narrowly conceived as a bricks-and-mortar approach to economic development. This calls exclusively for large-scale changes in land use patterns in or near central business districts that are financed, at least partially, by cities. Development of this type often exacerbates many of the social ills it is designed to address (Stoecker 1994; Taub 1994). Leveling low-income housing to make way for new developments continues to be such an approach (Logan and Molotch 1987; Wilson 1987, 1996).

Second, such growth makes some resources potentially available to fund social programs. But it typically includes no clear mechanism for the distribution of the revenue generated from the economic growth to the poor or other depressed segments of the community. Out of this sleight of hand has emerged "a tradition that historically has tied the fortunes of cities to the vitality of their private sectors and encouraged a reliance on private institutions (rather than on public control and planning for urban development)" (Barnekov, Boyle, and Rich 1989:213).

Finally, this bricks-and-mortar model ignores the fact that many community development corporations are also working to develop the social infrastructure of cities as well as to increase levels of human capital (H. Rubin 1994; Stoecker 1994). They are often pushed aside in the course of "development."

Corporate-centered development is not the only socially useful market-based strategy. Yet it has become the one most favored by official urban development planners. Mainstream (Clavel and Kleniewski 1990) or corporate-centered development thus reinforces the existing distribution of political power within the urban landscape.

Regardless, members of the Daley administration charged with addressing the "landfill crisis" were expected to work toward the creation of a "good business climate" for the city. To fulfill this condition, the mayor pushed for a program that would limit recycling's demands upon the city's future operating budget. But the city had to generate a contract that appeared beneficial to powerful firms who might be willing to run a large-scale recycling project that could provide new jobs. This project was supposed to help low-income communities, who had been hardest hit by the loss of Chicago's manufacturing industries. Expanding the job base from a large-scale recycling project would inject badly needed revenue into the city tax rolls and into employee payrolls. A renewed demand for local stores and local services would emerge with rising payrolls and increased employment. Small-business disinvestment in poor neighborhoods over the last twenty years (Wilson 1996) would be slowed, halted, and possibly reversed. While more of these objectives have been approached in later years of the program, the city lost valuable opportunities in failing to rein in Waste Management in the early years of the program. And it is our argument that in seeking this fiduciary protection, the city was also foregoing other opportunities to move closer to the three Es of sustainable community development through recycling.

Corporate-centered development is seductive because people need jobs. Almost any strategy that claims to create lots of jobs is appealing. The problem with corporate-centered development is that there are no mechanisms to ensure that the jobs produced come with a living wage, decent working conditions, or human development. Moreover, within this strategy, the firm makes few if any commitments to remain rooted in place for any period of time. Thus proponents of this strategy fail to recognize the difference between high-road and low-road development (Harrison 1994). Low-road development is driven by firms who seek profits by controlling their costs, usually through the exploitation of workers and the local environment. These firms are attracted to struggling urban communities by the potential to create a dependent relationship. A large employer can dictate labor conditions and local environmental ordinances, thereby controlling costs.

High-road development is driven by firms who seek profits through increased productivity. They employ the best workers and the latest technology. These firms are attracted to urban communities by the large pool of trainable workers. They see the potential to create a world-class workforce that carries out high-performance production (see generally Harrison 1994; Longworth 1998; Thurow 1996). The challenge for urban communities is to use the global economy to create a local economy constructed from high road firms and industries.[1]

---

[1] Note that we do not view "high road firms" as unproblematic or as businesses necessarily engaged in sustainable community development

By ignoring this distinction, municipalities are primed to generate a stream of disastrous compromises. Each separate action appears to make sense, but taken together, they constitute a socially and economically unproductive bidding-down pathway that leads farther away from sustainable community development. This was readily apparent in the history of the blue bag program.

1. The city of Chicago assumed that attracting a large firm like Waste Management would protect Chicago's development potential. Thus, they made a series of initial financial compromises to attract them.

2. The city of Chicago also assumed that a large program with huge MRFs would also lead to economies of scale. Thus, they invested massive financial resources into constructing four of them.

3. Finally, the city assumed that a large-scale program run with cutting-edge technologies by a large firm would naturally be positive. Thus, they followed the lead of Waste Management.

Retracing the rationale behind the decisions, we were struck by how powerless the city viewed itself as a market actor and by how much faith they placed in Waste Management to insulate them from market fluctuations in recyclable prices. These decisions came back to haunt the city in the first years of its recycling program. As we documented in the chapter 3, they did make changes to address the low recovery rates, poor recycling stream quality, and abominable labor conditions. However, they had limited degrees of freedom. The city was committed by contract to a corporate-centered strategy with Waste Management for at least seven years. Even beyond this, the city has committed itself by capital outlays for the MRRFs, and there is little they can do to correct many of the design flaws of its program.

Conclusion: Relationships in the Treadmill

One way of pulling these ideas together is to outline the nature of relationships in a treadmill-based political economy. Wayne Baker (1994: 44–47) has conceptualized the possible relationships into a classification scheme. He considers the motivation of each parties in a network of economic relationships, and traces the nature of the commitments between them that result. Chart 7.1 outlines these.

Baker notes that relationships 2 and 3 are "not sustainable because orientations are mismatched. Eventually, you protect yourself and withdraw from the exchange, or you convince the other side of the merits" (1994:45) of your own position. Communities are desirous of creating

CHART 7.1

Types of Connections between Communities and Remanufacturers

		REMANUFACTURER'S MOTIVATION	
		DEAL-ORIENTED	**RELATION-ORIENTED**
COMMUNITY MOTIVATION	DEAL-ORIENTED	1. Spot market	3. Exit
	RELATION-ORIENTED	2. Exploitation	4. Partnerships

sustainable relationships with remanufacturers, who want to utilize the community's recyclable materials. Community developers have often struggled to create a kind of "bootstrap" approach to remanufacturing. Municipal agencies gather and sort recyclable materials, on the one hand. On the other hand, they create mandates for the purchase of subsequently remanufactured products (especially paper products). They see their role as "market makers," stimulating both supply (curbside collection and MRFs) and demand (purchase of remanufactured goods).

Community agents ignore the discomforting reality that absent a given level of actual or anticipated profit, private organizations will be oriented only toward "deals." Firms are generally not interested in ongoing relationships to protect the community's environment through remanufacturing with locally gathered recyclables. Communities have attempted two approaches to this dilemma. One the one hand, they seek to avoid the undesirable outcome of being exploited by remanufacturers. On the other hand, they seek to avoid being seduced into creating MRFs and then being abandoned by remanufacturing firms when profits are too low.

First, community MRFs have selected only those recyclable materials that can find a somewhat-reliable market demand from remanufacturers. This essentially leads to a selection of materials for collection and sorting that is market oriented, and not ecologically oriented (what we have called "getting the materials right" [Weinberg, Pellow, and Schnaiberg 1996]). Unselected materials are disposed of in landfills or incinerated. For example, in the mid-1990s, many recyclers stopped collecting plastics because of their low market returns, despite their significant volume in the solid waste stream.

A second approach is for community MRFs to select remanufacturers who will reliably sustain a demand for the community's output from its MRFs. The MRFs attempt to find commodity brokers who become intermediaries between the community and the market of remanufacturers. Essentially, this establishes a relationship, rather than just spot transactions, between these brokers and community agents. Evanston is one example we found that uses both these strategies.

This latter process has been extended recently by the establishment of a national trading market for recyclable materials. This has been lauded by some recycling proponents, although its operations have not been very successful. Even with this development, though, communities remain vulnerable to market fluctuations. In neither case is there a relationship orientation with the purchaser of recyclable materials. Most of these community strategies have essentially created only a diversity of spot deals.

Communities hoped to benefit from having a less monopolistic market for their recyclables by finding "many buyers." However, with more than eight thousand U.S. communities recycling, the trading advantage redounds typically to the remanufacturer. This disparity exists in part because the remanufacturer sees recyclables as only a commodity, rather than as a means of achieving ecological protection or community revitalization. Remanufacturers are, de facto, forcing community agents to change their values for recycling from an ecological policy into more of a market exchange.

Some mutually beneficial relationships between community-based MRFs and remanufacturers have emerged, though. In the early 1990s, for example, increased market activity raised prices for newsprint and other paper recyclables substantially. This created more favorable balance sheets for community recycling agencies, on the one hand, and for remanufacturers, on the other. Unfortunately, this did not lead to a heightened ecological consciousness for either party. Rather, MRFs became temporarily visible as a potential revenue-generation center for municipal budgets. Likewise, recyclables gained more popularity as a feedstock for a growing number of paper remanufacturers.

As economic growth slowed somewhat in the middle 1990s, some of the older economic dilemmas of community MRFs reappeared. Costs of community collection and sorting became higher than revenues from remanufacturers. Demand was still high enough to prevent a return to the 1980s-style material glut of recyclable paper stocks. The rise of community recycling had in fact economically induced more large paper manufacturers to invest in remanufacturing facilities in order to take advantage of cheap and plentiful supplies of wastepaper feedstocks. Remanufacturers did not become more "ecological"; they simply applied their standard guideposts of profitability to the emerging scale of recycling technologies. Remanufacturers' economic shift further encouraged local community recyclers to actually become more, rather than less, "economic" in their orientations, further diminishing the vision of recycling as a form of ecological protection.

When market prices for recyclables declined, how did community agents respond? Most made some incremental changes in their local processes in order to adapt to new market conditions. They expanded recycling of some materials but condensed or abandoned other materials. They sought to find new brokers to help them. In a small number of cases, they began to think more aggressively, to try to become the market makers they desired to be. They sought out larger and smaller organizations to use evolving technologies in ways that could generate profits in remanufacturing goods out of higher-volume and lower-value recyclable materials, such as paper and old tires. As we noted in chapter 4, few of these projects have actually materialized. There were too many economic uncertainties for these remanufacturing organizations. Essentially, the "deals" have simply not been profitable or predictable enough for the market actors to take greater economic risks.

Recycling has thus become less ecologically and socially oriented over the past decade, despite (or because of) its nominal success. The diffusion of curbside recycling and community-based MRFs has actually oriented community political and economic officials to the behavior of the market more than it has induced these latter organizations to become more "green." People like Jim Burris and Ken Dunn are largely being removed from the industry's terrain. This is our sobering conclusion to both this chapter and the preceding ones. It poses a challenge for how to think about recycling and broader strategies of environmental reforms that will "do good" for communities rather than just "feel good" for citizens. In the final chapter, we take up this theme.

Eight

The Search for Sustainable Community Development: Final Notes and Thoughts

The Political Economy of Solid Waste Management

In July of 1997, we had the privilege to participate in an Internet conference focusing on solid waste management practices around the globe. During the course of the conference, a solid waste consultant, Anne Scheinberg, offered an evaluation of recent changes in solid waste management that shed light on our understanding of recycling. In this section, we present a summary and analysis of that evaluation because it paints a portrait of the industry that sheds light on the cases we have presented in the previous chapters.

In a paper posted on the Internet during the conference, Scheinberg argued that during the last twenty years, the Organization for Economic Development (northern) countries have witnessed a total paradigm shift in the rationale for and approach to municipal waste management. The new paradigm originated over a concern that waste dumping was causing groundwater contamination in many communities. Many of these nations have long recognized the need to introduce and enforce environmental controls over organizations and individuals that continue to bury wastes. In particular, she noted a growing emphasis on siting and constructing ecologically sound landfills, which would prevent wastes from leaching out of landfills and eventually into the groundwater.

The movement for safer landfills led to a shift upward in the economy of scale of solid waste disposal. Simply put, communities had to regionalize their waste streams in order to be able to cover the costs of constructing and operating "safe" landfills. Local unregulated dumps gave way to larger regulated regional landfills. This regionalization weakened the role of local government in the disposal process. Communities increasingly found that their only option was to pay large firms to pick up and transfer solid waste to the regional landfill. Initially, this led a rapid rise in the cost of solid waste disposal. Such costs tended to spike within the first two-to-five years of the transition, and then gradually decline as "modern" disposal capacity was constructed and brought on-line.

Scheinberg noted that as solid waste disposal practices modernized around landfills, there was a move at both the grass roots and the policy levels to require a range of source separation initiatives, such as recycling. The intent of these initiatives was to reduce both the volume and weight of waste materials requiring disposal. The second-order impact of this regionalization change was to transform existing recycling activities, which were actually informal scavenging operations, to more formalized recycling, reorganized in the formal sanitation sector.

This organizational shift is important because the formal sector is driven by a search for profits, mostly derived from the collection and removal of solid wastes. Thus, the private sector was motivated primarily by the lure of large contracts with local government for the collection and processing of recyclable materials. Such formal sector firms then sought to increase profits by expanding their control over the entire recycling process. They accomplished this goal in large part by purchasing other formal sector firms and by driving out informal scavengers. Most often this incorporation created the loss of livelihood for the community of scavengers, scrap dealers, intermediaries, and commodity-based buyback systems. It also created job losses when firms merged or were acquired and certain positions became redundant.

Scheinberg then provided longitudinal indicators of the resulting impacts on communities around the globe. For example, as the rise of private recycling firms continued, there was a temporary but relatively long-lived (three-to-seven-year) depression in the regional (and in some cases world) market price for the secondary (recycling) materials. The supply outstripped the demand. Eventually there was an expansion of the market for these secondary materials, arising from increases in the technical capabilities of firms to utilize the recycled materials. This tended to happen over a five-to-fifteen-year period. Following this, there was some restoration of price levels for these recycled materials, and the market often expanded to incorporate other recyclable materials — such as materials with a higher level of contamination or new mixtures of materials.

In turn, this change led to an explosion of technical innovation, first in collection and separation technologies, and, as a second-level result, in feedstock preparation and preprocessing. Finally, Scheinberg observed a diversification of publicly financed or publicly guaranteed disposition, processing, and final disposal options, such as transfer stations, separation plants, composting and anaerobic digestion facilities, incinerators, landspreading operations, mono-fills, long-term storage facilities, and the like.

Scheinberg's depictions are most revealing for us. Her comments about the "informal sector" are analogous to what we have termed "community-based" recycling operations (chapter 4). Her concept of "modernization" essentially relates to what we have termed "corporate-centered" recycling programs (chapter 3).

In particular, we note that in her analysis solid waste disposal is driven by formal organizations in search of profit. There is nothing in the analysis that suggests that the nature and pace of production are likely to be driven by ecological or social goals. Recycling enterprises may offer some environmental efficiency gains, but these are mostly minor deviations from the standard means and goals of formal organizations. Scheinberg has described a "business as usual" model of an industry that most observers view as quite unusual and unique: recycling will emerge in the form of large municipally based programs that are designed around the multiple needs of producers.[1]

Major equity and environmental threats are thus likely to emerge in this modernization process. First, the threat to the informal sector is essentially built into the process of modernization. Second, after the initial stage, environmental concerns are not the drivers in the modernization process. However, Scheinberg believes that there is some room to redirect the later process:

> The strategies for creating or supporting informal sector enterprises probably need to incorporate a service element into what has likely been a purely commodity-based income stream, with a resulting need to cultivate a service constituency with some degree of willingness to pay. . . . Examples [include] the community organizations, which become involved in collecting from underserved areas, [and] are developing both a service and a materials value component. (Scheinberg 1997)

Scheinberg concludes that at the policy level, there is a general need for more sophisticated tools for impact analysis of the effects of modernization and privatization on the existing waste infrastructure, both formal and informal, and on the institutions needed to provide sustainable services to poor or underserved constituencies. To deal with these potential risks, Scheinberg suggests the following approaches may be most politically feasible:

> Attempts to support the informal waste sector are most sustainable when there are clear links to the formal municipal planning and modernization processes, both at the local government level and in the planning work of donors, so that (for example) support for marketability of a particular materials stream is not rendered irrelevant by denial of access to those materials

---

[1] We underscore that corporations have multiple needs, despite the primacy of profit. Political goals and many other inter- and intraorganizational dynamics often displace, compete with, or complement the drive for profit. For a review see Dimaggio and Powell 1991.

through the introduction of compactors or restricted access to a "modern" landfill. (Scheinberg 1997)

To some extent, she suggests that the dead ends awaiting most community-based recycling programs may be avoided if their "access" to materials is maintained by local governments. Our view is that with the growth of a "modern" waste management system and especially a modern recycling industry, community-based recycling programs lack the power to achieve such access. This results, in large part, because modern waste management organizations simply lack the economic incentive to offer such access. They possess the political power to sustain their own operations at the expense of community-based or "informal" sector operations. We now turn to these issues more directly.

Critical Social Science: Power, Education, Community, and Politics

Both our analysis and Scheinberg's suggest that progressive attempts to implement recycling must be understood as intimately linked with much larger decisions about waste streams. As the blue bag example made clear, decisions that were specific to recycling were also made within much larger decision frameworks about how to create a viable solid waste management operation in the city of Chicago. For us, the central question is: Under what conditions can communities manage their waste streams in a fashion that embodies the three Es of sustainable community development?

Although it is customary in academic books, we will not propose here any glib answers to this difficult question. We will, however, offer a few good places to start thinking about this question. In particular, we believe that three issues have shaped our analysis. Paying attention to these issues is, at the very least, a reasonable point of departure in visions of potential contexts for achieving sustainable community development within a globalizing treadmill of production. The four issues are: (1) the role of *social movements*, (2) the role of *management training*, (3) the tensions between *labor and the environment*, and (4) the need for *shadow pricing*.[2] In the rest of this chapter we address these themes, paying attention to what they tell us more generally about waste streams and sustainable community development.

---

[2] "Shadow pricing" is the term given to those accounting practices that attempt to reflect the "true" cost or actual benefits embodied in the production and delivery of a good or service. So for example, while the price of a gallon of gasoline may be $1.50, if "shadow pricing" were employed, this figure would be much greater, to include the social and environmental costs of petroleum extraction, refining, and distribution.

Power: Environmental Movements, Recycling, and Sustainable Communities

Social movements played a major role in the emergence of recycling in the United States. This is especially true in the case of the Uptown Recycling and the Resource Centers, but it is also true in Maywood, Chicago, and Evanston. In each of these cases, these social movements were later overwhelmed by dominant economic players. Social movement organizations, in other words, had very little power to *maintain* existing progressive programs or to challenge regressive ones. Their power lay more in raising issues than in implementing new production policies (cf. Shuman 1998).

We should remember that modern waste recycling arose from efforts by progressive community groups in the 1960s to discover ways in which society could be environmentally responsible and still address equity issues. Thus, the Resource Center and Uptown Recycling emerged directly from social movement activity, and their leaders identified themselves as part of the ecological movement. They continued to operate largely as social movement organizations. Their mission was to bring about political and social change through the practice of recycling. However, despite their unusual ability to construct and operate smaller-scale recycling businesses, even these groups were not powerful enough to stave off the crippling impact of the blue bag program. In Uptown Recycling's case, this incapacity was fatal. In the case of the Resource Center, the result was the city's near total retreat from curbside recycling into entirely different types of environmental services.

The absence of enduringly powerful social movements in these cases denotes two shortcomings about modern environmental movements (Gould, Weinberg, and Schnaiberg 1993). First, despite the rhetoric of sustainable community development, most well-funded environmental organizations remain focused on more narrowly defined environmental issues such as wilderness preservation and natural resource protection. They tend to be far removed from the daily concerns of urban populations. Clearly this is not true of the legions of citizen-worker groups focusing on environmental justice (Bullard 1990, 1994; Bryant and Mohai 1992; Szasz 1994). In Chicago, however, environmental groups with resources were not the small-scale environmental justice organizations. Rather, they were the larger mainstream groups, such as the Sierra Club, the Audubon Society, and the Lake Michigan Federation. As their names indicate, these groups have little interest in directly operating alternative social and economic production systems, such as urban recycling.

This does not mean that mainstream environmental groups did not or do not support recycling. Many of the larger organizations have been active, or at least have offered vocal support, in the early phases of recycling. Thus, they were very important in pushing for municipally based recycling programs. These groups have also been active around regulatory issues such as mandatory recycling laws. Such policies induced communities to capture a certain percentage of the waste stream and induced firms to use a minimum percentage of recycled materials in their production processes. Mainstream national environmental groups such as the Environmental Defense Fund and the Natural Resources Defense Council have also supported efforts to require governments to purchase recycled materials.

We generally applaud the efforts by the mainstream environmental organizations to support recycling, but note that too many of their emphases has fallen prey to the "more is better" ideology. Of course, all else being equal, more *is* better. However, "all else" is in fact never equal, particularly when powerful interests are at stake. Mainstream environmental groups have missed the boat when it comes to pushing for certain types of recycling systems while being critical of others. Instead, they have largely pushed recycling of *any* kind, and at *any* cost. Our view of this tendency is that environmental groups have too often paid attention to the quantitative dimensions of recycling programs to the exclusion of the qualitative dimensions; they ask questions like "How much?" rather than "Under what conditions?"

This is not true of all environmental groups, which brings us to the second weakness of the environmental movement. When environmental organizations have attempted to exert pressure on shaping the process of the qualitative dimensions of recycling programs, they usually have been locked out. Here the best case is Chicago itself. Long before the blue bag system went on-line, three efforts among social movement groups had emerged. The Westsiders for a Safe and Toxic-Free Environment (WASTE), the Chicago Recycling Coalition, and Citizens for a Better Environment led the successful effort to shut down the Northwest Incinerator. This facility was owned by a Waste Management subsidiary, Wheelabrator Technologies. While the environmental movement was successful in closing down the incinerator, it was unsuccessful at promoting a progressive alternative. Waste Management quickly recovered from its defeat to develop the regressive blue bag recycling system (a pyrrhic victory for Waste Management, since the Chicago MRRFs have not proven to be a profit center for them).

The second social movement action was the attempt by the Resource Center and Uptown Recycling to enter the bidding process for the city's Request for Proposals in its search for a new recycling system. Their attempt was stymied as the city focused only on large private corporations and simply ignored the proposals by smaller nonprofit organizations. Social movement actors were simply barred from the beginning of this process.

At this point, the third effort emerged. This action was led by the Chicago Recycling Coalition and Citizens for a Better Environment. For many months before the blue bag program went on-line, they launched a major media campaign to discredit the program's environmental promises. The two main objections they raised were the projected higher costs of running the blue bag system versus a source-separated approach, and the anticipated high levels of material contamination (due to recyclables being mixed in with municipal solid waste). This framing of the problem struck a resonant chord with many taxpayers, but it was not enough to turn the tide of support from the Daley administration.

The solid waste recycling campaigns of these environmental movement organizations were plagued with problems, particularly the lack of funding from the philanthropic community. Additionally, there was no critical mass of Chicago residents associated with these organizations that could have facilitated their mobilization into an enduring political force. Environmental movement groups involved in recycling politics were thus neither powerful enough to sustain existing community-based recycling organizations nor able to prevent corporate-centered programs from taking hold.

Finally, the environmental community has been misled and co-opted by groups such as Keep Evanston Beautiful. These organizations claim to represent environmental causes. In the end, they reduce the impetus for mainstream groups to pay attention to the details of solid waste because it appears that somebody is already playing a watchdog role. But Keep Evanston Beautiful, Incorporated, is an organization partly funded by a larger national parent organization, Keep America Beautiful, Incorporated. Their primary mission is not to make communities more ecologically balanced, but to find ways to permit and expand the production of disposable containers for the packaging and bottling industries. Keep America Beautiful is best understood as a trade organization representing a variety of corporate stakeholders.[3]

---

[3] Rather, these KEB campaigns were both designed to find ways to reduce the negative social reactions to producers of disposable containers — initially by getting containers "out of sight" and later by getting them "out of landfills." The latter role seems somewhat compatible with "closing the loop" and getting container manufacturers to take some responsibility for the wastes their disposable products generate — a kind of life-cycle production approach consistent with ecological modernization. But unlike firms that directly collect their disposed-of products, container manufacturers require municipalities to pay

In part because of the absence of other careful monitors of solid wastes and recycling programs, we think environmental movements might have to play a larger role in the development of recycling policies and programs in U.S. cities. In previous work, we argued that social movements might be more successful were they to act as "canaries in the mines" (Gould, Schnaiberg, and Weinberg 1996). They are the only social force capable of keeping both industry and the state honest and accountable.

Any sustainable community development endeavor will confront institutional actors who possess narrow market interests. Such actors will constantly try to reshape programs to maximize their own narrow interests. A strong environmental movement presence may be the best way to prevent or at least minimize this pattern. For this to happen, however, environmental groups will have to pay closer attention to the qualitative dimensions of recycling programs. In the case of recycling, the evaluation process will have to be more inclusive than simply "tons of wastes diverted from landfills." Market actors will, of course, almost certainly contest these expanded efforts of movement organizations.

Education: Decreasing the Homogeneity and Linearity of Management Ideologies

Achieving and practicing sustainable community development requires that managers learn to think in a different way. The concept of sustainable community development is premised on developing projects that integrate the three Es: equity, environment, and economy. Mostly, though, we train people to think in a linear fashion that focuses on only one problem (one E), using a single technique to locate a solution, and then implementing a solution through an organizational structure. Within the treadmill, most actors are trained to concentrate on the economic dimensions of a project. This problem is associated with the curriculums found in our nation's universities. Commenting on economics and master of business administration (MBA) programs in universities, Michael Shuman (1998:189) states:

> The transformation of business schools and university economics departments is another imperative. These institutions now celebrate personal profit over community service. Lewis Mumford once observed that industrial society

---

for the collection and sorting costs. Thus they allow municipalities to absorb the uncertainties of the marketplace because the prices firms pay to recycling centers for recyclables vary. In contrast, European producers of disposable containers collect their own containers and recycle or reuse them.

transformed all seven deadly sins except sloth into a positive virtue. Greed, avarice, envy, gluttony, luxury, and pride are the driving forces of the new economy. A startling study at Cornell University found that graduate students in economics, when given an opportunity to contribute to charity, donated less than half what other graduate students did. Their charitable impulse actually declined as they logged more years of training.

We do not want to equate "charity" with sustainable community development. Instead, we want to note two ways that the treadmill of production becomes institutionalized as ideology through education systems. First, most people are trained to view social, political, and environmental problems in narrow economic terms. They believe that if the treadmill can be sped up just a little bit more, then society can better address its problems or they will simply disappear.

Second, even when we train people in environmental issues, we adopt a similar unilinear style that revolves around science, technology, and large firms. Each of the authors has watched several universities develop environmental science programs at the undergraduate and graduate level. Unfortunately, these programs focus mostly on ecological processes and pay little or no attention to the social, economic, or political contexts in which such processes are embedded. Thus, all of us teach at universities where the environmental science program majors learn next to nothing about globalizing markets or political processes.

Such narrow environmental thinking is apparent in the nonresponse of environmental activists to the loss of local scrap and waste dealers brought about by the onset of new recycling programs. Traditionally, scrap and waste material dealers were primarily driven by economic and not ecological concerns. They wanted to exchange scrap wastes for moderate profits. Yet, as we noted in chapter 1, scrap businesses were often dominated by particular ethnic groups and concentrated in particular urban neighborhoods. They were family run and often incorporated multiple family workers.[4] Scrap businesses continue to operate today, especially in the old manufacturing districts of large U.S. cities, as well as in some smaller communities. But, in a painful paradox, they have often been displaced by the new recycling industry.

As we noted in chapters 1 and 3, modern recycling was first implemented in the early phases of the 1960s environmental renaissance. In numerous cities and towns, local environmental groups established vol-

---

[4] Ethnic and class ties of these families helped facilitate the collection and sale of these waste materials. Jews who had often suffered downward mobility in the migration from eastern Europe to the United States, were especially involved as ethnic middlemen in this business, for example. They often relied on coethnics with lower-class positions as suppliers of waste or even as local workers. And they often sold their materials to coethnic small entrepreneurs involved in manufacturing activities.

untary drop-off centers for "disposable" products — especially aluminum cans, glass bottles, and bundled newsprint. They intended to transform these materials from their characteristic state as low use-value wastes into high use-value by collecting and transporting them from scattered consumers and selling them to local scrap dealers.

Although such scrap-waste materials had often been transported directly to local manufacturers, the changing scale of industry and the mechanization of manufacturing had often displaced many small urban manufacturers. Environmental movement activists felt that their task was completed when they diverted wastes from incinerators and landfills and turned them over to "someone" who had some use for them. It was the physical transformation (i.e., the remanufacturing) that was at the heart of this ecological program — and it did not matter where the remanufacturing was being done (or really, even if it were being done). In other words, environmentalists were trained to narrowly pay attention to ecological values, which were met when materials were diverted from landfills into recycling centers.

The displacement of local scrap dealers by new municipal recycling programs created a leakage in the social equity dimension of recycling as a form of sustainable community development. Local scrap dealers became "outmoded" in the new recycling programs largely because the volume of recyclable materials grew beyond what these small-scale dealers could handle. At that point, for example in Evanston, one local dealer (Valley Scrap) appealed to the city to provide him with funds to purchase new equipment to help process the higher volumes and new materials. Instead, the city decided — for a period of five or six years at least — that it could achieve more by establishing its own local MRF program. But the ultimate unsustainability of this decision was clearer when Evanston recently privatized its program. The scrap dealer had survived for many years by offering buyback and reuse services (much as the community organizations in chapter 3 had done) — sorting scrap for usable parts as well as sorting and bundling larger recyclable volumes. He had established local networks and hired local workers.

By failing to use the expertise and local commitment of its own scrap dealers, Evanston entered into a national market in which its director was only partly skilled (cf. Pellow, Weinberg, and Schnaiberg 1995). The new recycler, Groot, has no local commitments and will likely treat the program as only a market transaction, perhaps abandoning it after their five-year contract is up. In contrast, the previous scrap company had been in Evanston for over thirty years and had roots and commitments to local institutions. Ironically, then, the "success" of recycling programs has meant the demise of many scrap dealers in larger communities, even though they could have been part of a local industry. This too is part of the "consolidation" or "rationalization" of the recycling industry noted in chapter 1.

Achieving sustainable community development requires more systematic linkages between inputs and outputs, between economic and ecological gains, and between organizational units and logics. Most American managers are trained to think in a unilinear, causal manner that makes sustainable community development seem odd and threatening.

The new managerial science and management business programs have all supported management by technique. Thus, they produce a cadre of managers who apply rigid techniques to all problems. Managers have neither the analytic skills to think about interconnections among the three Es nor the humility to struggle to reconcile competing needs. (And, as noted above, the structural arrangement whereby remote stockholders seek maximum returns on their share reinforces this style.) Most problematic are economics departments and MBA programs that produce managers with the inability to recognize that the techniques are rooted in narrow laissez-faire ideologies and that these are hostile to environmental sustainability and social equity. A bright economics major once commented about our course on sustainable community development that "this course is really neat. I never thought much about the practical or ethical issues. We just learn technique." When we pointed out that the technique he had been taught had little to say about sustainable community development, the student replied, "I guess you are right. I just assumed the technique was good for anything." This is a troublesome statement for a liberal arts major who is likely to become a manager of an American firm.

The call of sustainable development is for a form of management that comes close to classic pragmatic forms of logic. Pragmatism presupposes a process of continual reflection on its own methods, theories, and standards of evaluation (for review see Anderson 1990; Selznick 1992). At the very least, pragmatic management entails

1. recognizing business problems as paradoxes that need managing, not solving. Since organizations are always trying to achieve multiple goals, any decision will move us forward in some ways and backward in other ways; rules should be treated as working hypotheses to be refined based on experience. Since managers are trying to meet paradoxical goals, they also need to continually reflect on their practice and change the rules (Anderson 1990). No decision or practice is anything more than temporary; and

2. employing moral and rational approaches to decision making through reason. By reason, we mean a form of decision making where

ends and means are reconciled through humility, evidence, and dialogue (Pellow, Weinberg, and Schnaiberg 1995; see also Selznick 1992). This stands in stark contrast to "rationality," which identifies a problem, uses an established technique to locate the appropriate decision, and uses organizational structure to implement the solution, thereby solving the problem. (Selznick 1992)

These issues are clearly demonstrated by juxtaposing the Evanston/PIC project with the blue bag program. The Evanston facility was designed to be profitable, but also to achieve a difficult social goal of reintegrating marginalized young adults into the workforce. In return for a hard days' work, the organization trained the employees and linked them to jobs with good career ladders. Because the profit margins in the recycling industry are small, this was a formidable task. Nancy Burhop and Herman Jackson found themselves caught in two binds. First, they needed to run an efficient production process but were permitted to hire only a group of workers who lacked the skills required by private-sector firms with high productivity standards. Second, they had to focus simultaneously on economic and social goals.

Burhop and Jackson recognized the tension between these two goals and learned to live with the paradoxes. In interviews with them, we raised questions about a few of these paradoxes. Some were noticeable, like the disparity between needing to produce a steady volume of product and closing the recycling lines for a half day every week to do job skills training. Other paradoxes were more subtle. At one point, we were talking to Nancy Burhop as she simultaneously put a Band-aid on a worker's finger, weighed a truck, and read faxes on changing market prices for items so she could decide which items the workers should sort that day.

When we pointed out these dynamics, both Burhop and Jackson would smile and laugh. They did not intend to try to solve the paradoxes. They had learned to live with these contrasting goals. They drew on humility and humor. Jackson once explained that somebody trying to run this type of program had to "get beyond" conventional ways of thinking. He or she had to be reflective and creative, always looking for places of synergy while also developing the capacity to reflect on places where synergy was not occurring and develop management styles that could move back and forth between goals (Pellow, Weinberg, and Schnaiberg 1995).

All of this stands in contrast to the blue bag program, which was run by people who were always looking for definitive and permanent results. They dealt with a similar disjuncture between poor worker quality and wages by setting up a dummy corporation (REM) that initially made workers part-time, thus allowing the company to drive wages down. When workers had grievances, they brought in a security team to control and monitor the employees. When methane gas fires erupted at the facilities, management gave workers fire extinguishers. Over and over again, they failed to recognize the inherent contradictions or connections between problems. They operated on a corporate-centered managerial style that sought quick and permanent solutions to common problems.

One way of thinking about this is to argue that sustainable community development requires getting past ideologies that force us to approach issues as if we are searching for fixed solutions to enduring problems. Sustainable community development requires an understanding of the goals of the three Es in an ongoing tension with each other, and an acknowledgment that the tension can be reduced (not eliminated) only through continuous and reflective innovation. Selznick (1992:58) writes that this is a "[continuous] change within a framework of limited alternatives and necessary trade-offs." This type of thinking will simply not come about through an education system that teaches a narrow way of viewing and addressing social problems. The unilinear model of problem identification, technique application to locate a solution, and the use of organizational structure to implement the solution will simply not work any longer.

The President's Council on Sustainable Development noted in a report on the educational system that sustainable development "should not be taught as an ideology or as a goal, but rather as an ongoing process: not as a set of irrevocable answers, but as a way of continually asking better questions" (PCSD 1994:5). This type of thinking is unlikely to take hold in our educational system as it currently operates. Economics departments teach mostly laissez-faire theories, while environmental science programs focus on a narrowly defined natural science approach to environmental issues. The result is that students are instilled with the belief that all environmental problems have a technical solution that requires fiscal tinkering or chemical engineering.

One obvious response to this critique is that social and environmental advocacy groups need to work with large firms to develop the technologies that solve the problem. After one of the authors made a presentation on the blue bag program at a university, an environmental science professor commented that increased federal funding for research could develop technologies capable of making the dirty MRFs (like the blue bag) run more effectively. This statement misses the point entirely because it ignores the resulting political and economic impacts of the treadmill.

Whose Community? Labor and Recycling

Exploring sustainable community development also requires paying attention to the interface between labor and environmental protection. This is particularly important given that despite their rhetoric, green industries are not necessarily labor-friendly (Pellow 1998a, b). The Chicago blue bag program makes this case abundantly clear. Reconciling the labor (or equity) problem with environmental agendas will require new thinking and strong political coalitions. In particular, we need to better understand and work toward ties between the environmental and labor movements in the United States and abroad (Dreiling 1998; Gottlieb 1993; Levenstein and Wooding 1997; Wooding and Levenstein 1999).

Our understanding of this issue is straightforward. As we have argued, in the current political economy conflicts and struggles over scarce resources are endemic and systemic. Our image of workers laboring within a treadmill of production allows us to understand that proposals by environmentalists to enact purportedly environmentally benign practices such as recycling are likely to be undermined by the private sector's interests in business as usual. "Business as usual" in this instance means that recycling's environmental and social goals are likely to be subsumed by producers' economic motives, resulting in nondistributive outcomes (Stretton 1976; Lowi 1972). These outcomes often include maintaining secondary labor market jobs that are racially-distinct and characterized by unsafe occupational environments. Chicago's recycling workforce, particularly in the early years of the MRRFs, was a good example. We have generally found the MRFs we visited in numerous states staffed by marginalized social groups (the desperately poor, minorities, the mentally challenged, and prisoners) working in fairly depressing conditions.

But the assertion that recycling is "environmentally benign" often permits environmentalists to get off the hook without interrogating the particular means and motives of recycling organizations. Workers and environmentalists both desire cleaner local ecosystems. Workers and producers also generally support sustained economic growth. However, most environmentalists and producers have little sustained interest in the eradication of workplace hazards, or in the redistribution of wealth and political power. Simply put, these equity (or social) issues are not high on their agendas.

Interests of workers and environmentalists are thus often marked by cleavages that tend to disadvantage both groups vis-à-vis capital-owning interests. More often than not, workers and environmentalists fail to collaborate. As a result, they approach ecological issues from the producer's perspective by default. Environmentalists agree to promote "market-based incentives" and "voluntary initiatives" to achieve "pollution prevention" — methods that essentially allow producers to pollute as long as they are willing to pay for it. These cleavages have made it nearly impossible to achieve sustained collaboration between environmental and labor movement organizations. Some important exceptions include the coalition that organized against the North American Free Trade Agreement (Dreiling 1998) and campaigns to improve health and safety in the oil, chemical, and electronics industries (Gottlieb 1993). However, largely because of the continued concentration of wealth and political power in the hands of a small number of corporations worldwide, both the environmental and labor movements have declined in strength and influence during the last decade.

For their part, workers are confronting several major dilemmas that may present barriers to effective collaboration with environmentalists. These include threats to occupational safety, wage declines, increases in work hours, and growing under/unemployment. However, most scholars and the media have paid attention only to the last issue (Rifkin 1995; Wilson 1996). Unfortunately, the focus on rising under- and unemployment has often been used primarily to promote policies that call for still further corporate-centered approaches to create economic growth. These claims are made despite considerable evidence that corporate-centered development is the engine driving structural unemployment (Rifkin 1995; Schnaiberg and Gould 1994). Ironically, as we complete this book in an era of "economic growth" and reduction of formal unemployment levels, only a few analysts (e.g., Longworth 1998) point to the continuing rise of the working poor, along with the decline in welfare benefits, in the United States.

The problem of increasing occupational safety and health hazards has been all but neglected by policy makers in recent years. One reason for this omission is that, unlike the recognition of rising underemployment, the acknowledgment of the growing dangers to workers might directly challenge the corporate-centered development agenda. As long as policy makers and politicians are convinced that unemployment can be remedied by increased investment in the private sector, occupational safety problem will remain both unsolved and unchallenged. To admit that the jobs that remain increasingly injure and kill citizen-workers would constitute a threat to current political-economic structures.

How does it happen that the safety and health of U.S. workers remains a nonissue? Political scientists Peter Bachrach and Morton Baratz provided us with the tools to answer this question over three decades ago.[5] In two influential articles they argued that "to the extent that a person or group . . . creates or reinforces barriers to the public airing of policy conflicts, that person or group has power" (Bachrach and Baratz 1962, 1963; Schattschneider). There is no reason to assume that only the most visible decisions or activities in powerful arenas are the most important ones.

We can briefly explore this dynamic in the case of recycling. The history of recycling is one of different stakeholder groups vying for dominance and voice. The institutionalization of a social movement's goals has, paradoxically, become a victory for large-scale private industry. Recycling's history is therefore complex and multilayered. There are four principal reasons why the plight of worker-stakeholders remains "organized out" of the discourse on recycling.

First, as noted above, the majority of environmental organizations–stakeholders wholeheartedly support recycling and have done so for years. They have been so focused on the environmental agenda that they have failed to even ask questions about equity and labor conditions.

Second, work hazards are invisible to people with the means to change them. They are, in common with a great deal of "dirty work" in this society (Hughes 1971), "out of sight, out of mind" (Szasz 1994). The socially visible face of recycling is the local collection of postconsumer wastes. The MRFs where the collected wastes are sorted are only partly visible. The MRF may be visible from the street; the huge stacks of paper or cans may even make people feel good. However, the "dirty" work of sorting and discarding takes place inside, a place entirely unknown to most people. Ironically, one of Chicago's major reforms of their solid waste operations was to enclose the four new MRRFs, thus removing waste and recycling operations from public view. The ostensible goal was to remove these activities as "public nuisances" (interview with a former official of Chicago, May 1999).

The third factor rendering workers unseen and unheard is the general socioeconomic malaise that has always plagued communities of color and poor communities. The benefits of the "information age" are certainly by-passing that segment of the population that Schwarz and Volgy (1992) call the forgotten americans—the growing ranks of the working poor. Structural poverty haunts more and more people who live in communities that engage in the "race to the bottom" in order attract private investment of any sort (Harrison 1994). As corporations

---

[5] Of course many other social scientists have also expounded on this point. However, it should not be lost that social scientists have long recognized and publicized these problems.

are dismantled and restructured, a similar process occurs in the communities where these industries are located: it is unlikely that recycling firms which bring with them the possibility of new jobs will be turned away. This may be particularly so because of recycling's public image as a clean process. Moreover, since many communities in dire economic straights have welcomed incinerators, landfills, and hazardous waste management facilities (Gould 1991; Gould, Schnaiberg, and Weinberg 1996; Schwab 1994), recycling facilities might seem highly desirable by comparison.

The fourth and final factor creating bias against illuminating the dangers of the recycling occupational environment has been the general political effort to pit economic growth against environmental protection (Kazis and Grossman 1982). Ronald Reagan's administration (1981–89) acted to thwart proposed environmental legislation and undermine existing regulations. Since then, political leaders have increasingly found it more expedient to support the "growth machine" (Logan and Molotch 1987) than to propose reforming the treadmill of production. Recycling represents a win-win case for political and private sector elite stakeholders because in fact, it fails to slow down the treadmill of production (Schnaiberg 1992a, b) *and* it satisfies the demands of consumers and environmentalists. Recycling has a "multistakeholder" quality because several interest groups simultaneously have pushed for its adoption nationwide. Given this constellation of interests, for anyone to acknowledge recycling's occupational dangers would be to raise the threatening specter of "jobs versus the environment."

In Chicago, these dynamics were played out as the environmental movement pushed for a recycling system that would make progress toward addressing the jobs-versus-environment dilemma. Unfortunately, these groups had little control over the city and Waste Management's decision-making process. Even when the occupational health dangers of the blue bag system made headlines, environmentalists were often more concerned with low recycling rates. And, finally, the traditional labor movement was a nonentity in the later stages of this process.

Politics: The Need for Shadow Pricing

The history of recycling has been shaped by poor accounting methods that mask the real value of the practice from municipal officials. The best example is the Evanston/PIC program, which was abolished because it did not "pay for itself." The outlays for picking up the recyclables (labor, trucks, bins) and operating the MRF (labor, capital, electricity, etc.) were not covered by the sale of the recovered materials to remanufacturing firms. From a *strictly* economic accounting this may be true. However, the *true* costs were certainly very different. From this true-costs perspective, the PIC program was a state-of-the-art job retraining program that saved the city money in many respects. First, it reduced crime (by placing young adults with prior offenses into a productive context), thereby reducing law enforcement costs (including court costs) as well as property damage. Second, parents and family members reentered the workforce, which likely reduced social stress and resulting social problems (child abuse, spousal abuse, drug and alcohol abuse). And all of these were socially and economically costly to treat and prevent. Third, the trainees earned a wage and later went on to higher-paying jobs. They brought money into the community, creating positive secondary effects in local stores, banks, home improvements and so forth. From our estimate, it is quite likely that the total revenue (the revenue saved from other expenditures and the secondary benefits) did exceed the direct costs of the PIC recycling program.

In the practice of public administration, the type of accounting we used above is referred to as "shadow pricing" (Schnaiberg 1980: chaps. 6–7). Many public administration theorists argue that a great number of social programs *do* make financial sense if the accounting is done correctly. Governments should in effect make transfer payments across different agencies when one agency's programs simultaneously serve those of other agencies. In other words, a government's budget is enhanced when the savings that one branch realizes for another branch are actually counted in the first branch. In waste recycling practices, the obvious first component of this accounting is the saving of "tipping fees" by the diversion of solid waste from landfills: this should also reduce property taxes because tipping fees are tied to them But beyond this, the ecological costs of landfills and incinerators are also reduced by recycling programs. And if the third E — social equity — is also present, recycling opens up job opportunities for impoverished and low-skilled residents.

The idea of shadow pricing is a localized version of a much louder cry for "green" accounting, green fees, social accounting, and a range of related ideas proposed by sustainable development advocates. The general call is for a shift in accounting practices, wherein all the benefits and costs of current production and consumption activities are factored in, especially the socially and environmentally damaging by-products of these activities (Geithman 1997; Daly 1996a; Hawken 1993). Geithman uses the example of a coal-fired power-generating station. The station produces both kilowatt-hours of electricity and tons of air polluting particulates. For economic rationality to work, the benefits from the electricity generation and the damage of the atmospheric emissions must be measured and balanced. Thus in addition to labor, production, and transportation costs usually incorporated in the price of electricity, the sulfur oxides contained in the pollution could cause crop losses, automobile damage, visibility loss, respiratory problems, and so forth (Geithman 1997: chap. 4).

Under green or true cost accounting, these other costs would be factored into the price of electricity. To a very limited extent, proposals for trading of "emission credits" — where global warming gas producers such as utilities can buy "surplus emission savings" of more efficient producers — operate on this principle. Unfortunately, though, this may further undermine sustainable *community* development, as the community being excessively polluted does not gain any compensation in this process.

In a sense, the city of Chicago also used shadow pricing for several years through its "diversion credit" program. By paying the Resource Center and Uptown Recycling for every ton of waste diverted from the landfill, they recognized that by diverting waste from landfill burial, the nonprofits were saving the city money. Apart from saving landfilling costs, the nonprofits were also preserving more of the state's ecosystems — which are not priced in market values. The diversion credit the nonprofit centers received was not a subsidy. Rather, it was a fair exchange and payment for services rendered. Payment was made for saving the tipping fees (for landfilling) and preserving natural resources.

However, the City of Chicago later abandoned this practice, and the city of Evanston never even started a similar process. A number of things restrain cities from practicing shadow pricing. First, local municipal governments are not set up to carry out shadow pricing. Divisions are arranged, operated, and evaluated based only on their own budgets. Thus, Solid Waste Management is evaluated based on its own budget, regardless of the savings accruing to another division. Therefore there is no incentive for personnel to spend the time and resources to set up a shadow pricing system. This indicates a deeper problem as well, one that reveals that different divisions, branches, and agencies of government have little reason to cooperate if there are few rewards for doing so.

This lack of coordination is exacerbated by the overall structure of government itself. Many of the real benefits are not borne directly at the local level. For example: if the PIC program kept six people a year out of prison, it would be saving an estimated $180,000 (at $30,000 per year to house a single individual in the prison system).[6] However, these

---

[6] This is a low figure. One would also have to factor in loss of income and the loss of future income, since somebody is less employable after he or she comes out of prison. If that person is a parent, there are other costs to be borne as well.

savings would accrue to the state, not to the city of Evanston. Again, there is little incentive for the city to run a program that saves the state money. This is similar to the emissions trading scheme we noted above.

Finally, as we noted in chapter 7, neither the state nor the private sector is oriented to think beyond the short term or beyond simple causal relationships. Thus, shadow pricing is an atypical way of conceptualizing programs and problems and is unlikely to emerge from the current organizational morass of the state.

As a result, we have the problem of power, community, and politics coming together to create a series of roadblocks for sustainable community development. The long and contentious history of waste trade reveals that these struggles are ongoing in all aspects of recycling and solid waste management (Pellow [forthcoming]). Despite resistances by industry and the state noted above, governments working with social movements have sometimes been somewhat successful at implementing progressive social, environmental, and economic policies in some of this nation's largest cities. For example, under the mayoral administrations of Ray Flynn, Bernie Sanders, and Harold Washington, the cities of Boston, Burlington, and Chicago implemented policies aimed at circulating resources within the community. They made significant efforts to stem the tide of deindustrialization and corporate-centered growth in ways that minimize social, economic, and environmental damages (Clavel and Kleniewski 1990).

These cities all had strong social movement infrastructures. The ability of social movements to achieve such successes hinges on their own internal organization of resources and the existence of a window in the political and economic opportunity structures. If neither or only one of these factors is operating, then social movement organizations will confront an uphill battle.

The Economic Geography of Waste: Generalizing beyond Chicago and beyond Recycling

Given the analysis presented, we can anticipate that recycling is likely to emerge in places where the costs to municipalities of continuing with conventional disposal systems is high (due to the rising costs of transportation and tipping fees). These costs, however, are likely to be driven by politics. Communities across the United States are increasingly voicing strong opposition to the transport of garbage and other wastes through their neighborhoods and to the siting of waste facilities. In the Midwest this does not really pose a problem. There is still a fair amount of open space. It is a more explosive problem on the East Coast.

For example, New York City mayor Rudolph Giuliani's administration has been embroiled in a series of controversies over a proposed garbage plan. The present arrangement is not sustainable because the available landfill space is rapidly declining and the city is producing more garbage than ever. The mayor has made several efforts to convince other states like New Jersey and West Virginia to accept the city's waste, creating a major interstate controversy over politics, culture, and garbage. Thus, we can suppose that in circumstances where landfill space is becoming scarcer and daily exports of "out-of-state" garbage begin to increase, there will be conflicts. These in turn will place growing pressures on local governments to embrace recycling as the economically and politically "least expensive" means of dealing with waste.

Efforts to simply increase recycling, however, do not really portend much about the future of sustainable community development. The driving forces are not ecological, but political and economic. For example, firms have not been motivated to change production practices to reduce packaging and other waste. For their part, municipalities cannot allow garbage to accumulate in the streets, as this would create immediate public health threats and would be tantamount to committing political suicide.

Working together, firms and municipalities are likely to create high-volume recycling systems. They are also likely to contract the system out to large waste-hauling corporations, with the expectation that such organizations can adeptly reduce the uncertainties associated with recycling systems. Thus, we are likely to see more and more systems like the dirty MRF blue bag program pioneered in Chicago, as table 8.1 indicates. This is more detailed version of the table offered in chapter 1. The table reveals three major patterns. First, there is a steady growth in recycling programs, recycling tonnage, and recycling capacity. Second, recycling is largely organized around an increase in the number and capacity of MRFs. And third, these MRFs are increasingly the dirty MRFs ("mixed waste"), such as those associated with Chicago's blue bag program.

Lest our analysis be dismissed as specific only to recycling, consider the political-economic struggle at a recent conference on climate change and global warming in Kyoto, Japan. Controlling global warming is one of the necessities for sustaining a production system, given the limited absorptive capacity of the atmosphere for "greenhouse gases" such as carbon dioxide. The following commentary about this conference was published on an Internet service:

The global climate change negotiations are just one of the many arenas which has been captured and is being controlled by the corporate sector. The culprits

TABLE 8.1
Indicators of Growth in the Recycling Industry and Recycling Programs in the United States, 1990–1996

	1990	1995	1996
Number of MRFs	NA	310	363
MRF capacity (in tons per day)	NA	32,000	29,400
Number of mixed waste MRFs	NA	34	58
Mixed waste MRF capacity (in tons per day)	NA	20,000	34,800
Total MRF capacity (MRF + mixed waste MRF) (in tons per day)	NA	52,000	64,200
Number of curbside recycling programs	2,700	7,375	8,817

Sources: USEPA. *Characterization of Municipal Solid Waste in the United States, 1996 and 1997*; and Carless 1992.

behind the imminent failure to deal with climate change in Kyoto are several coalitions of extremely powerful and influential industries. These lobbies, which include well-known oil, automotive, mining and chemical companies in the United States, Europe, Australia and Japan, use a number of different strategies in order to protect their climate-damaging profits. The boldest efforts have been carried out in the United States, and have ranged from monumental public misinformation campaigns based on bad science (for example claims that global warming is an illusion, or that a warmer planet will not be so bad, and even the creation of phony climate models) to the funding and promotion of climate-change-skeptical scientists.

North American, Japanese, and European industry has made use of several deceptive arguments in order to protect corporate interests. For example, urgent warnings are made of economic disaster, massive unemployment, and loss of competitiveness if climate commitments are accepted. Industry, moreover, insists that developing countries also commit to binding agreements despite the fact that developing countries emit only a fraction of global greenhouse gases, and the historical burden for emissions rests on the industrialized world. But at the same time, industry also hypocritically lobbies developing countries to reject any environmental obligations that might hinder their development. [Industry has also pressed for stronger reliance on] "voluntary agreements" . . . "tradeable emissions permits" . . . and other technocratic solutions. (EnviroLink, December 11, 1997)

Much the same pattern that exists in battles over global warming on the international political stage can be found in local recycling programs. This is no coincidence: the power and pressures of the corporate world and their political agents are central to both these outcomes.

The impact of corporate power in the globalizing market is considerable. In addition to social and environmental threats, the power of the nation-state has diminished. Ironically, though, the nation-state's role in facilitating globalization is greater (Schor 1999:172; Frank 1999:275). States now provide larger outlays and more incentives, infrastructure, subsidies, and legislative "relief" to the private sector than at any time in history (Longworth 1998). The state's other roles as mediator and as provider of public services and security thus have been substantially diminished. Likewise, communities and workers are becoming more disempowered as corporate-centered policies appear to have become the only game in town in most cities, as well as in many nations (but note the variations given in Longworth 1998).

This is certainly true in recycling, where we are witnessing a steady movement away from small-scale community-based centers toward larger market-oriented municipal programs. As this is occurring, we are also seeing a shift from clean to dirty MRFs. Again, table 8.1 outlines these changes.

Our argument should not be read as one intrinsically opposed to globalization or multinational firms. Rather, we are arguing that communities need to make conscious choices about the forms of economic activity they want, in terms of whether such activity will lead to desired social and ecological outcomes. Just as firms have repositioned themselves in the globalizing treadmill, communities also need to reorient themselves. Accordingly, we have used this concluding chapter to outline processes through which communities can begin this process of reorientation. We believe that sustainable community development will only emerge in communities where there are

1. strong social movements that may be able to empower communities to take control and make choices;
2. more accurate social accounting techniques that facilitate communities' rational decision-making about alternative paths; and
3. shifts in education, so that both economic agents and community residents will better understand what is entailed when communities "harness the power of the marketplace" for the common good.

In our case studies, there was a range of economic activity, types of firms, and social outcomes. Waste Management and the blue bag program did little for the city of Chicago. In contrast, Uptown Recycling, PIC, the Resource Center, Bethel New Life, and Ersatz attempted to create positive forms of economic activity in Evanston, Maywood, and other Chicago-area communities. Generally, however, those forms of recycling were politically unsustainable. Thus, they were driven out of the marketplace. Our overall argument in the last two chapters is that communities need to better understand the dynamics of the new political economy and to actively seek out those practices and organizations that will provide economic, social, and ecological value to the community. To this end the treadmill is a good analytic organizing concept and recycling is a good case study, to chart possible paths to sustainable community development.

Final Reflections

Central to our reconstruction of the history of U.S. urban recycling programs has been the relationship between local political structures and larger economic market structures. We examined how this was played out in the creation and destruction of local recycling programs in the Chicago area. We noted two shifts in the history of recycling. First, there was a shift away from focusing on the use-value of waste toward treating it as a commodity to be mined from the urban ore. Second, there was also a shift away from waste retrieval as an activity engaged in by marginalized social groups toward its control by large firms, many of whom now operate in global markets. Ironically, such firms now employ marginalized social groups as employees.

Our findings support other scholarship in documenting how such corporate-centered policies privilege capital-owning interests over the community, its labor force, and local government. We have documented how this process has actually produced little or no genuine advance toward sustainable community development. Thus, the interplay between recycling's economic and political dimensions underlies many other urban policies as well. Recycling's history and evolution were impacted by the same U.S. economic and social policies that have affected most urban communities, workers, consumers, and local governments.

The core intellectual question concerning sustainable community development remains: What are the conditions or practices that will actually enhance the local economy of struggling communities, while also rebuilding strong social systems and preserving the environment? In short, how is it possible for communities to actually achieve a balance among the three Es of economy, environment, and equity? This is a difficult question. Using the contemporary history of recycling, we have developed a theoretical understanding of the context from which sustainable community development will have to emerge. We refer to this as a political economy of sustainable community development.

Our analysis has been critical, in the theoretical sense. However, we should not be misunderstood. We believe deeply in the vision of sustainable community development. Each of us has been actively working to move our communities and a variety of institutions in this direction. As much as we are aware that the forces of resistance against sustainable community development are formidable, the reader should also be reminded that the treadmill is not static, monolithic, or all-powerful. The treadmill is a metaphor that allows us to arrange complex thoughts and actions in a cogent fashion. While the stakeholders involved in the treadmill's operation and its economic, social, and ecological impacts are real, they *are* capable of being challenged. Indeed, they are *being* challenged in some form or fashion every day.

Likewise, despite our critical analysis of recycling in the United States we should not be read as being "antirecycling." We have come to respect and admire many recycling operations. At the community-based centers, we met impressive individuals fighting against considerable odds to reach out to marginal people whom society would like to forget. Their perseverance was inspiring. Their responses to Chicago's blue bag program were creative and potentially significant to some groups in their communities.[7] Furthermore the advent of reuse programs at the Resource Center was even more promising. Likewise, the Evanston/PIC program and the recycling industrial parks were stumbles toward some genuine forms of sustainable community development. Each of these efforts was highly innovative and transformative in many ways.

Interestingly, as we finish this project, there is evidence of programs around the country beginning to emulate these innovative Chicago-area programs. In Seattle, at-risk youth are taking computers out of the recycling stream, learning to repair them, and selling them back to low-income Asian American families. In the process, they are acquiring marketable skills. In New York, a similar program is reclaiming old furniture for repair and resale. While these projects are laudable, the political and organizational challenges they face remain formidable.

The following example in rural New York sets a high standard. An innovative recycling program was operating at the county landfill. Recyclables were taken to a MRF adjacent to the landfill, where they were sorted by mentally challenged adults through a work training program. Tires were remanufactured on-site into building materials for energy-efficient storage sheds. White goods (appliances) were being dismantled

---

[7] In one discussion with a major environmental law activist in the Chicago area, he recommended that URI, the Resource Center, and the Chicago Recycling Coalition stay in the background and steadily build up their local neighborhood and political support. He also suggested that they keep researching new solutions for recycling, so that when Waste Management abandons the failing blue bag in a few years (as he predicts), these organizations will be ready to step right back up to the plate.

in a human skills enhancement program being run for inmates from Camp Georgetown, a nearby minimum security prison. Finally, part of the landfill had been capped and there were plans to turn the escaping methane gas into energy to be used in the county office building.

This project was unique in the range of things it sought to accomplish. Unfortunately, it met economic resistance. The regional utility company refused to let the county use their lines to run the energy from the landfill to the county office building. At this writing, a regional waste-hauling company had just purchased all of the local waste haulers. Moreover, the company is threatening to take waste and recyclables to another landfill. According to a county politician, the landfill and MRF are likely to be closed. This is a distinct loss, along both ecological protection and social equity dimensions.

This book has been our attempt to understand our disillusionment and anguish over the path of modern recycling. In crafting this narrative, we are aware that recycling's history reflects America's recent social history. Recycling, like many other socially productive activities, has moved away from intragenerational and intergenerational redistributive goals of a humanistic policy (Schumacher 1973; Lowi 1972). Recycling has become just another profit center. Yet perhaps this says more about the political-economic context of recycling than about the internal logic of recycling itself.

As we have noted repeatedly, the current trend in national recycling programs is a movement toward public contracting to large global waste-hauling firms such as Waste Management and BFI. By handing over a potentially sustainable community development project such as recycling to these economic agents, the city of Chicago's actions most resemble the fox supervising the chicken coop. In Chicago, Waste Management has essentially destroyed much of the infrastructure built by that city's community-based recycling organizations. Moreover, Waste Management has profited from running operations that have been costly and largely unproductive for the city of Chicago. To add insult to injury, it has achieved this profitable but unproductive outcome by recycling relatively little of the city's waste and by exploiting relatively powerless workers — especially men and women of color.

Recycling is thus a canary in the mine for those of us who would like to see sustainable community development become a reality. In theory, there are many ways of combining the positive efficiencies of market-based organizations with the social and ecological goals of communities. Yet in practice, this requires a difficult traversing of the current political economy and a confrontation with its many antisocial dimensions. Too often, sustainable community development ideas are likely to replicate the proverbial patterns of cooking frogs. If you throw a frog into boiling water, it jumps out. But if you put it into cold water and slowly raise the temperature, it fails to perceive the danger and is eventually killed and cooked.

All too often, sustainable community development proponents argue that some small compromises are necessary. In order to move their efforts along, they must "go with the flow." But, as with the case of the live frog, this practice resembles slowly raising the water temperature to the point where good ideas are killed by successive compromises. At some point, these small compromises culminate in the death of good ideas — as practices accumulate that totally subvert these ideal goals.

References _____

Anderson, Charles. 1990. *Pragmatic Liberalism*. Chicago: University of Chicago Press.

Anderson, Elijah. 1990. *Street Wise: Race, Class, and Change in an Urban Community*. Chicago: University of Chicago Press.

Audirac, Ivonne. 1997. *Rural Sustainable Development*. New York: John Wiley and Sons.

Auletta, Kenneth. 1982. *The Underclass*. New York: Random House.

Ayres, Robert. U. 1989. "Industrial Metabolism and Global Change: Reconciling the Sociosphere and the Biosphere — Global Change, Industrial Metabolism, Sustainable Development, Vulnerability." *International Social Science Journal* 41 (3):363–74.

Bachrach, Peter, and Morton Baratz. 1962. "The Two Faces of Power." *American Political Science Review* 56:947–52.

———. 1963. "Decisions and Nondecisions: An Analytic Framework." *American Political Science Review* 57:632–42.

———. 1973. *Power and Poverty: Theory and Practice*. New York: Oxford University Press.

Baker, Susan, et al., eds. 1997. *The Politics of Sustainable Development: Theory, Policy, and Practice within the European Union*. London and New York: Routledge Press.

Baker, Wayne E. 1994. *Networking Smart: How to Build Relationships for Personal and Organizational Success*. New York: McGraw-Hill.

Barlett, Donald L., and James B. Steele. 1992. *America: What Went Wrong?* Kansas City, MO: Andrews and McNeel.

Barnekov, Timothy K., Robin Boyle, and Daniel Rich. 1989. *Privatism and Public Policy in Britain and the United States*. Oxford and New York: Oxford University Press.

Barnet, Richard J., and John Cavanagh. 1994. *Global Dreams: Imperial Corporations and the New World Order*. New York: Simon and Schuster.

Beeghley, Leonard. 1996. *The Structure of Social Stratification in the United States*. 2d ed. Boston: Allyn and Bacon.

Bell, Michael M. 1998. *An Invitation to Environmental Sociology*. Thousand Oaks, CA: Pine Forge Press.

Bethel New Life. 1994. "Testimony by Mary Nelson." Chicago: Bethel New Life.

Bluestone, Barry, and Bennett Harrison. 1982. *The Deindustrialization of America: Plant Closings, Community Abandonment, and the Dismantling of Basic Industry*. New York: Basic Books.

Boulding, Kenneth E. 1971. "The Economics of the Coming Spaceship Earth." In *Global Ecology: Readings towards a Rational Strategy for Man*, ed. J. P. Holdren and P. R. Ehrlich, 180–87. New York: Harcourt Brace Jovanovich.

———. 1973. *The Economy of Love and Fear: A Preface to Grants Economics.* Belmont, CA: Wadsworth.

Braverman, Harry. 1974. *Labor and Monopoly Capital: The Degradation of Work in the Twentieth Century.* New York: Monthly Review Press.

Brown, Phil, and Edwin J. Mikkelsen. 1997 (1990). *No Safe Place: Toxic Waste, Leukemia, and Community Action.* Berkeley and Los Angeles: University of California Press.

Bryant, Bunyan, and Paul Mohai, eds. 1992. *Race and the Incidence of Environmental Hazards: A Time for Discourse.* Boulder, CO: Westview Press.

Budros, Art. 1997. "The New Capitalism and Organizational Rationality." *Social Forces* 76:229–50.

Bullard, Robert D. 1990. *Dumping in Dixie: Race, Class, and Environmental Quality.* Boulder, CO: Westview Press.

———, ed. 1993. *Confronting Environmental Racism: Voices from the Crossroads.* Boston: South End Press.

———, ed. 1994. *Unequal Protection: Environmental Justice and Communities of Color.* San Francisco: Sierra Club Books.

Bunker, Stephen. 1985. *Underdeveloping the Amazon: Extraction, Unequal Exchange, and the Failure of the Modern State.* Urbana: University of Illinois Press.

Buttel, Frederick H. 1985. "Environmental Quality and the State: Some Political-Sociological Observations on Environmental Regulation." In *Research in Political Sociology,* ed. R. G. Braungart and M. M. Braungart, 167–88. Greenwich, CT: JAI Press.

———. 1986. "Economic Stagnation, Scarcity, and Changing Commitments to Distributional Policies in Environmental-Resource Issues." In *Distributional Conflicts in Environmental Resource Policy,* ed. A. Schnaiberg, N. Watts, and K. Zimmerman, 221–38. Aldershot: Gower.

Buttel, Frederick H., and Otto W. Larson III. 1980. "Whither Environmentalism? The Future Political Path of the Environmental Movement." *Natural Resources Journal* 20 (April): 323–44.

Cabral, Elena. 1998. "Taking Microlending to the Next Level." *Ford Foundation Report.* 29, no. 2 (Spring/Summer): 6.

Carless, Jennifer. 1992. *Taking Out the Trash: A No-Nonsense Guide to Recycling.* Washington, DC: Island Press.

Casey, Patrick, and Stephanie Steen. 1998. "Recycling Center Analysis." Memorandum to Evanston City Manager. May 4.

Castells, Manuel. 1983. *The City and the Grassroots.* Berkeley and Los Angeles: University of California Press.

Catton, William R., and Riley E. Dunlap. 1989. "Competing Functions of the Environment: Living Space, Supply Depot, and Waste Repository." Paper presented at the Conference on Environmental Constraints and Opportunities in the Social Organization of Space, International Sociological Association, University of Udine, Italy, June.

Chakravarty, Subrata. 1993. "Dean Buntrock's Green Machine." *Forbes* (August 2).

Chicago Recycling Coalition. 1997. "Problems with the Blue Bag Program." Memorandum. Chicago: CRC.

Clark, John G. 1995. "Economic Development vs. Sustainable Societies: Reflections on the Players in a Crucial Contest." *Annual Review of Ecology and Systematics* 26: 225–48.

Clavel, Pierre, and Nancy Kleniewski. 1990. "Space for Progressive Local Policy: Examples from the United States and the United Kingdom." In *Beyond the City Limits: Urban Policy and Economic Restructuring in Comparative Perspective,* ed. John Logan and Todd Swanstrom, 199–234. Philadelphia: Temple University Press.

Clawson, Dan. 1980. *Bureaucracy and the Labor Process: The Transformation of U.S. Industry, 1860–1920.* New York: Monthly Review Press.

Cohen, Maurie. 1998. "Ecological Modernization: A Response to Its Critics." Paper presented at a roundtable of the American Sociological Association, San Francisco.

Conley, Dalton. 1999. *Being Black, Living in the Red: Race, Wealth, and Social Policy in America.* Berkeley and Los Angeles: University of California Press.

Daly, Herman E. 1996a. *Beyond Growth: The Economics of Sustainable Development.* Boston: Beacon Press.

——. 1996b. "Sustainable Growth? No Thank You." In *The Case against the Global Economy,* ed. Jerry Mander and Edward Goldsmith, 192–96. San Francisco: Sierra Club Books.

Daly, Herman E., and John B. Cobb. 1994. *For the Common Good.* Boston: Beacon Press.

Daniels, Steve. 1996. "Chicago Recycling Dispute Rages On." *Waste News,* December 16, 5.

Demes, Beth. 1998a. "City Delays Decision to Privatize Recycling." *Evanston Roundtable* 1, no. 20(November 11): 1.

——. 1998b. "City Council Closes Recycling Center." *Evanston Roundtable* 1, no. 21(November 25): 1,13.

Derber, Charles. 1995. *What's Left? Radical Politics in the Postcommunist Era.* Amherst: University of Massachusetts Press.

Deval, Bill. 1980. "The Deep Ecology Movement." *Natural Resources Journal* 20 (April): 299–322.

Dickson, David. 1975. *The Politics of Appropriate Technology.* New York: Universe Books.

Dimaggio, Paul, and Walter W. Powell. 1988. "The Iron Cage Revisited: Institutional Isomorphism and Collective Rationality in Organizational Fields." In *Community Organizations: Studies in Resource Mobilization and Exchange,* ed. Carl Milofsky, 77–99. New York: Oxford University Press.

——, eds. 1991. *The New Institutionalism in Organizational Analysis.* Chicago: University of Chicago.

Dougherty, Deborah, and Edward Bowman. 1995. "The Effects of Organizational Downsizing on Product Innovation." *California Management Review* 37:28–44.

Dowie, Mark. 1992. "The New Face of Environmentalism: As Big Environmental Organizations Dodder, the Movement's Energy Shifts to the Grass Roots." *Utne Reader,* July/August; 104–11.

Dreiling, Michael. 1998. "From Margin to Center: Environmental Justice and Social Unionism." *Race, Gender, and Class* 6:51–69.

Eastwood, Carolyn. 1992. "Sidewalk Sales: Remembering the Heyday of Jewish Street Peddlers in Chicago. *Jewish United Fund News,* May 22, 33.

Ehrenreich, Barbara. 1990. *Fear of Falling: The Inner Life of the Middle Class.* New York: Harper Perennial.

Emerson, Jed, and Fay Twersky. 1996. *The New Social Entrepreneurs.* San Francsco: Roberts Foundation

European Community. 1993. *Toward Sustainability: A European Community Programme of Policy and Action in Relation to the Environment and Sustainable Development.* Luxembourg: Commission of the European Communities, D-G XI.

Evans, Peter. 1979. *Dependent Development.: The Alliance of Multinational, State, and Local Capital in Brazil.* Princeton: Princeton University Press.

Evans, Peter, Dietrich Rueschemeyer, and Theda Skocpol, eds. 1985. *Bringing the State Back In.* Cambridge: Cambridge University Press.

Evernden, Neil. 1985. *The Natural Alien.* Toronto: University of Toronto Press.

Ewell, Miranda. 1999. "High Tech's Hidden Labor." *San Jose Mercury News,* June 27.

Ferleger, Louis A., and Jay R. Mandle. 1994. *A New Mandate: Democratic Choices for a Prosperous Economy.* Columbia: University of Missouri Press.

Frank, Robert H. 1999. *Luxury Fever: Why Money Fails to Satisfy in an Era of Excess.* New York: Free Press.

Frank, Robert, and Philip Cook. 1995. *The Winner-Take-All Society: Why the Few at the Top Get So Much More Than the Rest of Us.* New York: Penguin Books.

Franklin Associates. 1996. *The Future of Solid Waste Management and Recycling: Multi-Client Study.* Draft November.. Washington, DC.

Freudenburg, William. 1990. "A 'Good Business Climate' as Bad Economic News?" *Society and Natural Resources* 3:313–31.

Gamson, William. 1975. *The Strategy of Social Protest.* Homewood. IL: Dorsey.

Gedicks, Al. 1993. *The New Resource Wars: Native and Environmental Struggle against Multinational Corporations.* Boston: South End Press.

Geithman, D. 1997. *Economics and the Environment.* Dubuque, IA: Kendall/Hunt.

Gonos, George. 1997. "The Contest over 'Employer' Status in the Postwar United States: The Case of Temporary Help Firms." *Law and Society Review* 31:81–110.

Gordon, David. 1996. *Fat and Mean: The Corporate Squeezing of Working Americans and the Myth of Managerial "Downsizing."* New York: Martin Kessler Books.

Gottlieb, Robert. 1993. *Forcing the Spring: The Transformation of the American Environmental Movement.* Covelo, CA: Island Press.

Gould, Kenneth. 1991. "The Sweet Smell of Money: Economic Dependence and

Local Environmental Political Mobilization." *Society and Natural Resources* 4:133–50.

Gould, Kenneth A., Allan Schnaiberg, and Adam S. Weinberg. 1996. *Local Environmental Struggles: Citizen Activism in the Treadmill of Production* . New York: Cambridge University Press.

Gould, Kenneth A., Adam S. Weinberg, and Allan Schnaiberg, 1993. "Legitimating Impotence: Pyrrhic Victories of the Modern Environmental Movement." *Qualitative Socialogy* 16(3):207–246.

———. 1995." Natural Resource Use in a Transnational Treadmill: International Agreements, National Citizenship Practices, and Sustainable Development." *Humboldt Journal of Social Relations* 21, no. 1: 61–94.

Graedel, T. E., and B. R. Allenby. 1995. *Industrial Ecology.* Englewood Cliffs, NJ: Prentice-Hall.

Granovetter, Mark. 1974. *Getting a Job: A Study of Contacts and Careers.* Cambridge: Harvard University Press.

———. 1985. "Economic Action and Social Structure: The Problem of Embeddedness." *American Journal of Sociology* 91, no. 3: 481–510.

Green, Gary. 1997. "Self-Development as a Strategy for Rural Sustainability." In *Rural Sustainable Development in America,* ed. Ivonne Audirac, 175–90. New York: John Wiley and Sons.

Grieder, William. 1997. *One World, Ready or Not: The Manic Logic of Global Capitalism.* New York: Simon and Schuster.

Grove, Richard H. 1992. "Origins of Western Environmentalism." *Scientific American,* July, 42–47.

Harrison, Bennett. 1994. *Lean and Mean: The Changing Landscape of Corporate Power in the Age of Flexibility.* New York: Basic Books.

Hawken, Paul. 1993. *The Ecology of Commerce: A Declaration of Sustainability.* New York: HarperBusiness Books.

Hawkins, Keith. 1984. *Environment and Enforcement: Regulation and the Social Definition of Pollution.* Oxford: Clarendon Press.

Hays, Samuel. 1969. *Conservation and the Gospel of Efficiency: The Progressive Conservation Movement, 1890–1920.* New York: Atheneum Books.

Hoff, Marie. 1998. *Sustainable Community Development: Studies in Economic, Environmental, and Cultural Revitalization.* Boca Raton, FL: Lewis Publishers.

Horowitz, Tony. 1994. "Inside a 'Dirty MuRF': The Unofficial Part of the Recycling Boom." *Wall Street Journal,* December 1.

Hughes, Everett. 1971. *The Sociological Eye.* Chicago: Aldine-Atherton.

Hurley, Andrew. 1995. *Environmental Inequalities: Class, Race, and Industrial Pollution in Gary, Indiana, 1945–1980.* Chapel Hill: University of North Carolina Press.

Hutchinson, Colin. 1997. *Building to Last: The Challenge for Business Leaders.* London: EarthScan.

Interviews. Ethnographic documentation the authors completed during the years 1993–1999 in the metropolitan "Chicagoland" area.

IUCN (International Union for Conservation of Nature and Natural Resources).

1980. *World Conservation Strategy: Living Resource Conservation and Sustainable Development*. New York: IUCN, United Nations Environment Programme.

Jacobson, Timothy. 1993. *Waste Management: An American Corporate Success Story*. Washington, DC: Gateway Business Books.

Jelewski, L. W., T. E .Graedel, R. A. Landise, D. W. W. McCall, and C. K. W. Patel. 1992. "Industrial Ecology: Concepts and Approaches." *Proceedings of the National Academy of Sciences* 89:793–97.

Jones, Scott. 1996. "The Third Annual Waste Age 100." *Waste Age*, September.

Kacandes, Tom. 1991. "Market Development in New York: A Report from the Field." *Resource Recycling*, September, 53–60.

Kanter, Rosabeth Moss. 1995. *World Class: Thriving Locally in the Global Economy*. New York: Touchstone.

Kazis, Richard, and Richard Grossman. 1982. *Fear at Work: Job Blackmail, Labor, and the Environment*. New York: Pilgrim Press.

Kendall, Peter. 1997. "City Recycling as Much in the Bag as on Landfill." *Chicago Tribune*, December 16.

Killian, Dan. 1999. "Reduce, Recycle, Refuse? Despite a Recycling Rise, Chicagoans Still Aren't Going for the Blue Bag." *New City*, May 13, 8–10.

Kline, Alison. 1998. "City Council Postpones Contract Vote." *Daily Northwestern*, November 10, 1,12.

Korten, David. 1996. *When Corporations Rule the World*. West Hartford, CT: Kumarian Press.

Kuttner, Robert. 1997. *Everything for Sale: The Virtues and Limits of Markets*. New York: Alfred A. Knopf.

Lamphere, Louise, ed. 1992. *Structuring Diversity: Ethnographic Perspectives on the New Immigration*. Chicago: University of Chicago Press.

Landy, Marc K., Marc J. Roberts, and Stephen R. Thomas. 1990. *The Environmental Protection Agency: Asking the Wrong Questions*. New York: Oxford University Press.

Larane, A. 1995. "Lille Takes Lead in High-Tech French Recycling." *Waste Age*, November, 75–76.

Lele, Sharachchandra M. 1991. "Sustainable Development: A Critical Review." *World Development* 19 (6): 607–21.

Leidner, Robin. 1993. *Fast Food, Fast Talk: Service Work and the Routinization of Everyday Life*. Berkeley and Los Angeles: University of California Press.

Levenstein, Charles, and John Wooding, eds. 1997. *Work, Health, and Environment: Old Problems, New Solutions*. New York: Guilford Press.

Levitan, Sal, and Isaac Shapiro. 1987. *Working but Poor: America's Contradiction*. Baltimore: Johns Hopkins University Press.

Lindblom, Charles E. 1977. *Politics and Markets: The World's Political-Economic Systems*. New York: Basic Books.

Lindstrom, Bonnie, Ann Traore, and Marcia Untermeyer. 1995. "Evanston." In *Local Community Fact Book: Chicago metropolitan Area*, ed. Chicago Community Fact Book Consortium, 254–56. Chicago.

Lipietz, Alain. 1987. *Mirages and Miracles: The Crises of Global Fordism*. Translated by David Macey. London: Verso Books.

Logan, John R., and Harvey Molotch. 1987. *Urban Fortunes: The Political Economy of Place*. Berkeley: University of California Press.

Logan, John, and Todd Swanstrom, eds. 1990. *Beyond the City Limits: Urban Policy and Economic Restructuring in Comparative Perspective*. Philadelphia: Temple University Press.

Longworth, Richard. 1996. "New Global Economics Toss the Rule Book Out the Door." *Chicago Tribune,* October 20, 2.1.

———. 1998. *Global Squeeze: The Coming Crisis for First-World Nations*. Chicago: Contemporary Books.

Lounsbury, Michael. 1997. "Collective Entrepreneurship: The Mobilization of College and University Recycling Coordinators." *Journal of Organizational Change Management* 11:50–69.

Lowi, Theodore. 1972. "Four Systems of Policy, Politics, and Choice." *Public Administration Review* 32 (4): 298–310.

———. 1979. *The End of Liberalism*. 2d ed. New York: Norton.

MacIonis, John J., and Vincent N. Parrillo. 1998. *Cities and Urban Life*. New York: Prentice-Hall.

Marstrander, Rolf. 1996. "Industrial Ecology: A Practical Framework for Environmental Management." In *Business and the Environment*, ed. Richard Welford and Richard Starkey, 197–20. Washington, DC: Taylor and Francis.

Massey, Douglas, and Nancy Denton. 1993. *American Apartheid: Segregation and the Making of the Underclass*. Cambridge: Harvard University Press.

McAdam, Doug. 1982. *Political Process and the Development of Black Insurgency, 1930–1970*. Chicago: University of Chicago Press.

McAdam, Doug, John McCarthy, and Mayer Zald, eds. 1996. *Comparative Perspectives on Social Movements*. Cambridge: Cambridge University Press.

McAdam, Doug, and David Snow, eds. 1997. *Social Movements: Readings on their Emergence, Mobilization, and Dynamics*. Los Angeles: Roxbury Publishing Company.

McAdams, Cheryl, and Walter McAdams. 1995. "Computer Technology in the Waste Industry." *Waste Age*, September, 125–30.

McCarthy, John D., and Mayer Zald. 1977. "Resource Mobilization and Social Movements: A Partial Theory." *American Journal of Sociology* 82:1212–41.

Melosi, Martin. 1981. *Garbage in the Cities: Refuse, Reform, and the Environment, 1880–1980*. College Station: Texas A&M University Press.

Merton, Robert K. 1957. "Social Structure and Anomie." In *Social Theory and Social Structure*, rev. and enl. ed., chap. 4. New York: Free Press.

Milkman, Ruth. 1997. *Farewell to the Factory: Auto Workers in the Late Twentieth-Century*. Berkeley and Los Angeles: University of California Press.

Miller Freeman, Inc. 1996. "Pulp and Paper." *1997 North American Factbook*.

Mishan, Ezra J. 1967. *The Costs of Economic Growth*. New York: Praeger.

Mitchell, Robert C. 1980. "How 'Soft,' 'Deep,' or 'Left'? Present Constituencies in the Environmental Movement." *Natural Resources Journal* 20 (April): 345–58.

Mol, Arthur P.J. 1995. *The Refinement of Production: Ecological Modernization Theory and the Dutch Chemical Industry*. Ultrecht: Jan van Arkel/International Books.

————. 1996. "Ecological Modernisation and Institutional Reflexivity." *Environmental Politics* 5:302–23.

Molotch, Harvey L. "Urban Deals in Comparative Perspective." In *Beyond the City Limits: Urban Policy and Economic Restructuring in Comparative Perspective*. Philadelphia: Temple University Press.

Morris, Aldon. 1984. *The Origins of the Civil Rights Movement*. New York: Free Press.

Nilges, Darlene E. 1998. "Minutes, Special Administration and Public Works Committee, meeting of May 6, 1998." City of Evanston.

O'Connor, James. 1973. *The Fiscal Crisis of the State*. New York: St. Martin's Press.

————. 1988. "Capitalism, Nature, Socialism: A Theoretical Introduction." *Capitalism, Nature, and Socialism* 1:11–38.

Office of Technology Transfer. 1990. "Chicago Announces 1991 Recycling Plan." *Solid Waste Management Newsletter* 4, no. 12 (December). University of Illinois Center for Solid Waste Management and Research.

Oliver, Melvin L., and Thomas M. Shapiro. 1995. *Black Wealth/White Wealth*. New York: Routledge.

Pellow, David N. 1996a. "New Models for Struggle: Environmental Decision-Making through Consensus." Working paper WP-96–34. Evanston, IL: Institute for Policy Research, Northwestern University.

————. 1996b. "Recycling Waste, Throwing Away Labor." *Environment, Technology, and Society* 83:1, 4.

————. 1998a. *Black Workers in Green Industries: The Hidden Infrastructure of Environmental Racism*. Ph.D dissertation, Sociology, Northwestern University. Evanston, IL.

————. 1998b. "Bodies on the Line: Environmental Inequalities and Hazardous Work in the U.S. Recycling Industry." *Race, Gender, and Class* 6:124–51.

————. 1999. "Work, Race, and Health: The Social Mechanisms that Produce Unhealthy Work Environments." Paper presented at the Annual Meeting of the Robert Wood Johnson Foundation Scholars in Health Policy Research. Aspen, Colorado. June.

————. Forthcoming. "Framing Emerging Environmental Movement Tactics: Mobilizing Consensus, De-mobilizing Conflict." *Sociological Forum*.

Pellow, David N., Adam S. Weinberg, and Allan Schnaiberg. 1995. "Pragmatic Corporate Cultures: Insights from a Recycling Enterprise." *Greener Management International* 12 (October): 95–110.

Perry, Stewart. 1978. *San Francisco Scavengers: Dirty Work and the Pride of Ownership*. Berkeley and Los Angeles: University of California Press.

Peterson, Paul E. 1981. *City Limits*. Chicago: University of Chicago Press.

Pezzy, John. 1989. Economic Analysis of Sustainable Growth and Sustainable Development. World Bank Environment Department Working Paper no. 15, Washington, DC.

Phillips, Kevin. 1989. *The Politics of Rich and Poor: Wealth and the American Electorate in the Reagan Aftermath*. New York: Random House.

————. 1993. *Boiling Point: Democrats, Republicans, and the Decline of Middle-Class Prosperity*. New York: Random House.

Powell, Jerry. 1992. "Safety of Workers in Recycling and Mixed Waste Processing Plants." *Resource Recycling,* September 1992.

Preckwinkle, Toni. 1997. "Doubts Abound about City's Blue Bags." *Hyde Park Herald,* June 4, 4.

PCSD (President's Council on Sustainable Development). 1994. *Education for Sustainability.* Washington, DC: United States Government Printing Office.

———. 1997. *Sustainable Communities Task Force Report.* Washington, DC: United States Government Printing Office.

———. 1998. PCSD Town Meeting. Pittsburgh, PA, October.

———. 1999. *Towards a Sustainable America: Advancing Prosperity, Opportunity, and a Healthy Environment for the 21st Century.* Washington, DC: United States Government Printing Office.

Rachel's Environment and Health Weekly. 1997. "Waste Management Accused of Gangster Death Threats against New Orleans Officials." July 24.

Rathje, William, and Cullen Murphy. 1992. *Rubbish! The Archaeology of Garbage.* New York: HarperCollins.

"Recycling: How to Throw Things Away." 1991. *Economist,* April 13, 17ff.

Redclift, Michael. 1984. *Development and the Environmental Crisis: Red or Green Alternatives?* New York: Methuen.

———. 1986. "Redefining the Environmental 'Crisis' in the South." In *Red and Green: The New Politics of the Environment,* ed. J. Weston, chap. 4. London: Pluto Press.

———. 1987. *Sustainable Development: Exploring the Contradictions.* New York: Methuen.

Reddy, A. K. N. 1979. *Technology, Development, and the Environment: A Reappraisal.* New York: United Nations Environment Programme.

Reich, Robert. 1991. *The Work of Nations: Preparing Ourselves for 21st Century Capitalism.* New York: Knopf.

Resource Center. 1996. *The Art of Reuse.* Newsletter of the Creative Reuse Warehouse, Chicago.

Resource Conversion Systems, Incorporated. 1994. *The Maywood Story.* Report prepared for the Village of Maywood. June.

Rifkin, Jeremy. 1995. *The End of Work: The Decline of the Global Labor Force and the Dawn of the Post-market Era.* New York: G. P. Putnam's Sons.

Ritter, Jim. 1996. "City Urged to Give Away Blue Bags for Recycling." *Chicago Sun Times,* July 23.

Ritzer, George. 1995a. *Expressing America: A Critique of the Global Credit Card Society.* Thousand Oaks, CA: Pine Forge Press.

———. 1995b. *The McDonaldization of Society: An Investigation into the Changing Character of Contemporary Social Life.* Thousand Oaks, CA: Pine Forge Press.

Rubin, Beth A. 1996. *Shifts in the Social Contract: Understanding Change in American Society.* Thousand Oaks, CA: Pine Forge Press.

Rubin, Herbert. 1994. "There Aren't Going to Be Any Bakeries Here If There Isn't Any Money to Afford Jelly Rolls: The Organic Theory of Community-Based Development." *Social Problems* 41:404–24.

Rudel, Thomas, and Bruce Horowitz. 1993. *Tropical Deforestation: Small*

Farmers and Land Clearing in the Ecuadorian Amazon. New York: Columbia University Press.

Russell, John. 1996. "NYC Workers Find More Acid in Trash." *Waste News,* December 16, 5.

Sassen, Saskia. 1991. *The Global City.* Princeton: Princeton University Press.

Schattschneider, E. E. 1960. *The Semisovereign People: A Realist's View of Democracy In America.* Hinsdale, IL: Dryden Press.

Scheinberg, Anne. 1997. "Response to Inge's Paper: For Discussion." Internet message, July 30, to Solid Waste in Low-Income Communities Forum (ECOCT-P@SEAGATE.SUNET.SE)

Schnaiberg, Allan. 1973. "Politics, Participation and Pollution: The 'Environmental Movement.'" In *Cities in Change: Studies on the Urban Condition,* ed. John Walton and Donald Carns, 605–27. Boston: Allyn and Bacon.

———. 1980. *The Environment: From Surplus to Scarcity,* New York: Oxford University Press.

———. 1982. "Did You Ever Meet a Payroll? Contradictions in the Structure of the Appropriate Technology Movement." *Humboldt Journal of Social Relations* 9 (2) (Spring/Summer): 38–62.

———. 1983a. "Redistributive Goals versus Distributive Politics: Social Equity Limits in Environmental and Appropriate Technology Movements." *Sociological Inquiry* 53 (2/3) (Spring): 200–219.

———. 1983b. "Soft Energy and Hard Labor? Structural Restraints on the Transition to Appropriate Technology." In *Technology and Social Change in Rural Areas,* ed. Gene F. Summers, 217–34. Boulder, CO: Westview Press.

———. 1986." The Role of Experts and Mediators in the Channeling of Distributional Conflict." In *Distributional Conflicts in Environmental-Resource Policy,* ed. A. Schnaiberg, N. Watts, and K. Zimmermann, 363–79. Aldershot, England: Gower Press.

———. 1990. "Recycling Policy [Re]considered." *Environment, Technology and Society* 60:6–8.

———. 1992a. "The Recycling Shell Game: Multinational Economic Organization vs. Local Political Ineffectuality." Working Paper WP-92–16, Institute for Policy Research (Center for Urban Affairs and Policy Research), Northwestern University, Evanston, IL.

———. 1992b. "Recycling vs. Remanufacturing: Redistributive Realities." Working Paper WP-92–15, Institute for Policy Research (Center for Urban Affairs and Policy Research), Northwestern University, Evanston, IL.

———, ed. 1993. "Social Equity and Environmental Activism: Utopias, Dystopias, and Incrementalism." *Qualitative Sociology,* 16 (3) (special issue).

———. 1994a. "Plastics Policies, Prologue, and Parable: Reframing Recycling." *Environment, Technology, and Society* 77:1, 3–4.

———. 1994b. "The Political Economy of Environmental Problems and Policies: Consciousness, Conflict, and Control Capacity." In *Advances in Human Ecology,* vol. 3, ed. Lee Freese, 23–64. Greenwich, CT: JAI Press.

———. 1997a. "Paradoxes and Contradictions: A Contextual Framework for 'How I Learned to Suspect Recycling.'" *Humanity and Society* 21 (3): 221–39.

———. 1997b. "Sustainable Development and the Treadmill of Production." In *The Politics of Sustainable Development: Theory, Policy, and Practice within the European Union,* ed. Susan Baker, Maria Kousis, Dick Richardson, and Stephen Young, 72–88. London and New York: Routledge.

Schnaiberg, Allan, and Kenneth A. Gould. 1994. *Environment and Society: The Enduring Conflict.* New York: St. Martin's Press.

Schnaiberg, Allan, A. S. Weinberg, and D. N. Pellow. 1998. "Politizando la Rueda de la Produccion: Los Programas de Reciclaje de Residuos Solidos en Estados Unidos." *Revista Internacional de Sociología* 19 and 20 (January–August): 181–222.

Schor, Juliet B. 1991. *The Overworked American: The Unexpected Decline of Leisure.* New York: Basic Books.

———. 1998. *The Overspent American: Upscaling, Downshifting, and the New Consumer.* New York: Basic Books

Schumacher, E. F. 1973. *Small Is Beautiful: Economics As If People Mattered.* New York: Harper and Row.

Schwab, Jim. 1994. *Deeper Shades of Green: The Rise of Blue-Collar and Minority Environmentalism in American.* San Francisco: Sierra Club Books.

Schwarz, John, and Thomas Volgy. 1992. *The Forgotten Americans.* New York: W. W. Norton and Co.

Selznick, Philip. 1992. *The Moral Commonwealth: Social Theory and the Promise of Community.* Berkeley and Los Angeles: University of California Press.

Sheehan, Helen E., and Richard P. Wedeen, eds. 1993. *Toxic Circles: Environmental Hazards from the Workplace into the Community.* New Brunswick, NJ: Rutgers University Press.

Shuman, Michael. 1998. *Going Local: Creating Self-Reliant Communities in a Global Age.* New York: Free Press.

Siegel, Beth, and Peter Kwass. 1995. *Jobs and the Urban Poor: Publicly Initiated Sectoral Strategies.* Somerville, MA: Mt. Auburn Associates.

"The Silly Blue-Bag Mystery." *Chicago Tribune,* December 7, 1995.

Silver, Ira Daniel.1998. *Preventing Fires While Feeling the Heat: Philanthropists and Community Organizations Collaborating to Address Urban Poverty.* Ph.D. dissertation, Sociology, Northwestern University.

Skocpol, Theda. 1979. *States and Social Revolutions: A Comparative Analysis of France, Russia, and China.* New York: Cambridge University Press.

———. 1980. "Political Response to Capitalist Crisis: Neo-Marxist Theories of the State and the Case of the New Deal." *Politics and Society* 10 (2): 155–201.

Socolow, Robert H., et al., eds. 1994. *Industrial Ecology and Global Change.* Cambridge and New York: Cambridge University Press.

Solid Waste Technologies. 1996. Editorial, 45.

Sonnenfeld, David A. 1998. "Contradictions of Ecological Modernisation: Pulp and Paper Manufacturing in Southeast Asia." Paper presented at a roundtable of the American Sociological Association, San Francisco.

Spaargaren, Gert. 1997. *The Ecological Modernization of Production and Consumption.* Ph.D. thesis, Landbouw University, Netherlands.

Spaargaren, Gert, and Arthur P. J. Mol. 1992. Sociology, Environment, and

Modernity: Ecological Modernisation as a Theory of Social Change." *Society and Natural Resources* 5 (4) (October–December): 323–44.

Squires, Gregory. 1994. *Capital and Communities in Black and White: The Intersection of Race, Class, and Uneven Development.* Albany: State University of New York Press.

Squires, Gregory, Larry Bennett, Kathleen McCourt, and Philip Nyden. 1987. *Chicago: Race, Class, and the Response to Urban Decline.* Philadelphia: Temple University Press.

Stoecker, Randy. 1994. *Defending Community: The Struggles for Alternative Redevelopment in Cedar-Riverside.* Philadelphia: Temple University Press.

Stretton, Hugh. 1976. *Capitalism, Socialism, and the Environment.* New York: Cambridge University Press.

Szasz, Andrew. 1994. *Ecopopulism: Toxic Waste and the Movement for Environmental Justice.* Minneapolis: University of Minnesota Press.

Taub, Richard P. 1994. *Community Capitalism: The South Shore Bank's Strategy for Neighborhood Revitalization.* Boston: Harvard University Press.

"Thinking about Globalization: Popular Myths and Economic Facts."; 1997. *Economist,* 4–18.

Thompson, Paul. 1989. *The Nature of Work: An Introduction to Debates on the Labour Process.* London: Macmillan.

Thurow, Lester. 1996. *The Future of Capitalism.* New York: Penguin Books.

Tibbs, Hardin. 1992. "Industrial Ecology — An Agenda for Environmental Management." *Pollution Prevention Review* (Spring).

———. 1993. *Industrial Ecology: An Environmental Agenda for Industry.* Emeryville, CA: Global Business Network.

Tierney, John. 1996. "Recycling Is Garbage." *New York Magazine,* June 30.

Timmons, Jeffry. 1994. *New Venture Creation.* Burr Ridge, IL: Irwin.

United States Environmental Protection Agency. 1996. *Characterization of Municipal Solid Waste in the U.S.: 1996 Update.* Washington, DC: U.S. Government Printing Office.

———. 1997. *Characterization of Municipal Solid Waste in the US: 1997 Update.* Washington, DC: U.S. Government Printing Office.

United States National Commission on the Environment.1993. *Choosing a Sustainable Future: A Report of the National Commission on the Environment.* Washington, DC, and Covelo, CA: Island Press.

Uptown Recycling, Incorporated. 1996. *Executive Director's Report for Executive Committee Meeting.* February.

Useem, Michael. 1993. *Executive Defense: Shareholder Power and Corporate Reorganization.* Cambridge: Harvard University Press.

Vogel, Kimberly. 1995. "What to Do When the OSHA Inspector Cometh." *Waste Age* December, 75–81.

Walton, John. 1993. "Urban Sociology: The Contribution and Limits of Political Economy." *Annual Review of Sociology* 19:310–20.

Weinberg, Adam. 1994. "Environmental Sociology and the Environmental Movement: Towards a Theory of Pragmatic Relationships of Critical Inquiry." *American Sociologist* 5 (1): 31–57.

————. 1997a. "Legal Reform and Local Environmental Mobilization." In *Advances in Human Ecology*, vol. 6, ed. Lee Freese, 293–323. Westport, CT: JAI Press.

————. 1997b. "Local Organizing for Environmental Conflict: Explaining Differences between Cases of Participation and Non-participation." *Organization and Environment* 10 (2): 194–216.

————. 1997c. "Power and Public Policy: Community Right-to-Know and the Empowerment of People, Places, and Producers." *Humanity and Society* 21 (3): 241–56.

————. 1998. "Distinguishing among Green Businesses: Growth, Green, and Anomie." *Society and Natural Resources,* 11:241–50.

————. 2000. "Economic Development in Rural America: Globalism, Sustainable Development, and the New Political Economy." *Annals of the American Academy of Political and Social Sciences.* Forthcoming.

Weinberg, Adam, Allan Schnaiberg, and Kenneth A. Gould. 1995. "Recycling: Conserving Resources or Accelerating the Treadmill of Production?" In *Advances in Human Ecology*, vol. 4, ed. Lee Freese, 173–205. Westport, CT: JAI Press.

Weinberg, Adam S., David N. Pellow, and Allan Schnaiberg. 1996. "Sustainable Development as a Sociologically Defensible Concept: From Foxes and Rovers to Citizen-Workers." In *Advances in Human Ecology*, vol. 5, ed. Lee Freese, 261–302. Westport, CT: JAI Press.

Wellin, Christopher. 1997. "Liberation Technology? Workers' Knowledge and the Micro-politics of Adopting Computer-Automation in Industry." Ph.D. diss., Sociology, Northwestern University, Evanston, Illinois.

Westrum, Ron. 1991. *Technologies and Society: The Shaping of People and Things.* Belmont, CA.: Wadsworth.

Wiewel, Wim. 1990. "Industries, Jobs, and Economic Development Policies in Metropolitan Chicago." In *Creating Jobs, Creating Workers,* ed. Lawrence Joseph, Chicago: Center for Urban Research and Policy Studies, University of Chicago.

Willers, Bill. 1994. Sustainable Development: A New World Deception. *Conservation Biology* 8:1146–48.

Wilson, William J. 1987. *The Truly Disadvantaged: The Inner City, the Underclass, and Public Policy.* Chicago: University of Chicago Press.

————. 1996. *When Work Disappears: The World of the New Urban Poor.* New York: Knopf.

Wooding, John, and Charles Levenstein. 1999. *The Point of Production: Work Environment in Advanced Industrial Societies.* New York: Guilford Press.

World Commission on Environment and Development. 1987. *Our Common Future.* New York: Oxford University Press.

Zukon, Sharon. 1995. *The Cultures of Cities.* Cambridge, MA: Blackwell Publishers.